EMPIRE AND AFTER

Series Editor: Clifford Ando

A complete list of books in the series
is available from the publisher.

The Gods, the State,
and the Individual

THE GODS,
THE STATE,
AND THE
INDIVIDUAL

REFLECTIONS ON
CIVIC RELIGION
IN ROME

John Scheid

Translated and
with a foreword by
Clifford Ando

PENN

UNIVERSITY OF PENNSYLVANIA PRESS

PHILADELPHIA

Published by
University of Pennsylvania Press
Philadelphia, Pennsylvania 19104-4112
www.upenn.edu/pennpress

Printed in the United States of America on acid-free paper
1 3 5 7 9 10 8 6 4 2

Library of Congress Cataloging-in-Publication Data
Scheid, John, author.
   [Dieux, l'état et l'individu. English]
   The gods, the state, and the individual : reflections on civic
religion in Rome / John Scheid ; translated and with a
foreword by Clifford Ando.
      pages cm. — (Empire and after)
   Includes bibliographical references and index.
   ISBN 978-0-8122-4766-4 (alk. paper)
1. Religion and state—Rome. 2. Cults—Rome. 3. Rome—
Religion. I. Ando, Clifford, translator, author of foreword.
II. Scheid, John. Dieux, l'état et l'individu. Translation of:
III. Title. IV. Series: Empire and after.
   BL805.S3413 2016
   292.07—dc23
                                             2015016157

To the memory of Jean-Pierre Vernant

Non pas passer les universaux à la râpe de l'histoire, mais faire passer l'histoire au fil d'une pensée qui refuse les universaux.

—Michel Foucault

Contents

Translator's Foreword

John Scheid's *The Gods, the State, and the Individual: Reflections on Civic Religion in Rome* is an impassioned intervention in a contemporary debate in the study of ancient religion. It speaks for a method or, perhaps, a perspective, as well as a distinctive national tradition. In the book, Scheid himself contextualizes his work within a century's history of scholarship on religion in the ancient world. This foreword offers an additional perspective on the contemporary context in which Scheid intervenes and explains choices made in the process of translation.

Roman religion has long presented a number of challenges to historians of religion in the Christian and post-Christian West. Among others, one might single out the nonexistence in classical Latin of any term that corresponds to English "religion," and the similar absence of any vocabulary to discuss religious affiliation or acts of conversion that distinguish those phenomena from, say, acts of political belonging or changes in doctrinal persuasion in the study of philosophy. To these one might add Roman religion's lack of a sacred text that (nominally) offered a totalizing portrait of the religion's propositional content or foundational myth, as well as the Roman practice of describing relations with the divine using technical terms for social relations widely employed to discuss relations with other humans: *pietas*, whence English "piety," describes dutiful respect toward ties of kinship above all, but also other social bonds; *colere*, whence Latin *cultus* and English "cult," describes sustained acts of attention, respect, and cultivation toward things we cherish: social superiors, close relations, and the land whence one springs.

Building on a long tradition of scholarship, whose contours I trace below and in which he himself has played a leading role, Scheid confronts these challenges head-on. Proceeding with a profound respect for historical and philological detail, Scheid explores the functioning of a religious system tightly imbricated with other structures of social and political belonging. How shall we describe the situation of individuals vis-à-vis Roman religion, when the Romans themselves did not regard the individual as a primary unit of social analysis, freely making religious commitments that might emancipate or sunder oneself from other forms of social commitment? In addition, Scheid outlines and emphasizes the consequences of our accepting as historically primary features of Roman religion prominent in the sources (its emphasis on ritual action; its profound concern for the here-and-now), instead of seeking at Rome those features of Christian religious life that we would like to find, whose very lack then becomes at once an explanandum and the principal evidence for Roman religion's deficiency *as* religion.

Scheid describes the emergence of what he alternatively terms a sociological or secular perspective on Greek and Roman religions as a hard-won struggle on the part of researchers to set aside a priori commitments, derived above all from Protestant Christianity, about what religion is and how individuals and communities relate to religions. In his view, nineteenth- and early twentieth-century historians of religion derived from Protestant theology and Romantic philosophy an understanding of religion as, in essence, an interiorized sense of individual dependence and awe before some unseen and transcendent divine. In that historiographic tradition, such feelings on the part of individuals have historically found collective expression in institutions and shared practices. For a multitude of reasons, individuals and cultures have often lost their way and become estranged from their own feelings and thus from the divine; religious institutions and practices are then hijacked by elites, who put themselves forward as experts—as priests—and exploit popular devotion to ritual and their own control over particular spaces, materials, and institutions of knowledge production to interpose themselves between individuals and the divine. Scheid's work in this regard is part of a widespread and international tradition of self-critical reflection in the study of religion, and he is surely correct in the fundamentals of his diagnosis. An exemplary essay in the American branch of this tradition is Jonathan Z. Smith's "On the Origin of Origins," the first chapter in *Drudgery Divine*.[1] Focusing ultimately on Protestant historians of religion of the nineteenth century and their influence in the United States, Smith shows, among other things, how Protestant efforts at self-differentiation vis-à-vis Catholic ritualism led to the misrecognition and denigration of any religious tradition in which collective ritual action was a preeminent form of religious expression. Many similar and also excellent works of historiography, from a wide variety of perspectives, might be cited.[2]

Although the way was paved by a number of earlier, excellent books—including, as Scheid and many others in the field emphasize, the extraordinary work of Georg Wissowa, *Religion und Kultus der Römer*[3]—the emergence of a new consensus was the result of convergent work in France and England in the 1970s and Germany perhaps a decade later.[4] This new consensus had three features of importance here. First, contributors to it explicitly reflected on the need to identify and bracket assumptions about religion derived from the Abrahamic religions:[5] those regarding the centrality of "faith" as an epistemic category (that religions are founded on belief) and a bundle of propositions (that religions have doctrines); the assumptions that religions are revealed to humans by gods who communicate with them in human language, and some, at least, of the content of those communications remains available in books, with all that entails about etiology, historical self-awareness, capacities for fundamentalism, and the need for interpretation; the assumption that adherents to particular religions properly display their zeal by persuading others to share that zeal;[6] and so forth.

That said, Romans wrote books on religious themes and reflected both discursively and in figurative art on their own religious practices, and they performed rituals, even if they almost never attributed the content of those rituals to some originary moment of divine revelation. The second feature of the new consensus relevant to this sketch is thus substantive in orientation. Across a variety of domains, scholars have sought to craft frameworks within which to understand the role of religious literatures and other forms of aestheticized cultural production at Rome, including avowedly literary forms like myth as well as philosophical theology and figurative art: were they merely personal reflections on the meaning of ritual performance, which was somehow primary? Or can they serve as indices to interpretive or ideological agendas at their moment of production? How, in sum, should they contribute to the writing of histories of Roman religion?[7]

As a related matter, the nature of Roman ritualism has also been subjected to searching inquiry. If religion consists in nothing more than a set of gestures, is it devoid of theological or even ideological content? What does it mean to say that the Romans esteemed correct performance—that their religion was an orthopraxy, as doctrinal religions might esteem orthodoxy—when the evidence clearly suggests that performances might vary, one from another? How should we, and how did the Romans, understand religious change? Greeks and Christians rehearsed etiological myths; the Romans spoke in vaguer terms about the customs of their ancestors (whom they tellingly termed *maiores*—literally, their "betters"). How did these distinctive ideological positions find expression in patterns of fundamentalism and historicism in religious thought and practice?[8] On another plane, how should one conceive the relationship of religious sentiment and affiliation on the part of individuals in such ritual systems? What did it mean to "participate" or "belong" to a civic religion?[9]

The final feature of this work on religion concerns the broader theorizing that it provoked. Scheid and many others use the terms "polis-religion," "the civic model," or, to refer specifically to the work of Richard Gordon, "the civic compromise" to describe the relevant theories. In abstract terms, these were attempts to describe Greek and Roman religions as symbolic systems within particular social, material, political, and economic contexts. At the level of method, this ambition encouraged a scrupulous historicism in regard to the actual practices of ancient worship and its imminent theorizations by participants, even as it worked to disallow any un-self-conscious or unreflective imposition of anachronistic or etic categories. Researchers thus came to trace and study the homology one might observe within elite cultural production between the ordering principles and structures of authority of Greek and Roman cults and the political communities in which they found life. What is more, work in this vein regularly stressed—quite rightly—the extent to which the performance of cult penetrated the structures of everyday life: there was no sphere of one's civic or familial existence outside religion, nor did religion offer space or forms of authority or systems of knowledge from which to launch an immanent critique.[10]

John Scheid has played a major role in all these developments over the past thirty years. In part this results from his extraordinary technical expertise across the full range of subdisciplines within classical studies, and his use of those skills in the study of the cult site and inscribed records of the Arval Brethren, a priestly college active in imperial Rome. In consequence of Scheid's mastery of this material, his monograph on the cult of Dea Dia, the goddess venerated by the Brethren, and the social, political, and material contexts of the institutionalization of the Arvals, is perhaps the most fully elaborated study now in existence of an ancient cult as it was conceived, developed, practiced, and sustained. What is more, his careful theorizing about the rules and meaning of Roman ritualism, developed out of enormously detailed engagements with the data, must stand as paradigmatic for what can be achieved by this method.[11]

For all the rigor of its method and proper regard for historicism at its core, the theory of *polis*-religion and civic cult has never actually been hegemonic in the field.[12] Although dissent and revision now proceed along a number of lines, no one has done more to provoke concern about the explanatory reach of the theory than John North. Commencing in 1979, North urged that the varieties of religious activity visible in the evidence already in the second century BCE could not be captured and explained by the theory. Focusing on the suppression by Rome of Bacchic worship, North urged that the action taken by state authorities could not be explained other than by postulating an awareness on their part of forms and spaces for religious activity that escaped not simply the actuality of their control but the form of their power. Never denying the prominence or importance of state cults, North has urged that we witness over time the development of a marketplace of religious choices, to which individuals repaired, sometimes in addition to their (at least nominal) participation in state cult, and sometimes instead.[13]

In recent years, critique of the civic model has developed a rich literature, some of which has been empirical, canvassing forms of religious activity that one can interpret as unaccounted for by the civic model. Greg Woolf's "Polis-Religion and Its Alternatives" is a touchstone of this genre.[14] Others have attempted theoretical engagements with the model and its expositors. The earliest and most trenchant articles in this vein were produced by Andreas Bendlin, and others have now taken up his misgivings about the notion of "embedded" religion.[15] A number of scholars have advanced sociologically oriented accounts, of now startling variety. Some have taken up the metaphor of the marketplace and sought to explain large, long-term changes as aggregates of individual choices, susceptible to comparison with other similar historical developments. Here, a massive failing of the field overall has been its assumption that the one great historical change experienced by antiquity in the domain of religion was its Christianization, and a systematic flaw of a subset of the sociological literature is its employment of comparanda consisting in the spread of Christianity among other non-Christian populations.[16] I have myself suggested that the phenomenon truly demanding explanation is not the conversion of the ancient world to Christianity, but its conversion to an understanding of self and religion in which "conversion" was meaningful; and I have attempted to provide a historical sketch of the dynamics that made this possible.[17] Finally, still others are trying to reorient inquiry away from public authorities to households, and most notably to the individual as irreducible historical agent.[18]

This is the context in which Scheid seeks to intervene. Indeed, *The Gods, the State, and the Individual* should be understood as motivated by this turn in contemporary scholarship. It represents, at least in part, an intensive response to contemporary anglophone scholarship, and it deserves to meet that audience head-on. What is more, the debate now raging has all along existed in something of an echo chamber, because as influential as Scheid has been among experts, his work remains largely untranslated. That said, Scheid does more than attempt to diagnose some limitations of theory and method among critics of the civic model. He also offers a powerful and elegant restatement of major components of an orthodoxy that Scheid himself helped to bring into being. This translation thus provides a sustained account in English of an important position in historical research by its most prominent advocate.[19]

Regarding this translation, let me say a word about language and another about passages quoted by Scheid. The Latin term *civitas* and the French term *cité* are essential terms of art in Scheid's text. The primary meaning of *civitas* is "citizenship," it being an abstraction from *civis*, "citizen." By metonymies standard in the classical period, it could also designate the collective that shared citizenship and was united by it—namely, "the people" of a given polity. It could also refer to the urban center that housed the political, legislative, and juridical institutions through which that people governed itself: *civitas* as "city." And it could refer to the territory in which that people resided: *civitas* as "territory" or, perhaps, "state."[20]

French *cité* occupies a correspondingly important role in Scheid's text. The primary meaning of *cité* is, of course, "city," but its metonymic and associative reach is quite different from English "city" and much closer to Latin *civitas*. For example, *cité* is the term commonly employed to translate English "city-state," meaning that it can render *civitas* in those contexts when *civitas* refers not simply to an urban center but to the totality of territory on which a given political collectivity resides. Likewise, *droit de cité* (literally, "right of the city") is a term of art in French and particularly Swiss citizenship law designating not simply one's status as a legal resident of a given city; in many contexts it forcefully implies the possession of citizenship that follows upon legal residence within a constituent polity of the national state. Hence, although their patterns of association have different centers of gravity, Latin and French concepts in these lexical complexes map each other much more closely than any set of English terms can map either of those languages. In correspondence, Scheid has suggested that one render *cité* as city-state wherever possible, and I have followed that suggestion.

Scheid quotes texts from Greek, Latin, and German, nearly always in French translation. In every case—including, of course, texts whose original language is French—I have provided translations into English. Where possible, I have made use of published translations, but often enough I have had to prepare my own. In a single case—namely, the discussion of Foucault in chapter four—I have provided references to, and quoted from, works of Foucault and Paul Veyne beyond those cited in the French edition of this book, in an effort to clarify both what was at stake for Foucault in the remarks quoted by Scheid, and likewise the import to be assigned to Veyne's reading of Foucault in the work cited by Scheid.

In closing, let me thank John Scheid for his cooperation in reading the English text and discussing several problems of translation. I am grateful also to the Notre Dame Institute for Advanced Study, where I read the copyedited text.

Preface

In a world disturbed by conflicts that sometimes pit religions against states, it is not easy to define the respective weights one ought to assign to one or the other in public decisions or private choices. The major religions have a tendency to claim an absolute position, regarded as conferring upon them an influence over social and political life that borders on exclusive. There are cases in which religious authorities exercise public power directly, and others in which they reserve the right to control the state, even to challenge the foundations of its sovereignty from within.

This raises a number of questions. Should a religion necessarily penetrate all levels of society and the state, as is envisaged by the monotheist religions? Is it legitimate that its doctrines and obligations be imposed on all individuals? These are problems for all faiths, albeit not always in the same terms. Can one compare the situation that obtains in Christian countries with those known to peoples who adhere to Islam? And what of those regions that do not know the revealed monotheisms, such as China and India? How do they manage diverse religions? How do they treat minorities?

These are central issues in contemporary politics, and not only in states struggling with religious antagonism and absolutism. Is the situation in our democracies totally clear? In some of them, religions are in principle separate from the state, public actions and individual conscience being alike freed from any religious obligation. In others, by contrast, there exist concordats. And what should one say about the special relationships that American democracy maintains with a number of its principal religions?

Confronted with the multiplicity and complexity of situations, is secularity (so often praised!) the most appropriate solution and the best guarantee of freedom of conscience? Is there not a risk that this will be seen as interfering in the life of individuals in an intolerable manner and likely to provoke dissent from certain sectors of society? Moreover, is otherness in religious matters an obstacle to civil peace, as it is understood in liberal democracies? Is diversity by its very nature going to create obstacles to good relations within the citizen body of any given nation? Finally, are secular democratic societies truly devoid of religious influences? Answers to these questions necessarily vary in the very different contexts of the many states and regions of the world.

Hence the need to take a step back in order to reflect on, among other problems, the questions now being posed regarding the principle of secularism that constitutes, in its diverse forms, one of the foundations of our democracies.

Undoubtedly, the study of texts and inscriptions in Latin does not provide the ancient historian with any particular legitimacy to intervene in this most contemporary debate. But when he or she takes the trouble to step outside this specialization in order to question the methodological principles that guide research, it may in consequence be possible for such a person to enrich that debate. For the past half-century, in fact, numerous scholars have toiled to bring to light and to explore the otherness that characterizes the religious conduct and behaviors of our ancestors. In ancient Rome, at least up until the fourth and fifth centuries CE, when Christianity became the sole religion, religious practice was conceived as a form of social conduct, without any claim to dominate the conscience. As Fontenelle said, "Do as the others do, and believe what you want."[1] In contrast to Fontenelle's dismissive tone, and indeed, to that of many modern historians, ritualism without dogma is neither as ridiculous nor as decadent as is often claimed.[2] That said, the progressive bringing to light of its specific qualities could not have occurred absent the operation of a principle of secularism: every researcher endeavoring to overcome his or her own convictions and personal practices, in order to confront behaviors and beliefs that are definitively other. It is this very approach, together with the results that it has produced, that is today being contested, even denied, by certain recent approaches that struggle to accept the results of this well-known principle of secularism, which is to say, of religiously disinterested research.

In fact, this overall debate encompasses a wider range of questions than that provoked by the image one might provide of civic religion, the religion of the citizens that the ancients called "public religion" (*sacra publica*). Rather, it concerns more generally every religion, whether ancient or modern, to which one cannot apply the principles of Christianity. Indeed, it is a question that

reaches beyond the domain of the specialists and is taken up in texts directed
to the public at large. Thus, a great public journal recently devoted an issue to
a theme dear to the cognitive sciences, "Brain and Spirituality." In that issue,
an editorial proclaimed, "spiritual experiences in all their diverse forms—
prayer, shamanic trance, meditation—have a bodily inscription in the brain."
It marveled to discover that this spirituality, which "is first of all, and above
all, a lived experience that affects the mind as well as the body," always has
"as its common aim to provoke a shock to a state of being, an enlargement of
consciousness and, often enough, of the heart." In other words, the editorial
asserts, seemingly without self-consciousness or irony, that inscribed at the
center of the human brain one finds the very principles of Christian piety. To
be sure, in the course of history there have been disbelievers. Sometimes, too,
it happens that the sense of the sacred is lost and religion is reduced to a social
or cultural dimension. Ritual gestures are delegated to priests and "religion
thenceforth takes on an essentially social and political function." In reaction
to "this overly exterior and collective" (observe in passing the "overly"—why
"overly exterior and collective?") "spiritual currents" transformed these religions, by renewing their ties to "the most archaic forms of the sacred." In
this perspective, Pythagoreanism and the mystery cults that arose in ancient
Greece are to be considered as essentially reactionary forms, which came into
being in opposition to the soulless polytheism of official religion.[3]

In this historical reconstruction of the emergence of "true" religiosity, the
reader familiar with German philosophers and theologians of the Romantic
era will recognize without difficulty the influence of Schleiermacher, Hegel,
and others. There is nothing new here: what is extraordinary is the return
(yet again) to an ancient thesis in the history of religions, based now on evidence supposedly furnished by psychology. The scanner becomes the means
to arbitrate in the human sciences, between older theories heavily marked
by Christianity, on the one hand, and the history of religions as it has developed over the past century, on the other. The editorial places in perspective
the endless alternation between some movement of the "truly sacred" toward
the institutionalization of religion and its opposite, as it is reproduced in our
own day, to wit, in "the need for experience and transformation being felt by
numerous individuals." Religion, community, individual. These are the terms
of this historical dialectic, which seeks without end to attain the "truly sacred"
essence of Christianity. In the eyes of the editorial, the role of the individual

in this process is that of an engine, driving the rediscovery of some originary revelation.

This kind of theory, deriving from theology, finds articulation not only in magazines and general remarks. One finds similar ideas in specialized works of history, even in sociological treatises from the nineteenth century to our own day. We are in fact under continuous threat of denying the right of otherness to those who, in the past and even in the present, do not possess the same ideas about religion as those who live in monotheistic cultures. So, certain contemporary works aim to show that religions based on ritual and closely tied to particular collectivities are but marginal phenomena in the history of Religion (with a capital R), which according to them is properly inscribed in the heart of the individual. The result is to classify these as non-religions, in contrast with a single religiosity deemed worthy of the name. How many contemporary religions correspond to the type of Roman religion? Ought one refuse to name them "religions"? As regards religion existing in our own states, including the monotheistic religions, ought one exclude any behavior that does not correspond to the paradigm of Christian "religiosity"?

My essay is devoted to those theories that attack, under the names "civic religion" and "*polis*-religion," historical and anthropological approaches to the religions of classical antiquity, and, in addition, to the practice of a research method attentive to a priori ideological and confessional commitments. It is not the aim of this essay to demonstrate that such theories are false, but merely to assign them their proper place, to wit, within a Christian theology of history, and to show that the data are susceptible to very different evaluation within a history of religions that tries to be secular. For the rest, I will try to show that certain critiques of the traditional religions of the Romans actually transgress the facts and are sometimes simply wrong. By means of these corrections, this book can at the same time give more precise description to certain important features of the religions of Rome. We will not linger at some very general level of the history of humanity; rather, we will focus on the Romans, referring to the people of Rome itself and of the Roman world. The Romans are a good object of study because, since the nineteenth century, their religion has been regarded as the most characteristic of those non-religions that populated the world after the loss of "true" piety and before the necessary synthesis in Christianity. Beyond the particular case, however, the reader will readily recognize arguments that are employed equally today, in contemporary conversations about religion and secularism—and will learn that the data of the past do nothing, in any way, to support those arguments. On the contrary, the Roman case may be able to provide new perspectives on our way of thinking about others and, to the extent that the Roman Empire had to solve problems that are not so far removed from the European situation today, also on possible forms of relation between the two levels of community.

Introduction

The model of civic religion, which was born in part from the recognition that religious practice is always exercised in a specific social context, has been called into question by a number of researchers in England and Germany. The challenge that they pose to the model of *polis*-religion is that, according to them, it does not take account of the religion of the individual, of religiosity viewed as a universal phenomenon, everywhere and always identical and present. In their view, religion exists fundamentally in the relationship—emotional, individual, and direct—that exists between God and human, without any need whatsoever for social institutions. In Germany, this model is bound to the history of Protestant theology and was diffused inter alia by Romantic philosophy, and it remains very powerful. It has always prevented other currents, based on modern Anglo-French social anthropology, from spreading, even if the so-called Frankfurt School, of which the historian of Roman religion Georg Wissowa was a precursor, was relatively close to an anthropological approach.[1] But this school was practically extinct after the Great War, and this left the field to those methods strongly inspired by Christianizing phenomenology.

The attack on *polis*-religion is therefore not surprising. Interpretations of ancient religions in their historical and social contexts have always provoked the same attack in their traditional milieu, whether that milieu is Christian and merely one that adopts its ideas from the Christian tradition. More surprising is the critique advanced by English colleagues, graduates of Cambridge and Oxford, universities where the *polis* model has been defined in opposition to a Eurocentric one. This development may have something to do with a generational reaction, or perhaps with the influence of British liberal thought, which tends to reduce all events to the free choice of individuals while denying any deterministic role to the social or institutional frameworks within which those choices are made.[2] Above all, however, one has the impression that in England, at any rate, the critique is an avatar of deconstructionism, which allows one to appear progressive and brilliant at very little cost. One deconstructs modes of analysis or the models of a science for the beauty of the gesture itself, and on this basis critiques this or that argument for its supposed ties to this or that ideology. Attention is often drawn to the problems posed by an ancient evidentiary regime, which is of course easy for an ancient historian to do, and then the site is left in ruins. It's a fun game, but it is altogether as free as it is dangerous, especially for the humanities. If we ourselves insist that our studies are nothing more than bourgeois or petty-bourgeois amusements, hampered by their certitudes and discourse, perhaps our colleagues will one day persuade the taxpayers who finance these amusements to direct their tax dollars to more serious pursuits.

To defend the disciplines of the humanities and social sciences, to justify the utility of history, and also to check whether a collection of researchers has indeed been working for twenty or thirty years under the influence of a collective illusion, it suffices to take up the same armaments: one must deconstruct the deconstructionists. This is not a difficult task: scholars of the ancient world are long habituated to investigate the history of their subject and to evaluate the contribution of their predecessors. For example, for a series of seminars in 1987 organized by Francis Schmidt, François Héran, Catherine Weinberger-Thomas, Jean Kellens, and Clarisse Herrenschmidt, I myself analyzed the influence of Romantic and Hegelian thought on the arguments of Theodor Mommsen and Georg Wissowa.[3]

We will therefore examine the arguments deployed against the model of civic religion, pointing out errors and misunderstandings, and we will try to show that the deconstruction of *polis*-religion has actually consisted in reintroducing to the history of religions extremely traditional points of view—indeed, exactly those points of view that the model of *polis*-religion was devised to combat and overcome.

The arguments formulated against the model of civic religion seem to me above all to misrecognize—to ignore, even—essential data that all those who study the Greco-Roman world ought to understand well: what was the city-state and its society, what was the individual in his epoch, and what was his involvement in the city-state? One must, in the end, understand the religion of the ancients without reducing it to some simple function of self-fashioning or identity creation.

I will try to show that deconstructionist theories typically pass to one side of the problem and neglect the sources. In opposition to the critiques formulated against civic religion, I will also try to reconstruct some important features of this type of religiosity, which seems to us so strange. In particular, I will draw attention to the fact that, in the Roman world, the entire community functions and expresses itself in a collective mode. This was not true simply of city-states or political communities. I will emphasize, moreover, that one should not reduce Roman religions to some communal anchorage for the expressing of piety. This was only the framework of religious practice, which was in itself essentially ritualistic and rested upon ancestral custom, devoid of revelation, of dogma, and of centralized authority. It is strange that the detractors of public religions never discuss this aspect of it.

Do not misrecognize the purpose of this book. I do not seek to deny that forms of expression or religious conduct other than those of the Greeks and Romans are possible. A Christian interpretation of historical facts is perfectly possible. But it will be viable solely for those who accept that the Christian point of view is the only one possible. For my part, I wish simply to observe that in the Roman epoch, as today among many religions, religious emotion had another dimension for the majority of practitioners. I will not deny that historians today are formed by ideological and other a priori commitments. Naturally, I accept this about myself, too. But unlike the deconstructionists, I admit and speak openly about my thoughts on matters of religion. Although I was raised Catholic, I have for a long time been agnostic, even if I am aware that I was formed, like every Westerner, in the Christian tradition and Christian culture. And so, I claim the right to analyze a religion independently from contemporary religious views and opinions. I want to be able to regard relations between the ancients and their gods as possibly more rational than Christian-Romantic theory can imagine, and thus I want also to be free to assign emotion to another place in polytheist ritualism than the one it occupies in religions of revelation. Finally, I do not believe that Roman religious history has today as its sole function to explain the transition from pagan religions to Christianity, and I refuse to reverse the argument but retain the problem by thinking that, before the Christianization of the world, everything was already the same and that, fundamentally, there is a single true religiosity, the "true religion" of the Christian Minucius Felix, which transcended the decadent institutions of *polis*-religion.[4] The reader will judge the objectivity of my position. And if I have failed in this regard, at least the failure will have been a knowing one.

That said, I see essentially three major problems, as the title of this book suggests. The first seems to me to be a neglect of what the Greek and Roman city was; the second is a poor comprehension of what one might call the individual in the ancient world; finally, the third is a limited and distorted understanding of the religions of this world of city-states. But before entering into the thick of my topic, it is appropriate to make an inventory of the critiques advanced against the model of civic religion.

Chapter 1

The Critique of *Polis*-Religion

An Inventory

Hegelian dialectic made a profound impression on historians of the nineteenth century, including, where Roman history is concerned, Theodor Mommsen and his successors.[1] This form of thought projected Western religious concepts into the past and on this basis explained the evolution of religion up to and including the Christian religions. It was relatively easy, since (by definition) no great rupture was expected. It sufficed for each generation of humanity to separate the wheat from the chaff before arriving at the enlightened Christianity of the modern age. Many historians took this route, including Ulrich von Wilamowitz-Moellendorff, Theodor Mommsen, and from a certain point of view Georg Wissowa, Franz Cumont (who invented the celebrated concept of the oriental cults), and Jules Toutain, to name the most representative figures.[2] The phenomenology of religion was also inspired by this historical-theological dialectic.[3]

Against this comparatism or reduction of all religion to a precocious manifestation of some religiosity approaching Christianity, other approaches have emphasized the religious alterity of the ancients. This alterity is, of course, not total. The Romans employed in part the same vocabulary for religious matters as we, and their conduct resembled ours. But if one looks closely, one cannot fail to observe numerous small differences that are, in fact, essential. To begin with, their conception of divinity was fundamentally different. The Romans, too, believed that their gods lived eternally at the heights of heaven and that they intervened in the lives of mortals, but their religion was not concerned in any way with the metaphysical space proper to the gods; it concerned itself solely with relations between gods and humans on a terrestrial plane. The rest was not relevant, so to speak, to the competence of human imagination. The Romans thus appear on one side very near to us, and on another, they are very much unlike us. It is for this reason that I affirmed, in the conclusion of my inaugural lecture at the Collège de France, the necessity to work on details:[4] not rejecting theories and models, but recommending that one practice one's research while in continuous contact with the sources, remaining attentive at once to otherness and to that which is difficult for us to understand. It is precisely in the unintelligible that the proper originality of the ancients reveals itself. If we think purely through abstractions, working from syntheses or general studies far removed from the sources, or by means of theories not continually subjected to empirical verification, we inevitably impose ideas and concepts of today on the civilizations of the past. Strongly inspired by what was once called sociology, such as it was understood by Georges Dumézil and Louis Gernet, which has become social anthropology, this project adopts as a fundamental principle the obligation to take the otherness of the ancients as a point of departure—in other words, to refuse to assimilate them to us. Or, if we compare two types of religion, to proceed with great caution, knowing that in matters of religion we are all of us directly or indirectly formed by 1,600 years of Christian thought. We are thus concerned with a method whose relevance extends beyond religion and reaches all other aspects of ancient culture. It calls for caution and the deconstruction of all modern interpretations before returning to the ancient sources.

It has been possible to exaggerate this affirmation of otherness, and it is appropriate to criticize such excesses. At the end of the nineteenth century and start of the twentieth, a certain number of historians of religion were already affirming the alterity of the ancients, when explaining their religious behaviors in light of practices observed in Africa or Australia. Their approach was tied to a grand objective: as philosophers, sociologists, or historians, they aimed to explain the birth of religion. Such was the aim in philosophy, as in sociology or history. The sociologist Émile Durkheim, like the philosopher Hegel before him, or his contemporaries, the so-called Cambridge ritualists[5] and the historian William W. Fowler,[6] sought the origin of religion or, at least, of particular religions. The comparativism practiced by Durkheim and Fowler did not differ on this point from the explicit approach of the Romantic philosophers.

Notwithstanding numerous useful observations, regarding, for example, collective behavior, their interpretations often resulted in theories of historical evolution necessarily oriented toward Christianity. The celebrated essay on sacrifice of Henri Hubert and Marcel Mauss is a case in point, as a comparative analysis of sacrificial rites in many types of religions issues in a Christian theory of the rite.[7]

All this is well known. Why, then, this return to an already old method of the history of religions, which was applied under the name of religious anthropology and taught in handbooks and monographs, and which appears to be a scientific achievement? It is of course entirely normal for a given mode of explanation to be criticized, not least one that is today more than fifty years old, if one refers to the works of Louis Gernet, Georges Dumézil, Marcel Detienne, or Jean-Pierre Vernant. Their works, and those they inspired, may contain errors and distortions, notably in their use of structuralism, which is often difficult to handle. The problem is rather that the objections now made to their work do not themselves seem relevant to the data at all and appear merely to recycle very old methods of explaining religious alterity in terms of our own religious categories, instead of seeking to understand it in its historical context.

The topic has not only general relevance. It applies also to a specific concept, that of the religion of the city, called *polis*-religion by those who criticize it. In the pages that follow, I will try to deconstruct this new theory, being unable to criticize ancient religions as the deconstructionists imagine it: one still awaits from them a convincing reconstruction of the religion of the ancients.

To speak frankly, opposition to the model of civic religion has gone on long enough and, at its basis, it consists always of the same arguments, dressed in new clothes. Already in 1912, in the introduction to the second edition of his handbook, Georg Wissowa responded to a critique that had been directed at him on the occasion of the first edition of his book, published in 1902.[8] Although the author of this review—in all likelihood Ulrich von Wilamowitz-Moellendorff[9]—recognized the value of the work, he found Wissowa's presentation excessively juridical: it exteriorized religious concepts and forms in conformity with the point of view of pontifical law; and it betrayed an obvious lack of sensitivity toward religiosity.

In point of fact, Wissowa's handbook was an important watershed in the historiography on Roman religion. It is not, however, in its historical perspective that Wissowa innovated, because the first part of his book, which his correspondence reveals to have been finished in about 1890, is relatively disappointing. Overall, that part makes only small advances beyond earlier manuals, apart from corrections to references. On one hand, Wissowa finds himself still under the influence of Hegel and his historical dialectic, and on the other, he is indebted to the Romantic notion of popular religion, of *Volksreligion*, as a pledge of authenticity. He therefore seeks to distinguish in the tradition between that which is originally Roman, which belongs organically to the religion of the Roman people, and that which comes from outside, from Greece. As it happens, Wissowa's inquiry was less a frantic search for prototypically Roman elements than a reaction against the indistinct commingling of Greek and Roman elements in contemporary treatments of ancient sources, such as was then the rule: Jupiter was Zeus, and Minerva Athena. Basically, Wissowa did not want to speak about Roman religion while citing Greek myths, as one still did in his day. From this point of view, he recovered a more correct picture of Roman religion. Nevertheless, it is true that Wissowa exaggerated in his approach, to the extent that he admitted that there had already been a mixture of "typically" Roman and foreign elements in the reign of King Numa, shortly after the foundation of Rome. Here one sees clearly the influence of Romantic *Volksreligion*, the religion of the people, a concept dear to Herder, who was followed in this by Hegel.[10] I will not dwell on the influence of these theories, to which I drew attention twenty-five years ago.[11] A second disappointing aspect of the first, historical part of Wissowa's handbook rests in his acceptance of a dominant theory of his day, according to which Roman religion had entered a state of decadence by the dawn of the empire, at the start of our era. This understanding was shared in that era by all specialists and also recalls features of Hegelian dialectic, according to which ancient Rome was characterized by a very impoverished degree of religious thought and at the same time by a fervent religiosity, which was prepared to accept any religious novelty. At the time, religious renewal took the form first of the so-called oriental cults, which were thought to prepare the way for Christianity. Thanks to the opening of the Mediterranean world by the Romans and their deep but "empty" piety, Christianity realized at last a union between the sensual and ecstatic piety of the Orient and the naïve but cool piety of the Greek variety. Apart from technical details, this entire part of Wissowa's handbook is therefore unsatisfactory, because the dialectical model that undergirds it has long since been abandoned, even if elements that supported that model have not themselves in turn been abandoned by all scholars, as we shall see.

However, Wissowa's book also contained a second part, which seems to correspond to the term *Kultus* in the title [*Religion und Kultus der Römer* (Religion and Cult of the Romans)]. Just as he finished the historical portrait, around 1890, Wissowa had discovered that this way of studying Roman religion could no longer suffice. At the request of Mommsen, Wissowa was reading the proofs of the second edition of the first volume of the corpus of Latin inscriptions, the one that contained the Roman calendars.[12] In doing so he realized that one could not continue to write religious history by confining oneself to speculation about archaic rites whose names are written in big letters on the calendars, relying on the similarly speculative interpretations of poets and mythographers. He appears to have realized that there existed an entire other part of Roman religion that had theretofore escaped study, that of the festivals and rites of the supposedly cynical and decadent era, which were also recorded on the calendars.[13] A second influence confirmed him in this discovery: his reading of the volumes of Mommsen's *Römisches Staatsrecht* (Roman Public Law), which had appeared at regular intervals during the early part of Wissowa's labors.[14] It was at this time that Wissowa decided to devote more attention to rites, to all rites, and not just those of the archaic period, as well as to Roman sacred law. These studies, which took ten years to complete, effectively shape the second, most innovative part of his handbook, which has ever since constituted the foundation of all expert study on Roman public cults.

As it happens, it is precisely this part of the book that shocked, and not the historical one, which was extremely conventional, as I have emphasized. The common reproach was that he had reduced Roman religion to cult, and public cult at that. In so doing, ran the critique, Wissowa's manual came to describe collections of priestly rules, of festivals conducted by magistrates and the elite, but presented nothing truly religious. One detects in this reproach the odor of secularist criticism against small-minded, small-town religion of the sort that Mommsen had identified with Rome in its decadence: a religion of a people devoted to (one might even say "lost in") the counting of rites to be observed and benefits sought and received, but deprived of true religiosity. We will return to this point, because the attack is in itself revealing. Let it suffice for now to study Wissowa's reply, which is in my view excellent: he

responded that he claimed the right to pose the question whether the concept of "religiosity" was indeed "a concept wholly fixed and constant for all
times and peoples."[15] For his part, he thought that the reproach directed at
the book should in fact be directed at the object of study, which is to say, at
Roman religion, as if to signify that it was itself responsible for this quality of
his portrait. In so writing, he did not specify exactly what he thought *in petto*
of Roman ritualism. According to the first part of his handbook, decline had
already commenced by the dawn of the empire. Like his teacher Mommsen,
he was compelled to render a rather negative judgment on the ritualistic and
self-interested piety of the Romans, even if he also tendered them a little more
indulgence. For Mommsen, who was agnostic, Roman religion strongly resembled the Catholicism that he encountered during his travels in Rome and
Italy. Because of his education in the Lutheran tradition, he abhorred this type
of religion. The Catholic Wissowa ought to have been less radical, although,
at the base, he had to share Mommsen's opinion. He nevertheless claimed the
right to study Roman religion and piety in their historical context, even as he
thought that all people had a right to their own beliefs. Perhaps his Catholic
conscience had been affronted by the Lutheran bent of the critique. We will
return to the confessional subtext, to Wissowa's choice, and to the critiques
leveled against his work, and to those that are still leveled today against his
wish to emphasize the alterity of Roman religion and against those who defend the same position.

Beyond the possibility that "religiosity" did not have the same form everywhere and always (the quotation marks are Wissowa's), and bracketing his
desire to separate out the influences exerted on Roman religion and place
them in historical sequence, the major contribution of Wissowa consists in
his description of Roman religion under the republic, from the fifth to the
first century BCE. He basically describes public religion, because it is about
this above all that the ancient sources speak and which in any event deserves
closer study. At times, when the sources permit, Wissowa remarks equally on
private rites. Overall, he recuperates a description of the religion of the Roman
people under the republic in the same terms as Roman historians, orators,
and thinkers, by seeking to reconstitute the rules and behaviors that can still
be reconstituted. The imperial era does not concern him except insofar as it
still adheres to this normativity, at least in the first century of the empire.
Moreover, it is important to observe that Wissowa did not align himself with

the ethnographic comparativism developed by Wilhelm Mannhardt or James G. Frazer, who proposed an alterity of a different type.[16] I cannot say whether Wissowa imagined a different form of comparativism, or if he rejected for whatever reason the way in which Anglo-French ethnology of that era analyzed ethnographic material, but the overall tone of his handbook appears to invite such an explanation.[17]

The Main Objections to the Theory of *Polis*-Religion

What are the modern criticisms of *polis*-religion? A first fact surprises. The term in question is always Greek *polis*, a surprising fact, and not the Latin term *civitas*. The explanation for the use of this terminology surely lies with the criticisms directed at an article written by Christiane Sourvinou-Inwood, published in 1990 in a collective volume, that summarized the chief aspects of the religion of the Greek *polis* as it had been analyzed in Paris and Great Britain over the previous two decades.[18] The strange neglect of the term (and concept) of *civitas* and also of the Romans is due to the fact that, according to conventional representation, the *polis* was dead by the third century BCE and the Roman *civitas* had already been left behind by the political, institutional, and demographic developments of the imperial republic. In any case, to apply the term *polis*-religion to a religious domain that was in fact much larger and which underwent an important evolution after the birth of the Greek *polis* is reductive and would seem to imply that historians of Roman religion who use this approach implicate themselves in an archaic model of limited chronological applicability.

A first criticism addressed to the works of such people concerns the social context of the rituals of public cult.[19] *Polis*-religion is described as a "civic compromise" that sought to establish a close link between sacrifice, euergetism—a form of public charity, or private funding of public goods—and domination. This model of priesthood and cult was imposed by the elite on its inferiors. The rural population would not have known the sacrificial system of the elites, which is to say, the cultic acts and distributions of meat in which all members of the *polis* were supposed to participate. Such a view is extraordinarily reductive. It signally neglects a fact that, indeed, critics of the civic model of religion always pass over in silence, to wit, that the population—the *entire* population—understood perfectly this system of sacrifice, because they practiced it in their families, in villages as well as the rural territories of city-states, and in the grand rural sanctuaries.

A second criticism urges that the masses would not actually have accepted the religious model of the elite. The gods who manifested themselves to ordinary people would have been more disquieting, more dominating than those of public cult, who worked for the well-being of all. The rapid expansion of the cult of Asclepios/Aesculapius is taken as testimony in favor of this argument, as well as the appearance of healer-heroes, the proliferation of small oracles and private mysteries, and the miracle workers and magicians. This expansion of the religious marked the limits of acceptance on the part of the masses of the cultic model imposed by the elite.

Such views must be qualified. First of all, the religious opposition between masses and elites, which hints at the importation of much later, Romantic ideas of Herder and Schlegel on the hidden riches of popular belief and folklore, must be questioned, because many of the cults in question were in fact introduced at Rome by the elites themselves. It was the Roman Senate that caused Asclepios/Aesculapius to come to Rome, and it was through the creation of Roman colonies—a statal act par excellence—that his cult was spread in northern Italy and through the Danubian territories. This devotion rapidly became a standard part of the cultic life of the Roman city. Second, and most important, to interpret the appearance in the third and second century BCE of immediately "useful" divinities (which is to say, divinities honored in exchange for expected services, such as healing or prosperity) as an important change in the religious life of the ancient city appears an over-interpretation of a simple fact: what is merely a consequence of an overall trend toward better documentation is taken as evidence of a profound historical evolution. It is only starting in the last two centuries BCE that we have sources available of sufficient detail and volume to get to know general aspects of religious life a little better, which is to say, the religious life of city-states, and also the religious life of subgroups within those city-states. As a correlate, this does not mean that the mere appearance of written evidence marks the appearance of a new "religiosity." Nothing precludes the possibility that similar cults—of Apollo, for example, or of Minerva—had existed already at an earlier period.

Moreover, in the eyes of Richard Gordon, the advent of new forms of religious behavior does not cast in doubt the model of civic religion, since in general they lay within its framework. They reveal, however, opposition to the dominant model, insofar as they demanded of their participants religious commitment and development.[20] It is at this juncture that the implicit and anachronistic opposition between civic and new religions is revealed as a theoretical postulate of critical scholarship. It is true, of course, that Greek and Roman authorities did not like secret cults, which imposed more or less stringent requirements on their followers, although it also needs to be emphasized that the "faithful" of these cults were not simply "the people," but often well-integrated and well-off citizens. All that to one side, when one reads that these new practices represented "a revalued conception of piety," questions are begged. A conception of piety is revalued in relation to what? In relation to a true "faith," more ancient, original, in greater conformity with the Romantic model of "religiosity," pure and true to its origins? Or in relation to what Minucius Felix called *vera religio*, "true religion," which is to say, Christianity? We return to the criticism directed against Wissowa.

Other criticisms of *polis*-religion are more global.[21] For example, *polis*-religion as described in the handbook of Louise Bruit and Pauline Schmitt-Pantel or the article of Sourvinou-Inwood granted a central place in the religion of city-states to cults shared among all the citizens.[22] These cults were directed and controlled by priests drawn from the elite, which retained religious authority on this basis. From this point of view, Greek and Roman city-states were identical. The most perfect realizations of this model were located in the city-states of archaic and classical Greece and at Rome. Later, the notion of *polis*-religion being diffused together with that of the city-state, the history of ancient religion was implicated in the fall of the classical city. After the decline of the ancient city, religion would no longer be a form of conduct tied to the city-state but became one choice among many groups who offered their own doctrines, experiences, and discrepant myths.[23] Here, again, one needs to nuance these claims. For one thing, it seems to me overly fast to date the decline of the city-state from the battle of Chaeronea in 338 BCE. This theory, which dates from the nineteenth century, has been successfully contested and overcome, first through the work of Louis Robert and Philippe Gauthier[24] and by many other historians of the second half of the twentieth century, to the point where one could now qualify the Hellenistic Age as a golden age of the classical city. One might likewise point to a remark of John North, who in the course of his argument refers to the third century CE: one cannot be said to prove much about broad changes in the history of religion in preceding periods through interpretive claims about evidence of that late date.

Finally, the chief reproach voiced against advocates of the model of *polis-religion* is that they ascribe everything to politics and overstate the historical salience of Romanization as well as Roman resistance to foreign influences.

Alongside these supposed characteristics of Roman cults, further weaknesses and failures of the model of civic religion are enumerated as follows:

- It is difficult on the basis of such a model to account for the complexity of ancient religion. According to this critique, the model cannot explain why successive layers of deities and cults were not syncretized by the religious authorities, so as to realize a certain order and harmony within the pantheon. For the moment, let it suffice to emphasize that in a polytheist regime the collective has no need to rationalize its pantheon, because diversity is its raison d'être.
- The model does not leave space for other aspects of religion that were important for some, such as myth or popular cults like those of Silvanus or the so-called Mothers in Germania. The problem here is that, in the Greco-Roman world, myth was not part of religion. Moreover, there existed domestic and private cults (like that of Silvanus) or local cults (like that of the Mothers). There was no reason to introduce them into the civic pantheon of Rome. Once again, these cults were tied to their social context and to the very structure of polytheism.
- The model is not able to explain change. It responded to changes that took place within some Mediterranean koinê. Thus, if the changes arose principally in the private sphere, every perspective that marginalized non-public cults was perforce incapable of taking those changes into account. The difficulty here is that, even if a single one of such private cults turns out to have been the start of a religious revolution, the mode of analysis of the other private cults proposed by critics of civic religion offers no better means to understand the reasons for this revolution.
- Treating private cult as a secondary religious phenomenon does not allow one to explain why paganism remained popular even when public cult had been abolished. This fact is paradoxical only

in appearance and can be easily explained: for a long time, private cult was not subject to the same prohibitions, and so it could endure after the promulgation of laws that in the first instance forbade only public cult.

- Greek myths antedated the city-state and were panhellenic; they were thus available to be used by the city-states that inscribed themselves within a framework greater than themselves. The great sanctuaries with which the city-states contended prove that cult sites were independent from their function within a specific city. Also, the oracles prove that there existed a religion superior to that of the *polis*. Finally, the temples of Asclepios at Epidauros and Pergamon, like the mysteries at Eleusis, were chiefly concerned with cult as celebrated by individuals. On these varied points, it is necessary to observe that the existence of federal cults or oracles external to the city is a banal given in the world of city-states. Nonetheless, one should also note that in the framework of panhellenism, it was not the Greeks who existed in federal union, but the Greek city-states, and moreover the cults and oracles functioned in a fashion closely homologous with the model of civic religion.

- Pilgrimage is also invoked, as well as human mobility, which would have led to the existence within city-states of numerous non-citizen inhabitants or metics. Because *polis*-religion is based on citizenship, it would have been less and less able to integrate the totality of religious actors, since these did not have citizenship. We will return to this question.

- There would have been a gap between public and private cults, and it is this gap that would have been the reason for change. It is through this gap that foreign cults would have inserted themselves. The very idea of such a gap or lacuna itself poses a problem. It seems to me to amount to the importation of an anachronistic "religiosity" rather than to the detection of a historically verifiable dissatisfaction experienced by participants in ancestral religions.

Overall, this series of claims is thought to demonstrate that, whatever its strength, *polis*-religion never in fact fulfilled its function, neither in the age of the archaic and classical Greek city, nor, certainly, in the age of the Hellenistic and Roman cities. It was a concern of elites, who tried thereby to impose their domination on the lower classes, without ever successfully colonizing their private lives. Not only would there always be cults outside and beyond the city, but individuals would have possessed religious activities more dynamic and enduring than those of the city. In sum, one has the impression that, below political and social institutions, existed Religion-with-a-capital-R: not the religion of Zeus, Jupiter, Minerva, and their companions, but the Religion of Cybele, Mithra, Isis, Aesculapius, and of the God of the Jews and Christians, or the gods of the Gauls, who were thought to address themselves to individuals. There was thus an opposition between religion and Religion, in such a way that the latter spoke to the individual and was not the product of some manipulation of the crowd nor a means of social and political control.

"Religiosity"

Clearly, behind all these separate criticisms lies the notion of religiosity, whose status as a universal was refuted by Georg Wissowa. It appeared in the Protestant context of early nineteenth-century Germany.[25] It refers to the subjective dimension of Christian religious experience, marked by its interiorization. This experience is opposed to objective, exteriorized religion, which (according to its theorists) finds expression in the institutions and dogmas of the Catholic Church.[26] This insistence on the feelings and emotions of the individual, on individual perception of the infinite, is memorably expressed in the work of Friedrich Schleiermacher on Christian faith, published at the start of the nineteenth century.[27] Effectively, he placed primary value on the private religious experience of the individual contemplating the universe. This contemplation triggers and shapes religious emotion, to the extent that by this means the individual recognizes and feels supreme order and his or her own absolute dependence in spiritual matters on the divine creator who animates everything. In other words, piety in itself is neither a knowing nor a doing, but a feeling and certainty of one's dependence.[28] This foundational principle eliminated as much as possible any role in religion for religious institutions. The individual could thus take himself to an existing church or just as easily to one he himself created. Indeed, in Schleiermacher's theology there is a sense in which even the biblical tradition lost its central importance, since only pious feeling counted. This is a paradox in Schleiermacher's thought that theologians have debated extensively, but it is not what interests us here.

Schleiermacher's approach has shaped the study of antiquity since Hegel and his successors. One example among many is Richard Reitzenstein, a professor of philology at the University of Strasbourg who tried to interpret the Judeo-Christian tradition commencing from pagan antiquity, which is to say, commencing under the empire, as a monotheist religion of a savior originating in the Orient.[29] Reitzenstein identified in Roman antiquity, in the Secular Games of Augustus, for example, the birth of a new form of religion, a "religiosity" that he imagined as an interiorization of religion. Observe right away that nothing connected to this celebration in the ancient sources authorizes this gratuitous claim, which is profoundly marked by a Christian ideology. It is therefore not without reason that Jerzy Linderski once criticized a colleague for transforming the Augustan historian Livy into a member of a Protestant church.[30]

To be sure, it has been urged that, confronted with varied religious formalisms, the advocates of "religiosity" were often inspired less directly by Christian ideas than by Schleiermacher's definition of religion.[31] The essential point, however, is that "by introducing the subjective and existentialist component of 'feeling,' Schleiermacher reduced religion to a predominantly private spiritual experience of the divine."[32] Duly noted. But historiographic precision aside, what does this change? It is still a matter of a definition of religion provided by a Lutheran theologian and based in the tradition of western Christianity. It is not a neutral definition of religion, which can have many variants.

It is, moreover, insufficient merely to reject references to "religiosity" in order to free oneself from notions of faith and private "religiosity." For this, one would do well to employ other comparisons. This is the criticism that was addressed to Wissowa, for it turns out that research conducted with different points of reference calls into question the universal character of Christian definitions of faith and religiosity.

Another argument: the hesitation of ancient historians to refer to this Schleiermachian category of faith would be all the more surprising if one were to consider that no one has questioned its utility as regards Christian beliefs of the Middle Ages.[33] It would therefore be uniquely true of the non-Christian civilizations of antiquity that their interiorized emotion and private belief cannot be the objects of modern study. Is it necessary to respond to this argument at length? One could easily imagine that this Romantic category might actually be relevant to medieval religious practices, which were essentially Christian, although the historian might still wonder if reference to this Lutheran or post-Tridentine conception of faith really enhances our understanding of the beliefs of persons of the Middle Ages. In any case, applied to non-Christian antiquity, the concept does not work. This is what produced a universal consensus in the nineteenth century, to the effect that Roman religion was not a religion at all, and thus motivated the search for the seeds of a *vera religio*, a true religion. Nor is it a matter of arguing that adversaries of this theology of history ultimately refer, whatever they might say, to a Christian notion of faith, because this would be false. In fact, they take into account other models of belief and religious practice, that of the Jews, for example, of whom one never hears a word in such studies, or those of the Indians, the Chinese, or the Japanese, or those observed by anthropologists during the second half of the twentieth century in America and Africa. Even the volume in which Andreas Bendlin published the study that elaborates the ideas I have cited here includes a chapter by an anthropologist sufficient to illustrate my point.[34]

In consequence, the point of the disagreement does not concern the acceptance or rejection of the model put forward by Schleiermacher. It concerns, rather, the existence or nonexistence of a universal and timeless category of belief, as well as the possibility of reducing this universal category to the form given it by Schleiermacher. Adversaries of the model of civic religion essentially deny the existence of any other way of regarding religion and, as a related matter, insist upon situating religious practice in a different category than other forms of social conduct, just as a Christian science of religion does. Please note: this is not a reproach. I do not regard this position as erroneous. From a Christian point of view, it is entirely correct. From a neutral, scientific, and historical point of view, however, it is not the only possible one.

Finally, it is necessary to devote a few words to another criticism, which concerns how one understands ritual. In general, this issue has been wholly absent from critiques of the model of civic religion, although it is in fact central or, in any case, it has become such under the influence of contemporary anthropology. Critics sometimes allude to the issue, but only in order to contest that rites can be collective representations of communal identity. The criticism in brief runs as follows: such a status for ritual (as an expression of communal identity) is unworkable, since it would be impossible to create a common identity among practitioners who would have discrepant notions of what the ritual scene was playing at. Ritual would have been powerless to communicate meaning that could forge a community. This is a point to which I will return.

To set forth why I believe it is correct to see a powerful religious ideology behind the superficially deconstructive appearance of the theory attributed to Wissowa and his distant descendants, allow me to cite the recent thesis of a Protestant theologian produced at Tübingen.[35] The author there speaks bluntly about matters on which ancient historians are silent or speak only in half-truths. First, he makes an explicit choice between two possible modes of analysis, that associated with Gustav Mensching and Joachim Wach,[36] which understands religion as belonging to the individual as an autonomous being, on the one hand, and that of Durkheim, Numa Denis Fustel de Coulanges, and advocates of *polis*-religion, on the other, which accepts as foundational the possible existence of other religious systems. Second, it is clear that the author attaches himself to a Christian and theological mode of religious history. In effect, his objective is to understand Christianity and the difficulties it encountered in the Roman empire. One apparently finds in the confrontation between Christianity and empire an instantiation of "an always already extent religious dynamic" "of tension between individual and collective religion."[37] Why would this dynamic be always existent? In light of what historical necessity?

Finally, once again we encounter an argument that seeks to show that religions cannot have had as their sole object and effect the constitution of identity; rather, beyond this, ancient people would have sought and discovered in religion a deeper feeling, which responded to an inner need.[38]

Returning to the impact of the ideas of Schleiermacher, Hegel, and Protestant religious ethics, these were very influential up until the First World War. Nor was it only ancient historians who sought to explain the advent of Christianity in a Hegelian perspective. This ambition found expression also in the works of the sociologists Georg Simmel and Max Weber.[39] At the center of their work one finds not institutionalized religion, but "religiosity" understood as a fundamental psychological and emotional disposition that characterizes the individual. Sociological discourse in this vein therefore sees in the attitude of the individual, who recognizes his or her absolute dependence in respect of God, a decisive factor in the birth of the religious.[40] So it is that Simmel derives the sense of the divine from the fear of death, from metaphysical enigma and from the need for consolation that these call forth. Religious feeling is therefore independent from organized religion: it is rather a feeling of piety and a need to believe that forms part of a disposition that is constituent of the human. In Simmel's words, "If one looks very closely, all ostensible attempts to trace the origin of religiousness always tacitly assume its preexistence; it will thus be better to recognize it as a primary quality that cannot be derived from anything else."[41] In other words, it is a human universal. Two aspects of this approach seem essential, to the extent that they would permit the method to respond to problems of a general nature: on the one hand, the possibility it holds out to explain all social action on the basis of this famous individual psychological datum; and on the other, the capacity that this approach claims for itself, that of superseding particular cultural specificity-states in order to speak to some multidimensional or universal level. One can see how this approach contrasts with that of Georg Wissowa, who in the first instance studied institutionalized religion and assigned himself the task of understanding the otherness of Roman understandings of religion, such as they were. In particular, he insisted upon a dichotomy between personal "religiosity" and exteriorized religion. For the critics of the concept of civic religion, the goal of inquiry should be to surmount this traditional dichotomy of subject and object, or, one might say, to apprehend conjointly the domains of culture and of emotion, of institutionalized religion and the dimension of individual psychology.[42]

This claim has the merit of being clear. In itself, it does not shock, because it is what we all try to do. Wissowa's was the first attempt. Since then, there has been some progress, provided, however, that one does not assess every individual behavior against the model of modern Western individualism, nor every form of religious conduct in light of Christian "religiosity," as it is conceived and promoted within certain milieus.

It should be noted in passing that this debate over civic religion occurs neither in comparative studies nor in social anthropology. It is easy to see why: those disciplines are opposed to universalist claims of the sort advanced on behalf of phenomenology or "religiosity" as it has been understood since Schleiermacher claimed universal status for it. This is how it offers historians a means to infallible interpretation. For the same reason, Wissowa presents a clear challenge to advocates of this interpretive scheme because of the rigor with which he interrogates the evidence. According to Andreas Bendlin, Wissowa was motivated to this rigor by a desire to defend his discipline, Latin, as a scientific domain in its own right and not, that is, by any concern for principles of interpretation in the history of religion.[43] Regardless of how one trivializes Wissowa's way of interpreting and analyzing the available sources, it is methodological madness to reduce the understanding of patterns in the ancient sources in the historical study of Roman civilization to claims about Latinists defending their place in the world. Does this mean that when one practices the history of religions, it is better to oppose the documents supplied by one's objects of study and rely instead on one's own personal (supposedly universal) conception of the religious and religion? Does this mean that philologists alone are obliged to yield to their sources? To regard the matter thus is ultimately to deny history the status of method or science, in favor of some sort of philosophy or Christianizing theology.

We will rediscover and revisit these arguments throughout this essay, when we examine the difficulties supposedly encountered by the model of civic religion as it has been employed by some number of scholars in Paris and England.

Chapter 2

Polis and Republic

The Price of Misunderstanding

One precondition for the study of a problem like the nature of religion in the Greco-Roman world is to know well the historical context of the object of study. This is not a matter solely of contextualizing one's analysis by situating it within some field of academic debate, but also, with equal rigor, of contextualizing the ancient sources that one cites. No one would be so ridiculous as to explain the findings of archaeologists in their samplings by reference to contemporary material culture, but this is what happens in certain studies of ancient religion. The resulting misinterpretations are numerous, and I will consider some examples of this kind. They concern not only matters of detail, of the kind about which this or that specialist or group of specialists might disagree, or disagreements about method. They concern, rather, fundamental and general disagreements.

These errors are frequently attributable to the separation between different fields of scholarship. The Greeks of the philosophers are not those of the historians; the Romans read by patristic scholars and theologians generally have little to do with those of the historians and archaeologists. During the 1960s, Jean-Pierre Vernant had such an impact because, in order to treat a question, he drew upon the different sciences of the study of antiquity: philosophy, history, philology, the history of art, economics, social history, and anthropology. Nor was his research on religion detached from more recent scientific developments. He encouraged comparative study, by inviting all scholars who worked on antiquity to participate in a given research project.

This methodological advance has not found an opening in certain areas of study: in philosophy, literature, or theology, and in the German university system, for example, it is largely unknown and always provokes surprise and perhaps even suspicion. The results of Vernant's research of this kind are today judged by one or another discipline, such as philology or epigraphy or theology, and often the specialists do not find anything to interest them, quietly regarding the social conduct of the Greeks as brought to light by Vernant and his collaborators as of little interest to their own projects or little relevance to the history of Greece in general. This is because they do not understand what Vernant was talking about.

What Is a Roman City?

It is the same with the problems that I am seeking to explore. The main contributors to the debate have only a very vague idea of what an ancient city-state was and, hence, of the way in which individuals integrated themselves in society. It is not a particularly innovative methodological move to suppose at the outset that this is not a historical problem, or to say that this question is not one that needs to be posed, because the form of the civic community has no particular relationship to actual society. If we deconstruct the arguments used to defend this position, we find once again the old theory of the decadence of the ancient city after Chaeronea, after the fall of Athens under the blows of Macedon and the advent of the Hellenistic age. Thereafter, the city as civic community would have dissolved into larger structures. It is significant that all authors admit that the system of *polis*-religion was in fact able to function in the framework of the archaic Greek city-states and in Rome of earliest times. Later, in each case, the world and society would have changed to such an extent that city and citizen would no longer have been the principal units of social interaction, but the individual confronted with a distant power.

Often, historians establish a direct link between the Hellenistic and Roman empires and the form of religious practice.[1] And always, *polis*-religion is relegated to the archaic period. In the Hellenistic and Roman periods, by contrast, *polis*-religion would have been weakened and defeated at the same as the traditional city-states were, and the lonely individual would have henceforth made his or her own religious choices from among the totality of cults and gods offered thanks to the opening of the Mediterranean. More precisely, it would have been from the fourth century BCE that the evolution and differentiation of religious choices in the Mediterranean world would have led to the collapse of civic religion, which would have been unable to integrate the new options.[2] Then, commencing with the triumviral period through the last quarter of the first century CE, deviations in public life from earlier norms in public religion would have become obvious. These deviations revealed the diversification of the religious system and provoked ongoing reevaluation of the role of cults in society. Put another way, according to these people, the history of religion in antiquity is actually the history of the destabilization and dissolution of civic religion, which was unable to coexist with social structures that exceeded a certain level of complexity.

The Myth of the Decline of the City

Let us examine these claims in detail. For the moment, it suffices to recall that the modern myth of the decline and disappearance of city-states in favor of more complex systems was long ago denounced and corrected by Louis Robert, Philippe Gauthier, and numerous other historians. One can admit without difficulty that one phase in the history of city-state civilization ended when foreign kings, in the form of Philip of Macedon, Alexander the Great, and their successors came to dominate Greek lands. Henceforth, city-states were no longer able to have an autonomous foreign policy or, in other words, to make war and choose their enemies and allies on their own. Also, for a while, it was equally impossible for them to freely choose their own magistrates. But beyond these restrictions, Greek city-states continued to be Greek city-states, functioning and evolving according to the model of the so-called classical city. The Macedonian and Hellenistic monarchies did not have the means wholly to control the city-states, and the citizens of the Greek city-states did not become members of the Macedonian or Seleucid monarchies to which they were subordinated. They remained citizens of Athens, Thebes, Rhodes, or Ephesus, and they conducted themselves as such. What was terminated in the fourth century BCE was the age of the myth of the Greek city. One could compare what happened to the Greeks with that which occurred in Europe after the First and even more after the Second World War. The age of the absolute preeminence of Europe was then ended. The myth of Europe, the leader of the world and of civilization, still exists and, from time to time, particular European states pretend that nothing has changed. But the facts are there. Henceforth, world politics and economic life are shaped by other states and continents. And yet, who would say that the European states have been dissolved? That they are in full decline, together with the entirety of European culture? That one can no longer analyze France, for example, in light of its constitution, society, and culture?

Similarly, the Greeks continued to the end of antiquity to live in city-states and to order life according to this model. City-states evolved, as they had evolved from the sixth to the fourth century BCE; they came to employ a backwards-looking rhetoric and lamented the passing of that glorious age when they had dictated terms to the king of Persia. But this did not prevent them from being passionate about the political debates that took place in their city-states, before and after the Macedonian or Roman conquest.

Nor was Roman experience any different. Its ascension to the status of world power over the course of the six centuries before this era, between the period of the Etruscan kings and the advent of empire, is well known. From the start of the fifth century BCE, Rome organized itself as a *respublica*, a city-republic, with citizens, magistrates, Senate, and laws, and it evolved greatly over the next centuries. Over time, it conquered Italy; later, at the head of an alliance combining the city-states of Italy under its power, it discovered how to resist Carthage, before spreading both east and west while subduing nearly the entirety of the known world. This imperial phase had two consequences at an institutional level. First, the Roman republic had to adapt to the demands of its imperial project, to endow itself with magistracies capable of waging wars permanently on all fronts and to build institutions that combined at the same time effectiveness as well as the defense of essential civic liberties. This prepared the way for the general-magistrates who would contest with each other for power in the last century of the republic.

The second grand change that took place at Rome and in Italy over this period concerned a central element of civic life: the definition of the body politic. In the archaic period, many city-states had known a degree of horizontal social mobility—a circulation of elites—and thus a relatively easy policy with their citizenship. But, over time, the Greek city-states gradually imposed strict limits on grants of citizenship. For this reason, their civic bodies were relatively small, which from a military point of view constituted a clear disadvantage, because the armies of city-states were composed of citizens. From this perspective, Rome remained an archaic city. Oligarchic, yielding the franchise based on tax status, Rome had a much more open conception of citizenship. It progressively integrated the populations of city-states that submitted to it, as citizens of full right or of secondary status—the famous Latin citizens, who possessed only some of the rights of a Roman citizen. It was these who offered to the Romans a virtually inexhaustible supply of soldiers, the famous allies, the *socii*, of whom the alliance with the Latins of the fifth and fourth centuries BCE constituted a prefiguration. At the same time, it was perfectly normal for Romans to free their slaves, who on this basis became citizens. Magistrates could equally well grant citizenship to people whom they favored. This does not mean that the Romans treated citizenship as a cheap commodity, even in Italy. The process was slow and took centuries before becoming an important phenomenon. In the period of the Second Punic War (218–202 BCE), at the end of the third century BCE, its effects were already making themselves visible, and they would be one of the reasons for Roman victory. The major change came after the Social War, the war with the *socii*, the allies, when in 90 BCE the Italians, citizens of the second category and the principal bearers of the toils of war, revolted against Roman hegemony. The Romans prevailed, but in the course of the years that followed the victory, all the citizens of the Italian city-states became Roman citizens of full right.

From then, the *respublica* of the Romans counted more citizens than any other city or civic polity in the world: in 70 BCE, after the Plautian–Papirian law of 89 BCE, which conferred Roman citizenship on all Italians, one is given the figure of nine hundred thousand male citizens; at the beginning of the principate of Augustus, in 28 BCE, the count is four million citizens, including women and children. Such a number of citizens had previously been unimaginable. But this spectacular expansion, which constitutes a profound change to the Roman world, in no way caused the city-states of Italy to break down. On the contrary, it reinforced them, by incorporating them in the very definition of citizenship.

It is essential to understand how the system of the city-states functioned after the Plautian–Papirian law, which distributed citizenship throughout the city-states of Italy, which gradually became either *municipia*, to wit, autonomous municipalities, or colonies of Roman right. Every Italian had to make a declaration before the urban praetor, at Rome, to indicate the city of origin in which he wished to be enrolled. It is by virtue of his city-state or political community of origin, his "little fatherland," that he became a Roman citizen, and it is there that ever after he had his *origo*, his legal place of origin. From this time, a Roman citizen had a double belonging, to his natural fatherland or fatherland of birth, and a universal fatherland, Rome. A number of authors seem to me to confuse everything when they reduce this double belonging to a simple hierarchy of the duties of loyalty, higher to Rome, lower to one's local polity.[3] Of course there is a hierarchy of duties, but the two types of duties and, indeed, of rights are not exclusive of one another. Each is as strong as the other.

It is not necessary to conclude that, after 89 BCE, Roman citizenship was granted by the separate Roman city-states. Nothing could be more incorrect. Roman citizenship was acquired by birth or adoption, by manumission and enfranchisement when one was a slave, or by a grant of the Roman people, generally through the intermediation of magistrates, and under the empire by benefaction of the emperor. This means on the one hand that Roman citizenship remained under the control of the central power, and on the other that the site of registration for citizens who did not live at Rome was the Roman city-states of Italy and the provinces. The city became an indispensable level, or perhaps locus, of Roman citizenship. Indeed, the legal system was so arranged that a Roman citizen of Italy or a province who found himself at Rome was not legally absent from his domicile of origin. On this entire topic, one should have recourse to the works of the lamented Yan Thomas, which some historians have ignored, to their loss.[4] The Roman jurists studied by Thomas naturally had their own ways of reasoning, in virtue of their particular objectives, but one cannot simply regard the evidence of the jurists as fantasies. Their arguments take into consideration the question of whether one does or does not have citizenship as well as privileges or obligations as regards liability for taxation—in brief, extremely important details about daily life—which endows their legal deliberations with highly concrete aspects.

To this must be added the fact that Roman origin could be acquired not only by birth or manumission by a citizen of full right, enrolled in a Roman colony or municipium, but also in communities of Roman citizens legally recognized by Rome and installed in foreign city-states. It is always through a place of Roman origin, through a Roman community, that Roman citizenship was conferred. And if the emperor gave citizenship to an individual, which happened often, he always enrolled that person in a Roman city of the empire.

After the Social War, the presence of Roman citizens in the city-states of Italy ceased to pose a problem, because all those city-states were henceforth Roman. In the provinces, where peregrine, which is to say, city-states alien in respect to Rome, were the large majority, the presence of Roman citizens could create strong inequalities. Indeed, citizens of these communities who also possessed Roman citizenship could profit from the privileges of being Roman and, with the complicity of the provincial governor, they could commit abuses, not least regarding jurisdictional rules, which were a potent source of conflict. Augustus tried to resolve this problem with the edicts of which we possess the version addressed to the province of Cyrenaica, in North Africa.[5] One there finds in outline what will become the rule in the imperial era. The changes made by Augustus concerned above all fiscal exemptions and exemptions from other local obligations that Roman citizens—particularly the wealthy—tried to escape. These abuses were most problematic in alien city-states, but they could also affect Roman city-states and place in peril the system of obligations and duties in these small civic communities, because it was possible to obtain immunities at Rome that were then extended to the city-states where the persons concerned were resident. The reform enacted by Augustus drew a strong distinction between Roman citizenship and exemption from charges and duties in one's community of origin. In particular, fiscal immunity had to be expressly conferred, and it was limited to goods owned at the moment the grant was made. In this way, local city-states were not voided of their most important taxpayers and candidates for elected offices essential to their functioning. Later, the principles visible in the Augustan texts become clearer still. Thanks to an array of documents, we know that in the second third of the second century, for example, an alien's obtaining of Roman citizenship implied no diminution of taxes, fees, or duties arising from the customs or laws of one's city of origin.[6] The new citizen saw no modification as regards his situation interior to his little fatherland. He retained his obligations there and benefited in return from the possibility of living according to local law. Christopher Jones has written about Athenian Roman citizens of this era: they were local magistrates, preserved the family law of aristocratic families of Athens, and settled some of their disputes before local tribunals, according to Athenian law.[7]

In spite of all these changes, the world of the city-states continued its life and development under the Roman Empire, and it is absurd to continue to speak of the decline, the implosion, or the disappearance of the city as one did in the nineteenth century. Such talk has no meaning once one breaks free from the artificial dialectical structures in which it was embedded. Every free inhabitant of the empire lived in a city-state or, for the marginal populations, in a tribe. Regardless whether any given city-state was of alien status, a *munici-pium*, or a Roman colony, they were all autonomous. They were of course subject to the power of Rome and provincial governors, to whom they paid taxes if they were not freed from them, as were some Roman colonies—Cologne and Carthage, for example—but they all administered themselves by means of their own institutions. Only the colonies, which were Latin or Roman, were obliged to function according to Roman law and to use Roman institutions. A colony was a city founded directly by Rome, whether or not colonists came directly from the metropole. A colony was like a district of Rome transplanted to the empire, sometimes on territory where there had been no Mediterranean city, as, for example, at Narbonne or Lyon, or superimposed on a preexistent city, as at Carthage. Colonies were classified as either Latin or Roman. Latin colonies were composed of Roman citizens and former aliens belonging to the local population. Persons of this latter type, who benefited from an inferior form of Roman citizenship, the so-called Latin right, could accede to full Roman citizenship by holding a local magistracy. In Roman colonies, all citizens were Roman citizens, and Roman public and private law were imposed on everyone. These colonies were not free and were subordinate to all the laws of Rome.[8] *Municipia*, by contrast, maintained a continuity with their pre-Roman alien past: the institutions created at the moment of their foundation as a Roman city were therefore not necessarily Roman and might perpetuate preexisting traditions. Municipal citizens therefore had the right to live according to local institutions and local law, even though they were all Roman citizens.[9] Again, there were both Roman and Latin *municipia*. As for city-states alien in respect to Rome, which were very numerous in the empire, nothing whatsoever prevented them from functioning according to their own traditions and institutions.[10]

We are therefore far from the disappearance of city-states and the erasure of local customs and institutions, another myth of modern historiography. Even when, in 212 CE, the famous edict of Caracalla (the so-called Antonine

Constitution) granted citizenship to all free persons of the empire, this juridical elevation changed nothing in their daily life. They continued to live in
their city-states, in conformity with local institutions, even if, henceforth, all
benefited from what had theretofore been a privilege: double citizenship, local
and Roman. Even then, one cannot speak of the end of the city-state—for as
we have already seen, free persons of the empire were not registered abstractly
with Rome even in their capacity as Roman citizens. There was no "citizenship
of the empire." As before, they acquired even Roman citizenship in their city
of origin, and it is always through those city-states that they were registered at
Rome. Moreover, as Claude Lepelley demonstrated twenty years ago, the city-
state survived as the framework for daily life for the population of the empire
until the fifth century CE, and it was only under the blows of the Alamanni,
Vandals, and Goths that, little by little, the world of the city-state sank into
the Middle Ages.[11]

It is therefore necessary to distance ourselves from the old historiographic
model that fixed the end of the age of the city-state in the fourth century
BCE and understood the Roman Empire as a fundamentally different, even
superior form of political life, in the same way in which, in Prussia, the great
historians who diffused this model—Johann Gustav Droysen and Theodor
Mommsen—called for the unification of Germany and the surmounting of
the world of small principalities, which they instinctively identified with the
city-states of the ancient world.

Moreover, one should not assume that the institutions of the city-state
were uniquely strong in Italy and in Rome. They were strong throughout the
provinces. There were of course differences between contexts. The Greek east
included a large number of old city-states that enjoyed great prestige among
the Romans. Apart from some colonies founded by Augustus after the civil
wars, all the *poleis* continued to exist, in a more or less brilliant fashion according to their historical evolution. In the West, the Romans encountered a
different landscape, including several entire regions, in Gaul and the Iberian
peninsula, where there existed as yet no city-states of the Mediterranean type,
and others where they took over earlier city-states, as in Africa. Everywhere,
however, they impelled or promoted the emergence and development of city-
states. And when it was a matter of Roman city-states, whether colonies or
municipalities, the institutions were always the same in all the provinces. A
city was always a conurbation with a territory that could be more or less grand:

"One used the term *civitas* for a place and a town and also the legal status of a population and of a population of human beings," writes Aulus Gellius.[12] The term thus possesses multiple meanings. The city was a material reality, a town with a territory; it was also founded upon a juridical idea: the right of a city; finally, the term designated the body politic of the city. The ensemble constituted the city, not simply the monumentalized urban core, as there was a tendency to believe in scholarship inflected by nationalist tendencies, in which the Gauls or Germans or Africans were imagined as resisting the Roman invaders and living peaceably among them on the territory of the city-states, but far from the towns that the Roman occupied. This approach makes no sense; there is no reason to believe that city-states were different in Gaul, in Iberia, in Italy, in Africa, or in Asia Minor. But this way of representing city-states, as towns of colonists, merchants, and Roman functionaries, like towns of the Middle Ages or the European colonial empires, is still widespread. Nothing reveals this better than terminology. In Germany, one always translates *civitas* by *Stadt*, "city," never by *Stadtstaat*, "city-state," in large measure because at the start of the twentieth century, the German scholars who set the tone could not accept that the city-states of Germany also embraced their rural territories, which were thought to be the framework of life for the Germans.[13]

These are all the differences between the modern political and social landscape that it is necessary to have in mind in order to reflect on the place of religion in a world of city-states.

Chapter 3

The Individual in the City

We have seen that criticism of the historiographical model of civic religion was in part indebted to a dated vision of the city and its supposed decline in the fourth century BCE. I have argued briefly that city-states continued throughout antiquity to constitute the material and legal framework for the life of individuals, in both the Hellenistic and Roman worlds.

I described the different types of city known under the Roman Empire and underlined that a city possessed a territory that might include dependent villages: it is the ensemble of this little state that formed the city-state. The city-states of the Roman Empire largely administered themselves, and there can be no question of imagining that Roman power somehow directed everything. Had it wanted to do this, its material and human resources would never have sufficed to the task. The Romans, which is to say, Roman promagistrates, governed the provinces at a very abstract level, by collecting taxes and maintaining the peace, making war, and holding assize courts. All the rest fell to the supervision of the city-states and their citizens.

What Was the Place of the Individual in the City?

The first general remark that one can make is that, after the defeat at Chaeronea in 388 BCE, after the creation of the Hellenistic monarchies, and after the conquest of the civilized world by the Romans, individuals remained integrated in a sufficiently dense network of occupations, responsibilities, and duties and did not become bored and seek refuge in individualist preoccupations and contemplation of the absolute. They could be magistrates or local officials and participate in one way or another in the administration of their city, of the provinces, or of the empire, according to their personal status. For many, Roman power could be distant, and they would find on the spot a strong and effective power, that of their city, which needed them—and to exercise this power through magistracies, there was, in fact, competition. Members of the elites competed with each other to hold office. Among Roman citizens, some rose progressively to equestrian rank and so belonged to a Roman aristocracy spread throughout Italy and the provinces. This aristocracy furnished judges for tribunals at Rome and one portion of the high administrative offices of the empire. Some equestrians achieved a senatorial career, if they had the necessary connections to have themselves chosen by their peers to fulfill one of the magistracies at Rome and then be chosen by the Senate and emperor for a post as governor of a province or commander of an army.

The situation was indeed different than daily life had been in the archaic and classical worlds, when day-to-day power was exercised in small city-states. To be sure, some lamented with nostalgia the passage of this age in the history of the city, as we regret the lost villages and small towns of yesteryear. But I do not believe that the inhabitants of the empire suffered in consequence of this evolution. On the contrary, I think the majority lived their relationship to power in a strongly traditional way, in relatively small city-states. This is actually a false problem. The city of Rome, which was extraordinarily large and complex, posed a problem that recurred in a few great metropolises of the empire: Carthage, Antioch, Alexandria. But one cannot situate Rome in hermeneutic relation to the rest of the world. At the provincial level, where Rome controlled only the upper echelon of power and justice, daily life resembled life in the past. Only in capital cases was jurisdiction reserved to the governor and, in certain cases, it could come about that even this power was delegated. For the rest, power was local, which means that the life of individuals did not change much compared with earlier eras. In the past, the autonomy of city-states depended on the goodwill of their neighbors and their own military power. Under Rome, the autonomy of city-states was protected by Rome and by its troops. This may have been less exciting, as individuals knew the next conflict in local politics was profoundly unlikely to change their life but, in totality, city-states realized more advantages than disadvantages, even if educated persons like Plutarch or Pausanias mourned the loss of some absolute freedom. But had such freedom existed even in the past? We are in the presence of a myth.

It is therefore not necessary to cite this modern historiographical myth, of the individual as a product of the imperialism of the Hellenistic monarchies and of Rome. The only effect of this historical evolution that one can discover is that the creation of the Hellenistic kingdoms and above all the Roman Empire permitted even less fortunate individuals to move throughout the Roman world without excessive risk. In this perspective, the individual had certainly earned a new liberty. The possible award of Roman citizenship in addition to one's local citizenship assured to each person a flexibility in relation to both local and Roman power that one's ancestors had never known, because Roman citizenship was granted more generously than anything comparable in earlier political regimes.

Let us consider precisely the situation of the individual in the city-states of the Roman era. My period is the end of the republic and the empire, between the third century BCE and the fourth century CE, because this is when the great changes that we are examining are supposed to have taken place.

The Individual and the Different Communities of the City-States

One of the most characteristic aspects of the ancient world is that the individual was not, as today, abstractly a member of the state to which he belongs. We are defined as French, German, or Italian, and our place of residence has only administrative and fiscal importance. Regarding our families, the topic matters only for fiscal reasons or those arising from social insurance. In the Roman world, one must stress, the situation was different. If all the citizens of a city shared the same rights and obligations—some more, some less—as is expected in a state with juridically determined ranks, the quality of being a citizen did not exhaust all the rights and obligations of individuals. Every citizen belonged to a family, and within that family citizens were subordinated to the power of the *pater familias* (the head of the family), who exercised real power over its members. A large number of delicts could only be judged within the family, with sanctions that could be capital. I cite as evidence the Augustan legislation against adultery, which intervened for the first time in the familial domain. Henceforth, in consequence of the Julian law on adultery of

18 BCE, if after sixty days a manifest act of adultery had not been acted upon by some family sanction, any citizen could bring a complaint before a tribunal against the guilty individual.[1] The power of the father of a Roman family was gradually nuanced and circumscribed, but the family always remained a site of power relations on which many aspects of individual life depended.

It should also be noted that there never was a unification of law. All the city-states possessed their own customs, and Roman conquest was never followed by the imposition of some totality of Roman laws and norms. This was not even the case in colonies, where reference to Roman law was automatic. Likewise in *municipia* composed entirely of Roman citizens. What is more, after 212 CE, when all free persons acquired the status of Roman citizens, there continued to be important differences between Roman customs and those of local communities. In the Greek world, for example, which is to say in Greek communities alien in respect to Rome, customs always remained local.

I have spoken of Romans and aliens. A word of explanation is necessary. A Roman is not anyone living under Roman power, but someone whose legal status derives from belonging to a Roman city. From this point of view, an alien is the equivalent of a foreigner. He or she is the citizen of another city or of another kind of community—a tribe, a kingdom—and does not possess Roman citizenship. It is not a defect to be alien, if one excepts the possible abuses to which one might be exposed abroad. Under the Roman republic, abuses were more frequent, as citizenship was less generously distributed and the conquest phase was much harder on non-Romans than the era that followed. Of course, while in one's own land, someone alien in respect to Rome remained subject to the customs of his or her homeland. Otherwise, in another city or at Rome, one depended on the power of local policing. The example of Paul of Tarsus arriving in the Roman colony of Philippi in Macedonia is a case in point. Arrested for disturbing local order, thrown in prison and beaten—things that were common when dealing with an alien—Paul caused great embarrassment for the local authorities of Philippi when he let them know that he was a Roman citizen, which saved him from being tortured.[2] The embarrassment derives less from the fact that he had been whipped, which could happen to a Roman citizen, than from the fact that this had occurred without any intervening judgment. When much later he was arrested in Jerusalem, Paul let it be known that he was a Roman citizen and desired to be judged as such, which saved him from being subject to local

laws, according to which he risked capital punishment.[3] A first meeting of the
Sanhedrin with the military tribune who had arrested Paul nearly became so
violent that the officer made his return to the fortress accompanied by soldiers. Next, he caused Paul to be taken to Caesarea, the seat of the prefect of
Judaea, along with a strong escort. The prefect interrogated him but reached
no decision. For two years Paul remained in prison, the time necessary for a
new prefect to arrive. According to the narrative in the Acts of the Apostles,
the accusers of Paul seized him immediately. And when the prefect wanted to
encourage Paul to bring himself to Jerusalem and to submit to a legal process
in his presence, the apostle appealed to the emperor, according to a privilege
of Roman citizens that developed under the empire. This appeal put an end
to this phase of the case, because Paul had to be sent to Rome immediately.
However, he could always have made the opposite choice and accepted to be
judged by the Jewish authorities. King Agrippa, who arrived at Caesarea some
days after these events, held a hearing in turn and concluded that he saw no
reason to reproach him. With the prefect, Agrippa thought that if Paul had
not made his appeal to the emperor, he could have been released to freedom.
This famous example shows that one must pay attention to the complex situation of individuals, because if they were Roman citizens, they could exploit
their status to achieve a maximum of guarantees. If they were aliens, they
could only be judged by their own courts, or possibly by a Roman governor, if
they had disturbed public order.

I have mentioned that there existed at Rome citizens of secondary status,
the freed. Freed slaves took the name and civic origin of their former owners
and continued to be under their power, now via the title of patron, and they
were marked by the stigma of servility. Hence, in the first generation they
could not present themselves as candidates for civic duties, even if they were
rich and their city needed local authorities capable of financing by private
means collective goods. There also continued to be slaves, who were numerous, although it is difficult to know their proportion of the overall population.
At the start of the empire, Italy might have had two or three million slaves; in
the second century CE, one-third of the population of the city of Pergamum
was servile. One cannot be more precise. But a phrase of Seneca, from his treatise *On Mercy*, informs us about their importance.[4] One day, someone thought
it appropriate, on the recommendation of the Senate, to compel slaves to wear
different clothing than free persons, but it rapidly became apparent that this

measure was dangerous, because there was a risk that the slaves would commence to count free persons. This extraordinary narrative also reveals another fact, beyond the great number of slaves. It shows that, under normal circumstances, slaves resembled everyone else. This must not be forgotten. In spite of the different legal statuses of individuals in the city-states of the Roman world, most of the time it was difficult immediately to distinguish persons of different status. The history of the arrest of the apostle Paul is evidence of this. The tribune Claudius Lysias, whose name shows that he had only recently been naturalized, checked whether Paul was a Roman citizen. He remarked to Paul that he had himself acquired Roman citizenship by payment of a large sum, as if to express doubt about the apostle's claim. Paul responded to this doubt by saying that he held Roman citizenship by birth. This is a typical exchange among inhabitants of the empire.

These differences of status were so common in the ancient world that our sources do not often remark specifically on them. Being better informed and habituated to this situation, ancient readers knew without difficulty how to identify to which category an individual belonged.

The Population of the City-States

Under the empire, individuals circulated freely inside its frontiers. It was the first time in the history of the West that one finds, on a grand scale, voyages undertaken for any reason whatsoever from one end of the known world to the other. Many of the empire's inhabitants removed themselves from their homeland and resided elsewhere. This information is perfectly well known. What interests us is the status of individuals in these different city-states, because in the criticisms directed at *polis*-religion, this topic is occasionally raised as though it presents a challenge to the model.

The topic concerns questions of identity and the bonds between public cults and the civic identity of this or that city. I will return to this matter in detail. For the present, I would like to recall that, even if full participation in civic life was generally reserved to citizens of the city in question, the *incolae*, the resident aliens, were considered an integral part of the city-states in which they resided. The municipal charters specify that not only registered alien residents, the *incolae*, but even guests and travelers could participate in collective activities.[5] The *incolae* were sometimes Roman citizens from other city-states, sometimes local citizens and beneficiaries of the right of a Latin city. In the case of colonies or *municipia* of Latin status, the *incolae* often represented the indigenous population, who had been integrated under this status in the framework of the new city. This population received lesser rights in their own city: they were assimilated to residents when they were elected to a magistracy that endowed them and their families with Roman citizenship. In each case, the *incolae* could exercise some responsibility in their city-states,[6] and vote in popular assemblies, as is attested in the municipality of Malaca.[7] They had their own seats in the theater[8] and were admitted to public meals.[9] Some even belonged to the *curia*, which is to say, the local Senate.[10]

Add to this the fact that city-states could grant their citizenship on an honorific basis to famous persons—celebrities—who added the new citizenship to that held in the city of their origin. But this situation does not interest us here, since from the moment that such "foreigners" coming from another city acquired the right of the city in a new one, they continued to be full citizens of full right in their city of origin, so long as we speak of Roman or Latin city-states.[11]

The same problem exists for Latin citizens, who did not possess full Roman citizenship and resided in city-states, whether *municipia* or colonies, of Latin right. Insofar as they were citizens of these city-states, they possessed part of the rights of a Roman citizen, but they also had duties and charges, notably that of holding a magistracy if they were elected, and likewise the right to vote in assemblies.

Those are the facts, but one must go further, into legal matters, in order to understand that the Roman Empire and the opening of the Mediterranean world did not destroy in any way the world of the city-states. The *incola*, the resident alien, who was registered in another local city than that to which he traced his origin, whether a Roman or a Latin city, could not abandon his local citizenship of origin. To do that, he would need express permission from the emperor, which was extremely rare. It is essential to understand this. The problem did not exist for a non-Roman. Registered on a provisional basis or even as a citizen in a Roman or Latin city, he remained an alien in respect to Rome, insofar as the Roman city that conferred local citizenship on an alien could not do anything more, since it did not have the power to make him a Roman citizen. That, only Roman magistrates or promagistrates and above all the emperor could do.

As for what is of immediate interest to us—namely, a properly registered *incola*—who had his residence in a city other than his city of origin: such a person was not only authorized to participate in civic events of the city of his legal residence; he was obliged to do so. And it did not suffice to install oneself in a city to be considered a resident. In order to benefit from the status of *incola*, he had not only to establish permanent residence in the municipality in question and keep there his business affairs and domestic cults; it was necessary to frequent the forum, the bath, and the spectacles; to participate in religious festivals; and to enjoy all the advantages of urban life, as the jurist Ulpian wrote at the start of the third century CE.[12] The ties were held so important by the legal authorities, to the point where someone who did not fulfill all his duties to his city could not leave it: so held the jurist Modestinus.[13]

The statuses of individuals in the city-states of the Roman world are therefore anything but simple and obvious. To imagine that, under the empire, there existed nothing but individuals enjoying a sort of imperial, universal citizenship or, better, to employ other terms, to think of the population of the Roman world as composed of individuals who circulated and acted as they pleased without regard for the administrative and political framework of the empire, is an anachronism. To sustain this kind of perspective, it would in fact be necessary to think of the world of the city-states as in wholesale decline and progressively effaced.

What is more, the city-states of the empire were anything but a trope of imperial discourse. On the contrary, even after 212 CE, when all free persons in the empire became Roman citizens, the city-states remained the framework of both daily life and of one's integration into the empire. In no way did the edict of Caracalla institute some sort of citizenship of the empire. The juridical status of the ancient *municipia* of Latin right, or that of numerous alien city-states, continued to exist. Even if at times we lack the evidence that would enable us to analyze in detail these aspects of individual life and of citizenship, their existence is nevertheless the object of a sufficient number of clear remarks to disallow any other interpretation.

A final remark needs to be made regarding the relationship between public and private in the Roman world. For those who know Latin and Roman literature, these terms do not pose any difficulty. They are legal categories. That is public that refers to the people; the adjective *publicus* being the equivalent of the genitive *populi*, "of the people, belonging to the people, concerning the people." A public activity is therefore in one fashion or another an expression of the will of the people and generally conduces its good. Here, a second specification is called for. What is called in Latin "the people" is the political community or citizen body. At times, one also speaks of the *respublica*, the republic of the Roman people, even under the empire, because this was even then the official name of what we would call the Roman state. It was not called the empire, but the republic of the Roman people (*Res Publica Populi Romani*). The term *public* must therefore in no case be confused with some concept like "in public," which renders the import of the term wholly banal. A public action could be accomplished by a magistrate, operating alone with a few assistants, as well as by the people as a whole. The taking of the auspices was performed by a consul, before the start of the day, in the company of two or three of his assistants, and this was a preeminently public act. A public act could be celebrated by representatives of the civic body, by groups of citizens and, in certain cases, by the great families, as well as by a collection of citizens. Moreover, one of the characteristics of such acts was that they were nearly always celebrated in public, before the eyes of everyone, on altars erected in front of temples and not behind closed doors. From this point of view, the juridical term and the social concept of the publicness of an act overlap.

What was private, by contrast, is that which accorded with private law, with the law of the individuals, families, or associations, in civil law. Private actions pertained only to private individuals and conduced above all their benefit, and if they had some public good in view, they were nevertheless entirely private contributions to that good and not public ones, in the Roman sense of the term. The only exception was when a city delegated one of its competences to a family or group of individuals. The problem, as always, is that the two types of action intersect—for example, in public spaces. A public space is under the regulation and governed by the will of the people. This does not prevent private individuals from acting there in a private capacity, but their presence in a public space does not suffice to render their action public.

What we call "private" in the present discourse, in opposition to that which is "public," are those things that fall under the juridical category of private. In other words, the term designates that which conduces the good of an individual or group of individuals. That which is public is that which belongs to the Roman people as a political entity, or it is collective, available to all citizens, and therefore *res nullius*, "the property of no one."[14] Also, under the term "private," it is not necessary to intend concepts like "individual" or "intimate." To be sure, the individual belongs in large measure to the private domain, and his or her conduct falls beneath this juridical category, but before being an individual, the individual is a member of a family, a district, or an association. All these collectivities subordinate to the city fall equally under the category "private." The private therefore does not have the same sense as individual intimacy, nor that connoted by the public/private distinction elaborated in socioeconomic life of the nineteenth century.[15] The individual therefore occupies a place in Roman society altogether different from that of the individual in late antiquity and especially in the modern era.

Do not err and regard these distinctions as belonging merely to pedants and jurists. It suffices to read the sources to establish that these rules applied to all. A dedication to a divinity, in the name of the city, by a public official having the juridical competence necessary to perform such an act, entailed consequences of an altogether different legal status than an offering made by an individual in his personal capacity, whatever his social rank. One knows the example of a sacred building, an altar, and a sacred couch dedicated in the space of a public cult by a Vestal, and thus a public priestess, but in private capacity: they were later wholly and simply removed.[16] Tolerated by the authorities so long as it did not cause a problem, the place of cult was treated as a profane object, which is to say, as not consecrated according to the sacred law that governed the space. In this way, the goods in Roman temples comprised two categories of objects: the first included sacred objects, which belonged to the inalienable patrimony of the temple and which normally were consecrated when the foundation of the cult building was laid; the second included the objects offered to the divinity in the aftermath. In law, the second category of objects did not possess sacred character and remained subject to the will of whoever controlled public spaces, to wit, the people—which is to say, the magistrates, the priests, and the local senate. It is clear that *we* often do not know the precise legal status of the dedicated objects that we recover and can today only guess. But when our sources are detailed, the situation that I have just described emerges. One is obviously free to think that Roman laws, the decrees of the Roman Senate, and the sources collected in the Digest merely articulate handsome pieties and that they formed part of a discourse that had nothing to do with day-to-day realities, where every individual simply acted as he or she pleased. But this is not my position. To be sure, everyone knows that social practice does not always correspond with the prescriptions and norms then in force. But to suppose that the norms themselves were an empty discourse and that one can therefore analyze the behavior of the ancient Romans outside of any normativity or legal framework, rather like the behavior of the English or French of today, this seems to me a fundamental error.

One ought also avoid insisting overly strongly on the subordination of the individual and the private to the state and the public. Wilfried Nippel has urged that the notion of the private constructed by historians of the nineteenth century is not founded upon the juridical and lexical tools of antiquity, but upon contemporary antirevolutionary ideologies.[17] For these liberal historians, the French Revolution and the Terror, with their strident references to antiquity, had demonstrated that in the ancient city the individual was subordinated to the collective. This is the reason why Numa Denis Fustel de Coulanges wished to distance himself from ancient Greece and saw the individual as having no rights in the ancient city: it was the city, for him, that held absolute power over the individual.[18] And so one arrives easily at the theory that the ancient citizen had no identity other than a civic one, which was expressed, for example, through his participation in civic cults. If the criticism of *polis*-religion related to this aspect of the historiography of the late nineteenth and early twentieth centuries, one could endorse it without hesitation. But the problem is that it treats the entirety of the model of civic religion as reducible to these exaggerations of another era.

By extending one's reading just a little, one finds behind the view of Benjamin Constant or Fustel de Coulanges the liberal understanding of private liberty. Indeed, in his *History of Greek Culture*, written at the end of the nineteenth century, Jacob Burckhardt proposed that it was only upon the fall of the Greek city as a mode of social life at the end of the fourth century BCE, beneath the Hellenistic monarchies, that the bonds between citizen and *polis* were so weakened that it was possible to have a private life.[19] Private life commenced with the Greek defeat at Chaeronea!

The concepts that I have just reviewed clearly do not provide any insight *in themselves* into the relationship between the individual and religion in ancient Rome. They merely constitute the framework within which and in light of which the investigation can proceed. To deny this context is to return instead to a historical practice founded on philosophy, transcending the domain of the contingent and intellectually colonizing antiquity. So it is with the theory of the city's decline, caused by the circulation of individuals, over an era when private motivations gradually won out against obligations incurred as a result of civic status: this theory strangely resembles older theories forged from antirevolutionary bourgeois ideology. Thirty years ago, Jesper Svenbro launched a call to decolonize antiquity. This project responds to that call, and seeks rather to contextualize the entire problematic.[20] As we shall see, the ancients were truly different from us, not least in the religious sphere: an alterity that is not enormous, which exists also in other civilizations, and which is due to historical transformations in our own conduct. To ignore these transformations leads inevitably to error.

Chapter 4

Civic Religion

A Discourse of the Elite?

Thus far, I have laid out a certain number of terms, concepts, and historical realities that seem to me poorly understood by those who write about civic religion: the city, individual status, the categories of public and private. We can now turn our attention to religion itself to examine the principal objections directed at the model of civic religion, in order to deconstruct the model of individual religiosity, redolent as it is of Christian theology and Christianizing phenomenology.

For me, four problems stand out. The first is the assertion that the civic model of religion was above all a discourse of the elite. The second is broader and consists of the opposition between civic religion and the "religiosity" of the individual. This opposition will be examined in numerous respects. For the opponents of *polis*-religion, it is essentially a matter of establishing that there was no link between citizenship and public cult, between civic identity and religion. To do this, they must prove that civic religion did not require individuals to participate in public cult and did not forbid other religious practices. As a related matter, they are concerned to cast in doubt the reality of popular participation in public religion.

I will respond to these arguments in turn, while adding a key element to my argument. As it happens, if one simply leafs through the ancient sources, one discovers that civic religion was not the only form of collective religious conduct in the Roman world. Rather, each time that the Romans got together for any reason, they conducted themselves in the same way as in their civic communities. In other words, they established a collective cult of the same type. In my view, therefore, the model is much more significant than one might at first glance suppose.

After the argument that civic religion was a discourse of the elite and that there is no reason to credit the civic model with true preeminence, the third problem raised by these theories is that of emotion. Emotion is declared indissociable from any religious activity worthy of the name, and civic religion is devoid of emotional significance. In discussing this problem, we will be drawn to discuss ancient ritualism, a topic almost never raised by the studies that I have mentioned. Finally, it will be appropriate to examine the argument according to which the religious changes that affected the Roman world were the product not of civic religion but of private religiosity.

The Arguments

For the idea that civic religion was a discourse of the elite, a foundational statement is provided by the article of Richard Gordon that I have already cited. Gordon describes the hegemonic position of the elite in the Roman religious system and underlines the tight relationship between sacrifice, euergetism, and the domination of the elite.[1] At the same time that the elite would have controlled and promoted one type of cult, it would have ridiculed and rejected other practices, such as magic, astrology, and *superstitio* in general. According to Gordon, the differences between religion and superstition were always negotiated, in such a way that cults that at one point lay outside the framework of civic religion, such as the so-called oriental cults or magical practices, could end up being integrated within the framework, and so could end up strengthening the public cults, to the extent that they tacitly accepted the cosmology of civic religion.

This approach, which does not arouse any particular reservations so long as one attempts only a limited analysis of Greek and Roman public cults, has in fact been elaborated, and the critique has gone much further. According to its developed form, the principal authors of *polis*-religion did not actually describe how religion was organized but how certain social groups tried to organize it.[2] According to this view, the religious works of Cicero—the treatises *On the Laws, On Divination,* and *On the Nature of the Gods*—which are elsewhere regarded more as prescriptive and technical writings than as disinterested efforts at systematizing norms, prove that the powerful did not consider their domination of *polis*-religion as totally assured. They describe not a historical reality but rather a discourse maintained by the elite. In particular, the distinction between public and private cults as it was drawn by the ancients and studied by contemporary scholars is arbitrary, just as is the emphasis placed on public cults at the expense of others. Stefan Krauter is a case in point. In his eyes, civic religion was religion as the elite wanted to see it, when they classified religious conduct as *religio* or *superstitio*, as positive or negative conduct. And so, he concludes, a very large domain, which he regards as essential for religious experience, was deliberately not taken into consideration.[3]

Civic religion, the manner in which the Senate, the consuls, and the other magistrates, at Rome and in the city-states of the Roman world, and indeed all ancient authors defined and understood relations with the gods, and the manner in which it seemed appropriate to them to organize those relations: all this was therefore nothing but a simple discourse, the discourse of the elite, which passed over in silence true religiosity, and that for more than eight centuries. Today as well, certain agnostic elites, influenced by Durkheim and Fustel de Coulanges on the one hand, and Wissowa on the other, adopt this same discourse because they did not understand what true "religiosity" is.

I will not repeat what I have already said. Behind these arguments one finds the same line of argument that phenomenology recuperated from Romantic philosophy. We will return to this point. If a scholar adheres to the belief that there exists no other form of religiosity than the Christian one, he or she will have difficulty understanding the ancients or, to put the matter bluntly, all others. Such an author might also rail against the idea that the ancients were such others.[4] Indeed, how could they be that, since in the field of religion they are supposed to be like us? And if one persists in postulating a transcendent, universal notion of religion and thus insists on their similarity to ourselves, then one might well conclude of defenders of the civic model what Ulrich von Wilamowitz-Moellendorff judged of Georg Wissowa: that he had no understanding of the texts, that he was far removed from a world in which this language made sense.[5] To explain the formulation of Wilamowitz-Moellendorff, I would say that in his eyes one can understand nothing about religion when one does not have an intuitive sense of the texts from the inside, in an immediate way, without any obstacle interposed by history or civilization. In short, from this standpoint, one cannot understand the religion of the ancients *except* through an anachronistic rather than a historical impulse. For my part, it seems to me more in conformity with scientific progress to try to understand the texts in a historical and rational way, and to try to be on guard against a priori assumptions. We will come back to this problem anew when we talk about religious emotion.

Let us return to discourse. Behind the argument that civic religion is nothing other than a discourse of the elite, one recognizes immediately the influence not only of Moses Finley but also of Michel Foucault. I refer to certain passages by Finley that take issue with the excessive subordination of historians to documents—though I would also emphasize that Finley himself, for his part, never ceased to insist on the otherness of the ancients.[6]

The distrust of ancient (elite) sources has been combined with the concept of "discourse" lifted from Foucault. However, I have the impression that the concept has not been well understood. Let me cite at this juncture a reflection on Foucault by my colleague Paul Veyne:

> For Foucault, as for Nietzsche, William James, Austin, Wittgenstein, Ian Hacking and many others, each for his own reasons, knowledge cannot be a faithful mirror of reality; . . . Foucault does not believe in this mirror, in this "mirroring" conception of knowledge. According to him, an object in its materiality cannot be separated from the formal frameworks through which we know it and which Foucault, in a badly chosen word, names "discourse." That is all. Badly understood, this understanding of truth as non-correspondence-to-the-real has generated the belief that, according to Foucault, the mad were not mad and to speak of madness was ideology.

Foucault himself complained that people made him out "to say that madness does not exist, indeed, that the problem was the other way around." He affirmed, on the contrary, "that madness, in order not to be that which the discourse of madness had said, is saying and will say about it, was not nothing, for all that." For Veyne, the best definition of the idea of Foucault's discourse refers to "the most precise, the tightest description of an historical situation in its nakedness; it is the bringing to light of the ultimate individual difference. . . . It is essential to strip the event of its ample draperies, which banalize and rationalize it."[7] In 1979 Foucault wrote, "Do not put universals through the grinder of history, but cause history to pass along a thread of thought that refuses universals."[8] Veyne comments: "Heuristically, it is better to start from the details of practice, from what was done and said, and to make the intellectual effort on this basis to explain the discourse. This is more productive . . . than to begin from a general and well known idea, because one risks being constrained by this idea, without perceiving the final and decisive differences that lead thence to ruin."[9] I fear that criticisms of civic religion are missing the problem. If we were to understand the definition of religion as cult paid to the gods in the city-states—both by the city and by private communities—as a discourse conducted by those who occupied the chief roles in the city, we would certainly be correct. Like all religious hierarchies in history, Roman authorities tried to assure their position and enable its continuation. To argue thus does not, however, require one to reject the model on the grounds that it was nothing but a simple, fleeting discourse, shaped by a cynical agnosticism or by an insensitivity to true "religiosity." Even if we employ the concept of discourse to describe the way in which the ancients viewed their relation to the gods, we would not thereby do away with their religious practice nor their legal definitions. As madness and sexuality were not hollow ideologies, the bringing to light of an ancient discourse on religion does not make *religio* and *superstitio* into empty or nonexistent concepts. Above all, this would not authorize us to regard some form of *superstitio* as uniquely expressing true "religiosity." Rather, we should emulate Wissowa and admit that the Romans really thought and acted in this way. The religion of the Romans is a reality that cannot be understood other than in its singularity, in light of their discourse, especially when that discourse is recovered by a collation of independent sources. Foucault's method here meets that of the twentieth-century anthropologists from whom the advocates for the model of civic religion took their inspiration.

Moreover, the use of the notion of discourse as a heuristic category sheds light on a truth inconvenient to critics of *polis*-religion: the Foucauldian approach is fundamentally opposed to universal concepts. Foucault recommended that one "cause history to pass along a thread of thought that refuses universals," as I recalled above. But where does the definition of religion as individual religiosity lead, if not to an affirmation that there is but one true religious feeling, that of "religiosity" as defined by Schleiermacher and his successors? I fear this is merely a theological stance and not a historical or anthropological argument. Nor will I cite at this juncture the perspective of Georg Simmel as an example of a method with sociological or empirical grounding, because that author has clearly defined religion as individual experience on an a priori basis.[10]

That said, which advocate of the model of *polis*-religion has ever denied that other types of cult existed in the city-states? Some, like Fustel de Coulanges, did go too far and distorted the model, particularly under the influence of severe political judgments regarding the totalizing power of the city.[11] In his *Roman History*, Theodor Mommsen settled his account with religion in general and the Catholic Church in particular, as he had known them in Italy, by denying the existence of any religion worthy of the name at Rome. Others, like the Englishman Edward Gibbon, whose personal mode was to attack Christian religion, were able thereby to glorify this way of organizing the religions.[12] It is correct to denounce these exaggerations, but to assimilate all recent research on Greek and Roman religions to this type of sloppiness is absurd.

Consider an example. No one has ever denied that the ancients speculated on occasion about the gods, rituals, and religion. In these texts, they sometimes entertain ideas about piety that sound modern and Christian. It is in the appreciation of these ideas that there exists a great difference. This is where the alterity of the ancients resides. For us, this type of reflection is located in—is contained by—religion, and one can hear reflections of this kind in the course of religious events. Among the ancients, such speculations and meditations were located to one side of religion, as, indeed, were the treatises of Cicero that I just mentioned. They participated in a learned culture under the same rubric as grammar or geology. For the Romans, religion was something other than or, perhaps, something apart from these more or less erudite reflections. Religion was the acts carried out in a given social context in order to express, as regards the divine partners in their community, courtesies indispensable for sustaining dialogue with them. A small nuance, perhaps, but all the difference; all their alterity is there. To restrict oneself as regards evidence, to make these learned or poetic speculations into the true manifestation of their religious sentiment, and to throw away a thousand and one institutionalized religious practices, is a grave methodological error. Likewise, to regard the model of civic religion as ignoring some vast domain, when it sets aside literary speculation as learned rather than religious, and to regard that domain as a decisive one for religious experience, is a point of view to which some are ideologically committed,[13] but it is an error.

The Discourse of Varro

Let us listen to an ancient author who clearly says just this. We speak of Varro, who was extensively cited by Augustine in *De civitate Dei*. In the introduction to his work entitled *The Divine Antiquities*, written toward the middle of the first century BCE, Varro defines precisely the relationship between institutions and personal convictions. Here is what Augustine wrote:

> We regret that Varro classed stage-shows among "Divine Matters," though this was not an expression of his own judgment. For though he assumes a pious role and exhorts men to worship the gods, as he does on many occasions, he acknowledges that he is not fol- lowing his own judgment in conforming to the customs which, as he points out, were established by the Roman state. Now he has no hesitation in admitting that if he had built that city at the beginning, he would have consecrated the gods and their names according to the rule of nature. But he asserts that he is bound, as a member of an ancient people, to maintain the traditional story of their names and surnames as it reached him, and to make it his aim, in his writing and researches, to encourage the common people to honor the gods, not to despise them.[14]

What interests us in this passage are three points that Augustine had no reason to distort. For Varro, who was deeply philosophical, speculation regarding the principles of natural order and regarding the gods could have no effect on an ancestral institution, even if it displeased him. Varro might elsewhere be cited as an example of a Roman who had at base the same inclinations as a Christian, but it remains that he clearly affirmed that interpretation or even speculation detached from cult had no place in religion.

Religion is therefore a product of institution-building on the part of the civic community: it is an institution. On reading this passage one is reminded of another, where Augustine cites the famous formulation by Varro: "The painter is prior to the painting, the builder is prior to the building; so, in the same way, city-states are prior to the things that are instituted by them."[15] Thus, the religion that he describes in his *Divine Antiquities* is that of Roman religious institutions, created by the city, and he will not go beyond this framework. One finds the same affirmations made by Cicero in his treatises *On the Nature of the Gods* and *On Divination*: one can speculate as much as one wants, but the only thing that counts is ancestral religious institutions, the same institutions as were treated by the book on *Divine Antiquities*. Elsewhere Augustine provides an analysis of this position, which takes into account Varro's preference and which helps to explain Roman ritualism. A little later on he writes: "It was not that Varro decided to rank human affairs before divine ones, but to give truth precedence over falsehood. For in his books on human affairs he follows the course of history, but his account of what he calls divine affairs is a collection of frivolous fantasies."[16]

The value of this passage for explaining the ritualism esteemed and enacted by the Roman elite is obvious. They made a choice not far removed from that of Plato[17] or, a millennium and a half later, by Maimonides: human institutions are the only ones that the human mind can know and explain; whatever is beyond needs remain unknowable. At the start of this era, the Christian Minucius Felix understood this position perfectly, as he puts an articulation of it into the mouth of the pagan Caecilius. In his dialogue, Caecilius is represented as saying that

> the mediocre abilities of man are quite inadequate for exploring
> divine matters. And we are, therefore, not privileged to know nor
> are we permitted to pry into what has been raised aloft, poised in
> the sky over our heads, or what has been plunged into the depths
> of the earth beneath our feet. These things it is sacrilegious for us to
> violate. Surely we are to be considered wise enough, happy enough,
> if we follow the old maxim of the sage and get to know ourselves
> more intimately.[18]

Moreover, for learned people who sought in private to probe the unknowable, there were many ways to achieve this. Four centuries later, in the course of one of the last great confrontations between traditionalists and Christians at the highest level of the state, the pagan Symmachus wrote: "Not by one way alone can one arrive at so great a mystery."[19] There are philosophical speculations; there are institutionalized rites; there is Christianity. A Roman could understand these approaches as parallel, without opposing them, one to another.

Who can say whether Varro, Symmachus, or their contemporaries knew other forms of relations with the gods? They knew institutions, and they gave them primacy. At the same time, they reserved, on a private level, a space for theological or metaphysical reflection. They did not ignore popular approaches to the divine, even if they disapproved of them, any more than they denied a right to exist to their own learned theorizing. If there is a discourse here, it is only in the hierarchy established between different types of practice. *Superstitio* refers to an excess of any kind, in ritual piety as well as interpretation, and the middle position recommended by elites since Aristotle is basically in accord with the ideology of the citizen, who ought not permit himself to be abased, by allowing himself to be dominated by fear and making a spectacle of himself, like a slave.

In any case, it is incorrect to say that the discourse of the aristocracy ignored other religious phenomena, or did not want to know them and stubbornly continued to promote that which had already been removed to the dustbin of history. A historian who knows the true nature of discourse and the facts can recommend only this, that one not look in the sources concerning the ancestral religion of the Romans for detailed information regarding the cultic practices of foreigners or new religious practices. Such information should be sought elsewhere, and that work has been done.

If we follow Varro, Cicero, and their friends, then religion, the gods, and piety are oriented to this world. All is in the institution. Please observe that Varro speaks not of public and private cult; however, to the extent that he speaks of the city-state, one may suppose that he treats public cult. One should remain alert to this point. As we will see, for Roman authors, every relationship with the gods occurs in an institutional framework, whether it is conducted in the public framework of the city or is pursued in the context of the family or in other collectivities of individuals.

Finally, one must maintain a correct understanding of elite discourse on public and private as these terms are applied to religious conduct: these are not simple tics of language belonging to a given discourse, but well-established legal categories that functioned for centuries. To deny this point is to treat the discourse of the elite not according to the method of Foucault, but as an ideology, which might be thought to veil some reality of social relations and social formations.

From this misunderstanding arise several subsidiary problems: one concerns the function of civic religion in identity formation; a second concerns the incapacity of this religious model for explaining the profusion of cults and gods, the forgetting of myths and popular gods, as well as religious change. Before considering the historical problem of religious change, let us take up these other points first, which are offered as criticisms of advocates of the model of *polis*-religion.

Chapter 5

Civic Religion and Identity

The intellectual approach of the inventors of *polis*-religion was largely functionalist. Under the inspiration of Durkheim and Fustel de Coulanges, they expected that religion would have as its sole and singular function the integration of individuals into the city and conferring upon them of an identity.

In general, critics of the civic model take as their point of departure a statement by Christine Sourvinou-Inwood, which was inspired by Fustel de Coulanges, though she does not cite him:

> The *polis* provides the fundamental framework in which Greek religion operated. Each *polis* was a religious system which formed part of the more complex world-of-the-*polis* system, interacting with the religious systems of the other *poleis* and with the Panhellenic religious dimension; thus direct and full participation in religion was reserved for citizens, that is, those who made up the community which articulated the religion. One belonged to the religious community of one's own *polis* (or *ethnos*, tribal state); in the sacra of others, even in Panhellenic sanctuaries, one could only participate as a *xenos* (foreigner).[1]

I will not justify or qualify this text about *polis*-religion, which is taken as fodder by adversaries of the model. They attempt to respond to it by emphasizing that civic identity was not defined by cult, since foreigners could participate, and that there existed religious structures beyond the framework of the *polis*. I will leave it to the Hellenists to respond as far as the Greek world is concerned

and concern myself with the Roman side of the question, which is also implicated in the debate.

The same objections are made to the descriptions provided in the handbook of Mary Beard, John North, and Simon Price, where one reads that, "in
the early history of the city of Rome, and in other states in the ancient world,
where political identity was defined by descent, and where access to religious
rites was coextensive with political rights."[2] Later, in the vast multicultural territory of the empire, attempts to provide a political and religious definition of
some normative Roman amounted to efforts to circumscribe what it signified
for citizens of diverse origin to be Roman. It was therefore still a matter of a
functionalist desire to define Roman identity.

Many arguments have been developed to show that the model of *polis*-
religion did not define civic identities, and we will examine these one by one.
We are concerned with how the Romans defined rites, with the extent of participation in Roman cults, and with the nature of religious authority among
the Romans. In correcting errors and responding to arguments, I will at the
same time provide a positive description of Roman religious practice.

The Religious Categories of the Romans

It appears to surprise Stefan Krauter that the Romans knew no term to designate what we call religion.[3] They had only terms to designate particular
religious phenomena, like *sacra*, which referred to specific categories of acts
performed for, or objects dedicated to, the gods; more on this in a moment.
This is one way among others to describe religious practices. A survey of
Roman usage, including the etymologies provided by ancient scholars, reveals
the Roman term *religio* to have been applied to religious phenomena—to religious phenomena and religious prescriptions, as well as to relations with the
gods, but it does not have the same meaning as it comes to possess in Christian
Latin and modern Christianity. To pass too quickly over this difference seems
to me to reveal a sectarian bias.

Consider the term *sacra*. It was used to designate sacrifices and prayers,
but not divination. It was therefore not a global category: but why should such
terms be comprehensive? Why should the Romans have had a unique term to
designate the totality of their religious activities? The response is clear: such a

term must exist, if one believes religion to be universal and that this universal religion is the equivalent of modern "religiosity," as it has been defined over time by Christian philosophers and theologians.

The famous definition of "public rites" of the grammarian Festus, writing at the end of the second century CE, is often treated as problematic: "Public rites (*sacra*) are those performed at public expense on behalf of the citizen body, which are celebrated for the hills, *pagi* [districts], *curiae* [constituent groups of the citizen body], and religious buildings; private rites are those celebrated on behalf of individual persons, families and kinship groups."[4] This definition is indeed interesting, and it is analyzed in all textbooks of Roman religion. Above all, its wording is legal, and it is essential to begin from this fact. It is not a simple discourse or ideologically motivated representation; it is a statement of law. In order to understand this fully, we must supplement it by consideration of a text by the jurist Ulpian from the early third century CE, which is reproduced in the first book of the *Digest*: "Public law embraces the *sacra*, the priesthoods, and the magistracies."[5] Public law, the law that governs relations among elements of the *respublica* of the Roman people—what we would call the state—therefore concerned, in order, religious acts, priests, and magistrates. In other words, it had three parts: sacred law, priestly law, and public law, in the narrow sense as it concerned secular activities of the *respublica* as these were enacted through magistrates. In a juridical perspective, public law was opposed to private law, which concerned private interests. In the same passage, Ulpian affirms that there are two domains of law, public law and private law. Public law is that which has under its supervision the well-being of the *res Romana*, the Roman state; private law is that which regulates the interests of individuals, the *privati*. Some affairs, he continues, are of general interest, and others are of more limited utility and private.[6]

One cannot act as if these categories were pure fantasies, invented by scholars or senators anxious to strengthen their power over society. They sought to give voice to a collection of principles and legal rules that applied to daily life and that had a reality, even if elites systematized them in some way. Of course, at all times, elites the world over have tried to strengthen and defend their power and authority, and they have used all the means at their disposal: profane, religious, legal, military, financial. But their strategizing does not rob the institutions that they used for this end of historical efficacy and meaning. The institutions existed and functioned. The problem is to assess whether the institutions were wholly artificial. Is it appropriate to regard the Church, the churches, or the Jewish or Muslim communities as artificial, on the grounds that elites in the separate societies employed religion to assure their preeminence? Or is it that this did not and does not happen in "true" religions? The religious principles of the religions of India, China, and other nations of the world, are they also artificial and nonreligious? Ought one ignore them when one studies religious life in these countries? I do not think so, and no historian, sociologist, or anthropologist would do this any longer.

Whatever the case may be, these questions issue in a series of claims that are supposed to prove that *polis*-religion did not in any way establish the Roman identity of its practitioners, but rather attested a baroque state of disorder. This disorder resulted at once from overreach on the part of the elite as well as the fact that true religion lay elsewhere, beyond the elite's normative imagination, in the new religions of the individual. Let us examine these issues, beginning with the assertion that there lay at the heart of civic religion a multiplicity and confusion, such that civic religion could not take account of all religious facts; we need also to examine the question of participation in cult.

The Alleged Failure of Civic Religion

When people aim to prove that civic religion never succeeded in constructing a clear Roman identity, the first thing that they cite is the great confusion that prevailed in the ancient city at the level of religion. The theory of civic religion, it is claimed, could never arrive at an explanation for the complexity of ancient religion, by which is intended the sheer mass of divinities, cults, and priesthoods similar to one another.[7] Why, one might ask, did the authorities of *polis*-religion not create even the appearance of order by suppressing redundant cults or "syncretizing" the superfluity of deities?

A first response might take the form of a question. What would it take to introduce order into the proliferation of gods and cults? One need only walk in a Catholic city to observe the same redundancy among cults and saints. And if one intends this as a critique of polytheism in itself, which was, of course, a fundamental characteristic of the religions of Rome and the Roman world, then we are no longer in the realm of historical study; we are in the domain of theology. Augustine could write along these lines, calling to account the alleged disorder of polytheism. Indeed, he wrote such, in his own way, perhaps with less naïveté, because he understood as well he might the logic of polytheism and played on it in order to show that it had been superseded by the arrival of Christianity and of a single, unique divine agent. As regards the numerous cults, they appear redundant when one considers them globally, in a panoramic fashion, like universal divinities divorced from any social or institutional context, as in Christianity, for example. Even then, if one makes the comparison between Catholic saints and Roman gods, the difference is less striking. In any case, the cults are numerous because they correspond to diverse levels of society and the state. Public *Lares* were not the same as the *Lares* of the crossroads or those of the different private households; Jupiter on the Capitol was not the same as Jupiter of a guild of artisans or of a Roman municipium. Moreover, these gods, although homonymous, had diverse historical origins, which conferred on them distinct identities.

We have spoken about the multiplicity of *sacra*, which (it is asserted) cannot have aided the establishing of identity through religion. We come, therefore, to the question of *ritus*, and the problems it poses.[8] In Latin, a *ritus* is not what we call a "rite." It is a modality for practicing cult, a *nomos*, as Greek authors would say, a custom, a general norm. At Rome, many *ritus* were known: the *ritus Romanus* [the Roman mode], *ritus Graecus* [the Greek mode], *ritus Albanus* [the Alban mode], and the *Graeca sacra* [Greek rites]. In a parallel fashion, the Romans speak of *patria sacra*, ancestral rites, and of *peregrina sacra*, foreign rites. Stefan Krauter cites my analysis of the *ritus Graecus* in order to claim that these categories were more or less artificial and that the Romans created them in order to affirm to themselves that their society was multicultural.[9] Finally, Krauter says that the Romans still set in opposition to one another Roman and non-Roman cults, their own cults and the cults of others, recognized cults and deviant ones, new and ancient cults, barbarian cults and civilized ones. He then draws the conclusion that all the categories through which the Romans tried to define their religion produced a troubling and contradictory plurality.[10] There was no frontier that would allow one to identify what was typically Roman. There was a limit to what was acceptable in the eyes of the Romans, but it included a Greek component, an Etruscan component, and so forth. If, therefore, the Romans defined themselves on the basis of religion, they did so in a paradoxical manner. To be Roman would have meant also celebrating non-Roman cults.

Presented in this way, the plurality of categories, of modes of cult practices, does seem paradoxical. However, it is rather the presentation itself that produces this impression, because it confuses things that could not be and does not give a proper account of the background of these cultic categories, which participate in a Roman discourse.

To begin with, Roman religious thought, or Roman religion, was not a global or totalizing doctrine, discussed, defined, and fixed in its dogmas by specialists down through the centuries. One finds only *sacra, caerimoniae,* and *religiones*, which is to say, ritual obligations. Priestly jurisprudence—priestly knowledge—could provide specifications regarding this or that rite in public cult, but the priests had no competence over private cults. There never existed a unified doctrine of the entirety of Roman religious practice. It knew no revelation, no dogma, no sacred book. What is more, the categories enumerated by Krauter are not contemporaneous. What the Romans called *ritus Graecus* dates, it seems, to the end of the third or beginning of the second century BCE. The category was mainly used at that date. I have proposed that it should be situated in relation to the Romans' imperialist ambitions, which introduced into their religious obligations rites taken from coveted areas like Sicily and the Greek states. A little later, the Carthaginians did the same thing with the Sicilian cult of Demeter and Kore.[11] The introduction of these cults at Rome and Carthage reflected not some mental confusion on the part of pagans, but rather the fact that they understood themselves now to be concerned with these cults and divinities because they now claimed and regarded as their own the regions from which they came. Notably, the Romans did not understand themselves as the metropole of Italy or the world, but rather very precisely as a Greek colony: a Trojan colony, practicing asylum and open to all city-states that wanted an alliance with them. This is why they felt their identity to have a foreign—a Greek—rather than autochthonous aspect, and why they created this cultic category. It was in fact an official discourse, because if one takes the trouble to read the texts that describe the rites practiced according to this modality, it rapidly becomes apparent that these were Roman rites with minor nuances designed to signal otherness. It testifies to an act of communication rather than mental confusion. The *ritus Graecus* entered into the system of religious obligations of the Roman republic in the same way as the so-called Greek rites of Ceres, which were nothing other than a Roman version of the cult of Demeter and Kore.

But the category of the *ritus Graecus* was scarcely productive after the Second Punic War. The cults recommended by the Sibylline Books, for example, frequently belong to the Greek modality, like those of the Augustan Secular Games of 17 BCE, which may have provided the last occasion for the application of this category within the definition of modalities of practice. I would say the same thing about the Etruscans. The Etruscan *haruspices*, who were members of the Etruscan aristocracy, were consulted under the republic like foreign oracles, like those of Praeneste or Delphi. This practice did not partake of some chaos in Roman religion, but was an approach traditional in all the city-states of the ancient world, to wit, to consult foreign oracles known to everyone to provide nonpartisan and incontestable acts of divination, which were not determined by immediate interests. Much later, from the first century CE, the Romans created for themselves an order of sixty haruspices who consulted with the Senate and magistrates. These haruspices were Roman priests of equestrian rank and were no longer all of Etruscan origin: the order was henceforth a Roman institution. Moreover, the totality of these different ways of venerating the gods was regarded as constituting Roman religion. If these religious obligations betray a certain complexity, that is for no reason other than that Roman religion never sought to create a clear identity for itself. This is because Roman identity tout court was and wished to be complex.

In addition, the categories employed by historians and grammarians in antiquity cannot be unproblematically assimilated to official cultic categories like *ritus Romanus* or *ritus Graecus* because, unlike them, the categories employed by the learned were often adventitious and reflected more the personal culture or opinions of particular Romans rather than their religion. Even a widely shared category like *superstitio*, a term that became current in the first century BCE, was not a religious category in the sense that it was applied officially by the priests to this or that form of excess in practice, including, notably, foreign and barbarous cults that were thought to conduct themselves in this way. This was a value judgment rendered on particular behaviors in ancestral cult as well as new or barbarian cults, and such judgment was not exclusive to the province of magistrates or priests.

I do not want to defend at all costs the idea that one was Roman by virtue of the practice of Roman public cults, but I think it is absurd to be surprised that the cults practiced according to the Greek modality could come to define Romanness. They made reference to the identity that the Romans wished to forge for themselves. Moreover, as we shall see, neither is it absurd to think that a Roman should practice the cults of his or her city and that, after a fashion, one is in a sense Roman if one practices these cults. In the same way, in the eyes of the French government, one has the identity of a resident when one pays for gas or electricity in French territory.

As to the alleged inability of civic religion to integrate myth or certain very popular divinities like the Mothers or Silvanus,[12] which is supposed to prove that the model of civic religion cannot account for the totality of Roman religion, this argument again derives from a modern vision of Roman religion.

Let us start with myth. This objection is strange, because all specialists of antiquity, whatever their position on the subject of civic religion, know that myth was never part of what the ancients called *religio, threskeia, sacra,* or *hiera.* Myths were narratives, more or less complex, more or less old, that circulated in society and belonged to the cultures of different communities. The versions of myths were innumerable, and study of the production of myths makes it clear that they were forever being reformulated in accordance with context and the narrator's intent. But suppose that these narratives were important for certain individuals, as is the case in religions that are founded on a myth and rehearse their foundational myths in cult. The fact is that nothing and no one prevented a Roman or Greek from understanding the rituals of ordinary cult in light of a myth, or speculating on this basis about its ancientness, its origin, and its meaning. In the very same cult, however, this was never an issue, because there was no sermon, nor was any mention of myth made in prayer. Myths might occupy a place in some ceremonies, either in the recitation of hymns at the end of the performance of some ritual action, or in the decoration of the built context of a cult site or of objects utilized by the celebrants, or in the theatrical games that were eventually joined to many great rituals. But even in those cases, it was only a complement to the ritual, an ornament designed to charm gods and humans. The role granted to myth was to bring pleasure at the moment of a ceremony's conclusion. Prayer and the actual gestures of ritual, meanwhile, made no allusion to myth, nor to any interpretation, whether moral or philosophical, of the ritual being celebrated. By contrast, the ludic phase that concluded the grand religious occasions, which were often called "Games" (*Ludi*), frequently employed myth, which is to say, one or another version of a myth. This should not be understood in any way as articulating the doctrine of a cult. During the Secular Games, for example, which constitute one of the best known ritual complexes of Roman public religion, the secular hymn was a commentary on the Games, which underlined certain of their aspects and also referred to myths, but myths were never mentioned during the prayers of the Games.[13] The hymn, moreover, was sung at the end, after the sacrifices and banquets, at the moment when the celebrants returned in procession to the Circus Maximus in order to conclude the entire celebration with races. The protocols of the Secular Games teach us in addition that the subsidiary games, joined on after the celebration, included also *ludi Graeci astici*, literally "Greek urban games," which seem to have included the performance of tragedies and therefore of mythic episodes taken from Greek mythology. But this was after the performance of cult.

In short, to claim that civic religion victimized those who wanted myth when they set themselves in relation to the gods is absurd, because myth had nothing to do with cult. It is also false, because myth could well have a place in the celebration of cult and in the private life of individuals, but that place was not the one expected by a modern person, habituated to religions founded on a great myth or to the teaching of Greek literature.

As regards widely worshipped divinities like Silvanus or the *Matres*, the Mothers, who never received public cult, the response is also very simple. At Rome and in Latium, Silvanus was a divinity worshipped above all in a domestic framework. Remember the rites as described by Cato the Elder. Slaves, for example, had a special relationship with this god. Like other private divinities, Silvanus did not have a public cult at Rome. And yet, when the Romans or Roman city-states found themselves in a space protected and managed by Silvanus—the frontiers of the empire, for example—the soldiers venerated him, and likewise the magistrates of the city-states, as in the colony of Philippi in Macedon: in that city, in response to his election as aedile, a certain Hostilius Philadelphus paid for the inscriptions decorating a small sanctuary of Silvanus.[14] The cult may safely be deemed public because, if a local magistrate finances a cultic building for an official reason, the building is of the political collective. At Lambaesis in modern Algeria, Marcus Aurelius and Lucius Verus built through the intermediation of the Third Augustan Legion a temple to Jupiter Valens, Aesculapius, Salus, and Silvanus.[15] The building is large and undeniably a public temple where the legates of Numidia regularly fulfilled vows.

In these situations, the god could well have become the object of public cult in other places, but apparently no one felt the need. In any case, nothing prevented anyone from worshipping Silvanus, but this would not have been done on a public level. As a corollary, it is not because a divinity did not have a public temple and public cult that it was not worshipped by the Romans.

It is true that such situations sometimes aroused conflict with the authorities. At Rome in 58 BCE, Isis and Serapis became the patron deities of groups of artisans, from among whom were recruited supporters of Clodius and other so-called *populares*. Their agitation was one of the foci of political trouble in Rome in these years.[16] These divinities had long since received from these groups an altar or a small religious building in the area of the temple of Jupiter Capitolinus. This small cult site had the legal status of a private cult. As such, it was tolerated by the authorities, because every citizen had the right to observe his personal devotions in spaces of public cult, so long as he respected public order. We must not forget that we are in a polytheistic context and that individuals established relations with divinities who were, for one reason or another, close to them, and between them and the titular deity of the temple. In this case, it seems that it was the sovereign nature of the Egyptian deities that inspired the political groups in question to establish this connection with the gods of the Capitol. Isis and Serapis could therefore perfectly well be worshipped on the Capitol by this sociopolitical group, at a place that was theirs.

Conflict came about one day when, by way of provocation, the *populares* who were attached to this cult asked of the consuls that their divinities be associated with the public vows for the safety of the Roman people that were undertaken each year on 1 January. This was an impossible claim. For one thing, it could not be done because the divinities who were involved in the public vow formed a tight group, including the Capitoline Triad (Jupiter, Juno, and Minerva) and *Salus Publica* [Well-being of the Roman People]. For another, it was impossible because no decision had been made to make public the cult of Isis. Hence, because it was ultimately a political provocation, it received a repressive response on the same, public plane: the altar (or building) was destroyed. It is regrettable that the history of this episode is known only because it served as an exemplary tale about the character of the consul who dared to lay his hand upon the altar. It was undoubtedly more complicated than this story suggests. Behind the provocation there may have been a request to change the status of the cult, which had existed at Rome since the second half of the second century BCE. The cult clearly had numerous adherents, which may explain the hesitation of the workers when they received the order to destroy the object at the heart of the scandal, and their hesitation compelled the consul himself to take up the ax. We are poorly informed about the procedures by which a cult became a public one. We know only that public status was granted to a cult by the Senate or possibly by a magistrate of the Roman people—for example, when he vowed a temple to a new divinity. Thus, a century later, Isis and Serapis seem to have received a temple and public cult on the Campus Martius as a result of the victory of Vespasian. According to an ancient procedure, it is highly probable that Vespasian promised a temple to those gods in a vow at the moment of his proclamation as emperor in Alexandria.

The second example, that of the *Matres*/Mothers, is also significant. The *Matres*, or *Matrones*, were divinities attested in the north of Italy and in Gaul, mostly in Belgica and in Germania Inferior. They were a group of three goddesses, who, according to what we know, were connected to clans and reached back to the Celtic era. Is it true that the *Matres* never received public cult? Yes and no. Yes, in Rome and in the other city-states of Italy, for the simple reason that no divinity originating in Gaul or Germany ever received an official cult there. The reason for this closure to the Celtic pantheon is not known, but apparently the Romans of Italy limited their public pantheons to Mediterranean divinities. No, because the *Matrones* received public cult in Germany. They were very tightly attached to the soldiers of Germany. The divine *Matrones* were notably so present in the City of the Altar of the Ubii that, when it was elevated by the emperor Claudius to the rank of Roman colony and became our Cologne, the goddesses clearly received a temple and public cult. We know, for example, that the temple of the *Matres Aufaniae*, which was located in the territory of Cologne, near the camp of the First Legion "Minerva," near Bonn, had public status. It received religious devotions from many magistrates of Cologne, including decurions, duumvirs, and even a provincial priest of Germania Inferior;[17] other dedications come from legionaries, officers, and legates of the legion.[18] In my view, all this proves not only that the cult of the *Matrones Aufaniae* was one of the important cults of Cologne and the region, but that it was also a public cult of the colony. In consequence, when the general context was so inclined, a city could perfectly well adopt an important local cult and obligate itself to the cult at the religious level. For Rome and for civic religion, the example of the *Matrones* therefore does not prove what it has been taken to prove.

As we have seen, all known cults and gods did not belong to public cults, either of Rome or of the city-states of the Roman world. Cultic obligations changed from city to city, and it would be absurd to want to find in the public cult of the diverse city-states or in that of Rome all cults known from all city-states of the Roman world. Roman religion was not a universal religion that had been put forward everywhere with the same pantheon and the same religious obligations.

The levels of practice differed, one from another. They communicated, to be sure, but not as the cult of a single, universal religion, which did not distinguish substantially between its different levels or in the solemnity of rites. In Christianity, every prayer is equivalent and is addressed to the same deity, wherever one might be. In the religions of Rome, prayers concerned variable groups of persons and invoked gods who were not always the same. At times, it was a matter of individual devotion, or the obligations of the father of a family to his domestic gods, or of a magistrate toward the divinities of the republic of the Roman people. And in a Roman city, there were also the local public divinities. Confuse these pantheons, or set them in opposition to one another, and you will deprive yourself of any possibility of understanding the functioning of Roman religions.

The Inclusion of Non-Citizens and Their Participation in Cult

Previously we spoke about the religious identity of city-states, and we have seen how oft-cited examples fail to prove that civic religion was an artificial and ineffective construction that ignored the "true" religion of ancient societies.

Three other arguments have been adduced to demonstrate that the political identity constructed by public religion was vague, if not nonexistent: that fact that the entire world could enter into all cult sites; that everyone could participate; and that there was no obligation that a priest be a Roman citizen.[19]

By dismantling these arguments one by one, we will have the opportunity to describe positively relations among the individual, the civic community, and religion. That said, it is really a matter for the adversaries of *polis*-religion, which is to say, religion of the city, to demonstrate that only the individual and one's free decision were determinants of religious life, and not one's social position or legal status. As before, I concern myself with Rome and the city-states of the west, leaving it to the Hellenists to respond to attacks on the religions of the Greek city-states.

Is it necessary to respond to the ridiculous claim that it is never specified that one must be a Roman citizen to be a priest? Let us skip over the fact that the priests were not the principal actors in civic religion: that role was clearly filled by the consuls, praetors, and even the aediles. About the hypothesis that there was no obligation that one be a citizen in order to exercise a priesthood: remember, there is also no text that affirms that it was necessary to be a citizen in order to be a consul, praetor, or aedile. For all these offices, which were subject to election, like the priesthoods, the principle is obvious. Is it necessary to repeat that there was no written constitution, no body of electoral rules as in our democracies? Prosopography, the aggregated data of actual holders of office, can help: we can debate this critique of civic religion on the day when we learn of a foreign priest or magistrate. Even the priestesses of Ceres, who were thought to be of foreign origin, received citizenship upon their entry into office. In addition, if one wants another positive argument, I observe that a priest who became a prisoner of war or was exiled lost his priesthood along with his citizenship, with the exception of the augurs and Arval Brethren,[20] who retained their priestly quality until death.

Access to Roman cult places was therefore not forbidden except in certain cults and for particular groups within society: according to the case, to men, women, or slaves, for example, but never to foreigners. This is true. We do not know of any general rule that closed all public cult sites to foreigners. Nor did there exist a global religious authority outside the Senate or the People. These released authority to those responsible for the cults and otherwise gave consideration to specific cults and not to cult in a general way. Decisions were formulated to apply to this or that practice and not to apply to all religious practices. Nor in any event is the problem posed in these terms by our sources. If available documentation does not mislead us, it did not matter who could *visit* a cult site, or at least its accessible parts. By contrast, it is in the description of actual cult acts that one finds indications of exclusions; the sites themselves, in themselves, were not the object of the rules. For example, women were excluded from cult acts performed for Hercules at the Ara Maxima, and men were banned from the cult of Bona Dea. One can imagine that on the days when no cult was performed, nothing would drive men or women from these two sanctuaries. In the etiological myth that explains the origin of these exclusions, Hercules would certainly have received water from the celebrants of the rites of Bona Dea if he had come at another time. On the holiday of Bona Dea, he was refused.

The insistence on participation in religious acts and the claim that a majority of *sacra publica*, of public rites, were celebrated in a non-public fashion, which is to say, without a large audience, signifies a certain ignorance about the functioning of Roman religion.[21] The people would not have participated except in certain rites and above all in the games on holidays.

The error seems to me significant, and we must pause to consider it. Two objections ought to be raised. The first concerns background: the need for an audience. The second bears upon the presence of a crowd, which was in no way limited to a few large ceremonies. Let us take up first the problem of limited audience, which would supposedly prove that all these rites were nothing but quasi-private cults celebrated by a few great families.

Who says that all the people or even a large part of them ought to attend the thousand and one rites of public religion? *Tres faciunt collegium*: three people make a college. This Roman principle establishes that it sufficed that three persons be present in order for the collectivity concerned to have been represented, in the same way that the Jewish *minyan* constitutes a community empowered to act collectively. Literally meaning "number," the minyan is the quorum of ten adult males required to hold a public service.[22] The Roman pontifex maximus, for his part, could not decide alone; two other pontiffs had to express the same opinion in order for his view to be valid. As Cicero explains in his speech *On the Responses of the Haruspices*, "what three pontiffs have decided has always seemed to the Roman people, always to the Senate, always to the immortal gods themselves sufficiently sacred, sufficiently august, sufficiently attentive to religious scruple."[23] The protocols of cult celebrated at Rome and in the Roman suburbs reveal that the twelve Arval Brethren were generally not all present, though they were charged with public sacrifice. We know as well that a number of ordinary citizens were present for the rites. But if it was necessary that a minimal number of celebrants be present in order for the cultic act to be valid, the addition of a fourth or a twelfth priest mattered not at all. This point deserves emphasis. In public cult, there was no need to judge the quality of a religious act by the number of celebrants present, and no further benefit derived in proportion to the number of citizens attending a cultic act, as if there were some necessary relation between the conviction and fervor of individuals and the size of the audience. In a religion that granted primacy to the obligation and the exactitude of ritual performance, piety consisted above all in observing ritual requirements, not in going beyond them. A Roman would have been tempted to describe as superstitious any superfluity of fervor.

In daily life, in addition to public cult, each resident of Rome and the city-states had a multiplicity of other cultic acts to accomplish, and each person was responsible for his share. The magistrates, priests, and other representatives of the people had supervision of public cult, and even if they were the only people present, their rituals would have appeared valuable to all citizens and been understood as celebrated in their interest. As a member of a guild, as a resident of a neighborhood, and as a member of a family, each person had his or her own level of religious responsibility, and it sufficed amply if he or she had also to pursue a professional activity. It was therefore not surprising if the crowd did not press around for certain celebrations, like the sacrifices offered on the Capitol by the flamen of Jupiter on the Ides of the month (the thirteenth or fifteenth) or those of the flaminica of Jupiter in the Regia in the Forum Romanum on the Nundinae (the fifth or seventh of the month). It is still important to know about participation, and I will return to this. Let me add only that, in public religion at Rome, an important problem was raised at the end of the second century and in an ongoing way to the end of the republic, when the civic body grew so rapidly that, whatever one wanted, it was no longer materially possible, in the course of a religious duty, to bring together the totality of the citizens, or minimally an important portion thereof. In contrast, in the little homelands of Roman citizens, things were very likely to be very close to earlier conditions and, indeed, to the idyllic condition of archaic Rome celebrated by the poets, when some shepherds gathered around an altar of turf in order to sacrifice one of the animals from their herd. I raise this problem, although the topic has not received attention from the critics of civic religion, because it is, at base, one of the major challenges presented to the Romans, and it remains so today for anyone who studies the sources. It

was in fact inevitable that this evolution in the civic body should have reper-
cussions on cultic deportment. Sadly, we know nothing precise about them.

By contrast, we can give ourselves a fairly clear idea of the participation
of citizens in cultic acts. I will give two examples. Although I will not discuss
the size of the cult sites at length, one can at least say that the great spaces
were clearly not intended to remain empty. Nor ought we forget that we are
in a polytheistic system, and the collective religious scene moved continually
from one place of cult to another. Some were frequented by the totality of the
community only once per year. The first example that I have chosen concerns
participation in sacrifices, the second the rites themselves and that which endowed them with their perfection, the prayers.

Public sacrifices at Rome offer an opportunity to ask in a concrete fashion
about how a large number of citizens might participate in rites. As I have said,
in the small city-states, participation was simpler and closer to the Roman
past. At Rome, we do not know exactly how things unfolded. The problem
is made difficult for us because the sources do not systematically specify that
the people participated in sacrificial banquets.[24] Keep in mind that sacrifice
was an act of offering food to a divinity, whether of living animal or vegetable,
which was subsequently divided and consumed by the divinity and also by
the celebrants—at least, so long as the divinities in question were not infernal,
because no commensality was possible for humans with them. In any event,
because of this, a banquet was a ritual necessity, as without it the sacrificial rite
would be rendered hollow and robbed of all meaning. The common sacrifice
celebrated every year on the Alban Mount by the delegates of the thirty city-
states of Latium was therefore invalidated and had to be restarted from scratch
if one of the delegates did not take his share of meat. Relatively numerous
sources teach us that the celebrants always consumed a banquet after sacrifices.
For example, at the Secular Games in 204 CE, the priests and the matrons
shared sacrificial banquets. These are described in detail for the sacrifices performed for Dea Dia by the Arval Brethren. Although we do not hear in these
protocols about other participants in the Arval banquets, the portions at these
are so large (one *amphora*, which is to say, about twelve liters per head) that it
is necessary to suppose that the parts received by the priests were destined to
be distributed to their entourage. As for the great ceremonies of public vows
for the well-being of the Roman people and the emperor, one must assume

a distribution of sacrificial meat. On that day, which fell on 3 January under the empire, the Arvals alone sacrificed nearly a ton of meat, according to the estimate of the archaeo-zoologist Patrice Méniel. And the Arvals were only one of the priestly colleges that sacrificed on this day, along with magistrates and undoubtedly other organized bodies. I have estimated that, under Nero, the sacrifices of all the authorities of Rome provided on 3 January on the Capitol around thirty tons of beef.[25] What became of this meat? The protocols of the Arvals do not mention a banquet on this day, any more than when the superior of the college, his assistant, and the administrator of the sanctuary offered in the sacred grove of Dea Dia a long series of expiatory sacrifices: two times fifty-one victims separated by some days, slaughtering the equivalent of two tons of meat. Neither do other sources mention banquets, other than the cult of Hercules, where everything that is sacrificed during the day is made to disappear by evening. What therefore becomes of the meat produced by the other public sacrifices?

Four answers are possible. One could suppose that collective banquets were so ordinary that the protocols and the other sources do not mention them. Perhaps. When we write that a mass was celebrated at Notre Dame, we do not specify how many persons took communion. If I were to play the devil's advocate, I would say that the priest who performed the duty would have noted in his succinct report about the service the amount of host distributed. But no indication suggests any such control in the practice of Roman public cult. The three other explanations appear to me more defensible.

First, the sacrificial banquets of 3 January were almost certainly not organized one by one, by the different bodies of priests and magistrates. In my view, the meat could have been gathered at a single large banquet sponsored, for example, by the consuls. As the Arvals did not have supervision over the ceremony of the banquet, they did not provide an account in their protocols. This is possible, but, as I have said, no source describes this great banquet. The next explanation is offered in light of the heightened number of Roman citizens at Rome, which made it impossible to organize a common sacrificial meal. One might imagine that the Roman people participated in this banquet through the intermediation of the magistrates and priests, which is to say, through those who represented them. Only these were able to take part and, for the reasons already mentioned, the different colleges of priests, including the Arvals, did not report the banquet, as it lay beyond their area of responsibility. But what then became of the enormous quantity of sacrificial meat? The priests and magistrates were too few in number.

The fourth explanation can respond to this question and builds on the third. It is supported by a letter of Pliny the Younger concerning the Christians.[26] We learn there that in Nicomedia, in Bithynia, Christianity had spread to such an extent that no one would buy meat at the butcher. This appears to have been the general rule in distributing meat produced in sacrifices. By means of butchers, all citizens, and all those who dwelled in the city, participated in public sacrifices. It may even be that those having the right to receive meat had tokens by means of which to collect their portion. We can therefore equally well suppose that the Arvals did not mention a banquet on 3 January because a distribution of meat was organized in this manner.

However, it is surprising that the Arvals do not mention the banquet over which they were in fact in charge—namely, that for the sacrifice to Dea Dia. As I have said, the protocols describe only the banquet of the priests. Does this signify that only the rites that the Arvals had to celebrate themselves were noted? The distributions of meat that took place on site or by some other means were simply not mentioned, because they were not relevant to this type of protocol, which recorded evidence solely for the acts of the priests. Perhaps there were activity reports of the assistants and slaves of the Arval college that recorded this type of information, because the distribution of meat and the organization of a collective banquet for those who attended the rite could have belonged to their responsibility. In other words, we may be asking of our evidence something that it does not contain, or which it could not provide, except perhaps exceptionally, as when there was some irregularity about which the priests had to make a decision.

In other words, the only thing of which we are certain is that there was an enormous quantity of meat available on the very same day. This quantity created a need: as there were no refrigerators in that era, it would have been necessary to use this meat immediately. Unless we imagine that the authorities had it salted for use in the army or public distributions, it would have had to be consumed very quickly. In the final analysis, whatever the means by which they disposed of the meat, we have to admit that many people were involved, and in virtue of this fact, they participated in large numbers in public rites.

In the more modest framework of the city-states of Italy and the Roman world, the modes of distribution were more immediate, and we possess many specifications in monetary terms of the amounts of meat and wine to be prepared for rites, these being the two regular components of Roman sacrifices. These documents mention the sacrifices that preceded the distributions only rarely but, in the majority of cases, one can suppose that they took place. Perhaps this was because every act of butchery was sacrificial in the Roman world—or so research on texts and the ongoing archaeological work of William van Andringa and Sébastien Lepetz would suggest.[27] In one fashion or another, animals were shared between gods and humans.[28]

For all these reasons, it is absurd to suggest that the regular ceremonies of public religion did not receive a large audience. I have discussed only one regular ceremony, the vows of 3 January, which were complemented all year long by the taking of a certain number of additional, extraordinary vows. It is necessary to add the other great festivals of the year, in connection with which the sources sometimes mention banquets, as for the Septimonium (11 December), which Suetonius describes in the age of Domitian, and which was tied to a distribution of food.[29] Nor should one forget the Compitalia, a public festival celebrated by the citizens in the districts of Rome, which certainly included banquets and brought together a large audience. Also, I have not mentioned, for the republican period, the triumphs, which involved, we are told, enormous sacrificial banquets. To receive, buy, and consume one's share at a public sacrifice amounted to participation in the rite in question, even if that participation was formal in character. In a ritualist religion, this is also what banquets or the purchase of meat at the butcher signified. The Christians were not wrong in this. Not to recognize the importance of this connection is to fall back into an antiquated way of talking about ritualism and the poverty of its religious content.

Chapter 6

For Whom Were the Rituals Celebrated?

It is one thing to question the effective participation of citizens; it is another to reflect on the composition of the community of those for whom cult was celebrated. But this community is never evoked in the debate that occupies our attention. As I have already indicated, in the rituals of a ritualistic religion, it suffices to bring together the required number of celebrants for a religious service to be valid and achieve its object. For this reason, the question of the participation of the people must be addressed in light of the modalities, both direct and indirect, of the people's participation. To deny the value that the Romans themselves recognized in the representation of the community by magistrates or priests amounts to a challenge of the depth of all religious ritualism.

Now we are concerned with perceiving the community of the faithful, as one might say today. This type of term embraces the collection of those who are members of the religious community in the name of whom and for whom cult is celebrated, regardless of whether or not they are physically present.

To address this question, we will examine different public prayers. We will not consider all known prayers, but only a few, whose signification seems to me perfectly clear. They derive from documents of cultic provenance and refer without ambiguity to religious practice, to cult as it was celebrated, and not to commentaries, to interpretations, or to discourse external to ritual. These examples will come from the imperial era, which is to say, from an epoch when civic religion is thought to have become wholly obsolete. I will analyze the sacrifice to Dea Dia by the Arval Brethren, the formula of consecration from an altar at Salona, the prayer of the public vows on 3 January, and finally the sacrificial prayer from the Secular Games.

On the seventh or eleventh of January, the college of the Arval Brethren announced officially the date of the sacrifice to Dea Dia, which was once upon a time not calendrically fixed. This announcement was made in the Roman Forum, before the temple of Concordia. It was therefore made in public, in a grand public space. Here is the formula as pronounced by an official among the Arvals. I have chosen the ceremony from January, 87 CE: "In the *pronaos* of the sanctuary of Concordia, which is next to the temple of the Divine Vespasian, the Arval Brother Gaius Salvius Liberalis Nonius Bassus, who officiated in the place of the *magister* Julius Silanus, with the Arval Brethren standing to one side, announced the sacrifice to Dea Dia for this year."[1] The dates and locations of the sacrifice followed. The temple of Concordia was a site bordering the Forum, which was not only public in a juridical sense, but also a civic space that was very crowded at midday. The Fraternity, or Brotherhood, which consisted of a dozen senators and even celebrated one part of the sacrifice to Dea Dia in the house of the official—a location that perforce did not allow a great concourse of people—had to announce the dates for sacrifice in public, before the people who found themselves in the Forum on that day. Among the dates announced was the date for the second day of the ritual, which included games (which is to say, chariot races) in a nearby suburb. I do not think the date was awaited with impatience because, under the empire, which is to say, under the Julian calendar, the date of the sacrifice, which had been mobile under the ancient astronomical calendar, had long been fixed. The Arvals maintained the ritual fiction of the former mobile date and made the dates of the festival to alternate from one year to another. What interests us is that the proclamation was made in public; the date was not determined in private and then communicated to a minority of the celebrants. Indeed, the decree of the priests may have been likewise posted before the temple or before the residence of the official.

A second point. If we read the formula of the announcement, we acquire the list of all those who were officially implicated by the announcement and the cult in question:

Let it be good, favorable, blessed, fortunate, and health-bearing
for Imperator Caesar Domitian Augustus Germanicus, pontifex
maximus, and Domitia Augusta, his wife, and Julia Augusta and all
their house, and for the Roman people and the Quirites, and for the
Arval Brethren and for me! The sacrifice for Dea Dia will be on the

sixteenth day before the kalends of June at home, on the fourteenth
day before the kalends of June in the grove and at home, and the
thirteenth day before the kalends of June at home.

The service therefore took place on 17, 19, and 20 May. The formula of announcement shows that the parties interested in the cult in question were
the emperor and his house, the Roman people and the Quirites (the citizens), and finally the Arvals. The official defines in a concise way the totality
of the Roman people, which we call the state: the emperor and his family,
the Roman citizen body, and, finally, as always in these formulae, those who
pronounce it, the collectivity of the Arvals and he who represents them, the
official (*magister*). The cult of the Arvals was therefore celebrated not for an
isolated group of aristocrats but for the entire Roman community.

The second example of a prayer is taken from the formula of dedication
inscribed on an altar of Jupiter at the colony of Salona, in Dalmatia, dating to
137 CE.[2] The formula first defines the properties and rules of the altar, before
concluding by asking from Jupiter that he be benevolent toward him who
dedicated the altar (to wit, the duumvir of the colony, reciting a formula dictated by a pontiff), toward his colleagues (that is, the other magistrates), the
decurions, the colonists, and the other residents (*incolae*) of the colony Martia
Julia Salona, to their spouses and children. Once again, the dedication is made
publicly, is inscribed on an altar visible to all and concerns all persons who rep-
resent and constitute the colony of Salona. One should note that the *incolae*,
the residents without local citizenship, are juridically part of the colony. They
participate in the cult as an obligation of residence, not by personal choice,
and their presence in the cult does not trouble the civic identity: on the contrary, their presence forms part of it.

Let us return to Rome. The votive formula from 3 January, which in the
first instance concerns the health of the emperor alone, specifies for its part
all the persons on whose behalf the vow is addressed to the Capitoline Triad,
Salus Publica Populi Romani (Public Well-being of the Roman People). Here
is the formula as it was recited by the superior of the Arvals on 3 January before
the Capitol, in some year when Marcus Aurelius was sole emperor:

Jupiter Best and Greatest, if the *res publica* of the Roman people
and the Quirites, the Roman empire, the army, allies, and peoples

who are under the sway of the Roman people and the Quirites, will
be unharmed on the third day before the nones of January which
will next be for the Roman people and the Quirites and for the *res
publica* of the Roman people the Quirites, and if you shall have
preserved [on that date] safe and unharmed from any dangers that
will be, whatever they are, Imperator Caesar Marcus Aurelius Antoninus Augustus, pontifex maximus, holding the tribunician power
<for the nth time>, imperator, consul for the third time, father
of the father land, son of the divine Antoninus Pius, grandson of
the divine Hadrian, great-grandson of the divine Trajan Parthicus,
great-great-grandson of the divine Nerva, the best and greatest emperor, whom we specifically name, together with Faustina Augusta
and Commodus Caesar and the other members of the Augustan
[that is, imperial] house, and if you have granted a good outcome
to them, such as we specifically say, and you do these things in this
way, then, we vow that there shall be for you two male bovines with
gilded horns [as sacrifice]. Juno and Minerva, in the terms in which
we have vowed there shall be for Jupiter Best and Greatest two male
bovines with gilded horns, which we have vowed this day, so as you
shall have done these things in this way, then for you in the same
words we vow that there shall be for you two female bovines with
gilded horns. Salus Publica . . . [The text is damaged].[3]

This formula cites in a very full manner all those who are counted as beneficiaries of the protection of the great gods of public cult, in order: the *res publica*
of the Roman people and the Quirites (the official name of the Roman state);
the *Imperium Romanum* (which is to say, Roman power); the Roman army;
the allies of the Roman people; the nations that find themselves under the
sway of the Roman people. In a second iteration, it is the emperor himself
and the other members of his family that are to be protected. Earlier votive
formulas do not specify all the beneficiaries. It is not possible to determine if
this formula was devised by Marcus Aurelius. It is not attested in so expan-
sive a form in the other verbal records of the second century of our era. Are
we obliged to conclude that this spectacular formula, which embraces practically the entire empire, the emperor, the Roman state, its army and allies,
and even the nations it dominates, is owed to the conditions under which it

was written—to the military situation as well as the plague that afflicted the empire from about 166 CE? It is possible. However, if we can trust the sacrificial formula pronounced by Scipio in 204 BCE as Livy reports it—included in its list of beneficiaries were "the People and the Roman plebs and the allies and those of the Latin name, who on land, sea, and rivers follow my lead and power of command and auspices, and those of the Roman people"[4]—then, we may conclude that the formula of the second century CE contained no novelty. Even if Livy's formula is not of the era to which Livy attributes it, it dates at the very least to the dawn of the empire, when the historian's work was written.

What interests us here, once again, is that the vows are formulated for the benefit of the entire Roman community, and even beyond. It cannot be a question of a ceremony that concerns only a few great families at Rome. I recall in passing that the vows were celebrated throughout the empire, in all city-states as well as in other official groups.

To object that, anyhow, no one attended these ceremonies changes nothing about their signification. The formulas prove that the entire community, political and human, was implicated. Moreover, we must not forget that the formulation of a new vow was preceded by the offering of the victims that had been promised the preceding year, if, that is, the divinities that had been invoked had in fact preserved safe and sound the beneficiaries of the vow. In other words, the new vow was preceded or accompanied by a sacrificial banquet or a distribution of meat that certainly involved numerous persons.

As for disqualifying these proofs by claiming that the vows, public sacrifices, and dedications were merely "political" rites: that amounts to revivifying an ancient reproach made against Roman ritualism by historians influenced by Romantic philosophy or more simply Eurocentrism. We will have an opportunity to return to this point.

A plausible definition of the community of celebrants and beneficiaries of Roman public cult is employed at the beginning of our era in the celebration of the Secular Games.

I will cite two prayers. The first was recited in the course of the official ceremony that announced the festival, between February and March of 17 BCE.[5] The quindecimviri, the members of the priestly college that celebrated the games, pray in archaïzing language to a certain number of deities in order that everything that they have accomplished in their college and will accomplish in the future shall prove favorable "for them, the people and the Roman *plebs*, in warfare and at home, [—lacuna—] and that they should turn out well and should be good for the Roman people [—lacuna—]." We can debate whether it is appropriate to restore the phrase "the allies and those of the Latin name" to the damaged text of this formula after the reference to the Roman people. Certainly, such language appears in the contemporaneous text of Livy as well as in later prayers. That issue to one side, it is nevertheless clear that the entire festival is organized for the Roman people in its entirety, in its foreign-military and domestic-civilian affairs. We heard a similar prayer in the mouth of the superior of the Arvals. Moreover, in the prayer proper to the Secular Games, which was recited before each of the seven sacrifices, as also during the rite of supplication performed by the matrons, we find the same elements.[6] The *magister*, the superior of the quindecimviri, prays to the gods or goddesses that they

> may increase the power and majesty of the Roman people and of
> the Quirites in war and at home; and that the Latin [people] should
> always be obedient; and that you may grant eternal victory and
> health to the Roman people and to the Quirites; and that you favor
> the Roman people and the Quirites and the legions of the Roman
> people and of the Quirites; and that you preserve the *respublica* of
> the Roman people and of the Quirites safe and make it greater;
> and that you be willing and kindly to the Roman people and to the
> Quirites and to the college of the quindecimviri, to me, my house,
> and my family; that you accept this sacrifice of nine female lambs
> and nine female goats, to be burned in their entirety; for the sake of
> these things be honored by the burning whole of this female lamb,
> being propitious to the Roman people and to the Quirites, the col-
> lege of the quindecimviri, to me, my house, and my family.

We thus find once again all the communities that compose the Roman world, a community over which the Romans summon the protection of the gods, whether it is a question of Roman citizens, Roman communities or allies, and even subjects.

Taken together with the votive formula from the age of Marcus Aurelius, does this prayer offer some indication of a universalization, or globalization of the effects of Roman religion? Is this an anticipation of the edict of Caracalla in 212, which conferred Roman citizenship on all free persons of the Roman world and which automatically made them worshippers of Roman gods? Perhaps, though one should not forget that this globalization may already be found, in statu nascendi, in the prayer of the Augustan Secular Games, more than one hundred and sixty years before the vow of the principate of Marcus Aurelius. At the same time, in order to appreciate in what way the Augustan formula does not accord with a globalization of religion, it suffices on the one hand to recall that active participation in the Secular Games was strictly restricted to Roman citizens and, on the other, to observe that the prayer contains an archaïzing formula, perhaps taken from an even older prayer in order to compose the Augustan one: "that the Latin should always obey" (*utique Latinus semper optemperassit*). Under Augustus, this formula has the air of the old republic, and of the difficult relationship Rome had with the Latin city-states of the area, and much later with the allies who were called Latin, who had an inferior form of citizenship. In the Secular Games of 204 CE, this formula was taken up again. In other words, the prayer put the allies and the subjects of the Roman people in their precise place. As good masters, the Romans prayed for the health of their allies and subjects into the next generation, but at the same time they prayed for them to remain in their historic role—that is to say, that they should obey their masters. This formula, which expresses with perfect naturalness a Roman imperialist mentality, resembles the prayer that the father of a family made for the safety of his household, which included his slaves, and in which he emphasized also that the slaves should remain in the place that was theirs. A formula of this type is recorded by Cato the Censor in his treatise on agriculture, written in the second century BCE. When offering sacrificial cakes to Janus and Jupiter, or *suovetaurilia* (a pig, a sheep, and a bull) to Mars, the father of the family asked of them that they should be good-willed and favorable to himself, his children, his family (*domus*), and his household (*familia*), which is to say, his slaves.[7]

I would therefore not draw too many or too strong conclusions from the votive formula employed by the Arvals in the years 166–170. The commingling of allies and also of subjects as beneficiaries of cult is, on some level, a correlate to the imperial practice of welcoming *incolae* and other temporary travelers in a city at grand festivals. By contrast, the prayers that we have examined show that those for whom religion was celebrated were above all the Roman people, enumerated by means of its hierarchical components. On certain occasions, one could join to them the allies and even the subjects, but it is important to understand the particular meaning of this extension of the benefits of the most official form of cult. About it, some have claimed that it neither united nor concerned anyone other than a smattering of aristocrats, who merely desired to *present* the rites as the center of religious life for all Romans. This view is, in my opinion, erroneous, in part because it does not take proper account of the conceptual framework of Roman ritual practice and in part because it misapprehends the importance of the rites.

In order to enrich this first finding, we can explore other aspects of the definition of the "body of the faithful," to use the modern expression once again. In particular, let us turn our attention to the formulas of exclusion that appear in certain rites, especially in the case of those religious events that are thought to have united a large audience—namely, the games.

The Public Character of Religious Acts and the Exclusion of Non-Citizens

The protocols of the Secular Games contain no formula explicitly excluding slaves. By contrast, the historian Zosimus, writing in Greek circa 500 CE, specifies that during the distribution of *suffimenta*, purificatory substances, with an eye toward participation in the games, slaves received none.[8] Only free persons benefited. But since the rite of purification was necessary in order to attend the games, this means that slaves were excluded.[9] Evidence connected with the *Ludi Megalenses*, celebrated in the year 194 BCE in honor of the goddess Cybele, the Great Mother, from 4 to 10 April, likewise signals that slaves were invited to exit the area at the start of the games.[10] The information regarding these two festivals has served as the basis for a double affirmation.[11] Their public character is immediately impugned, and it is suggested that the ritual exclusion of the non-free was not respected, and this is taken as demonstrating that religious practice cannot have aided in the constitution of identity. Both types of argument are erroneous. Let us begin with the public character of the games.

If we take a look at the verbal protocols of the celebrations of the Secular Games, we find that the *quindecimviri*, the fifteen priests who celebrated the games, call together the *liberi*, free persons, to come take the *suffimenta*.[12]

Consider first the term *liberi*: does it designate all free persons of Rome, or only Roman citizens? To learn the answer, one may read the letter sent to the *quindecimviri* by Septimius Severus and Caracalla in 204 in the context of a subsequent celebration of the Secular Games: they were convoked "in order to draw lots as to who would distribute the *suffimenta* to the people [*populus*], and in what place."[13] To verify that the term *populus* should not be interpreted in an anachronistic fashion as "the people," which is to say, the mass of human beings, but rather in a precise fashion as "the Roman people," which is to say, the totality of Roman citizens, it is sufficient to read the protocols regarding the actual distribution. On 26 May, "the emperors Severus and Antoninus Augustus . . . went to the Palatine, to the precinct of the temple of Apollo. After they had ascended a tribunal, . . . they gave the suffimenta to . . . as well as to the Equestrian Order, to the plebs and to the Roman people."[14] A little later, the other *quindecimviri* distribute the *suffimenta* to the people. One has the impression that the distribution was performed according to legal rank. I suppose that, in the lacuna recorded in the quotation above, some phrase such as "to the Senatorial order" was mentioned, preceded perhaps by "to the magistrates and priests of the Roman people." In other words, all the constituent parties of the Roman people were called together: the magistrates and priests and the senatorial and equestrian elite; on a second tier, the plebs, which is to say the part of the Roman people that received rations of free grain; and then the rest of the Roman people. Elsewhere, a little earlier in the protocols, the summons to the rites of the Secular Games is addressed to the *Quirites*, which is to say, to the citizens insofar as these together constitute the Roman people.[15]

The Secular Games have been characterized by some as announcing in a spectacular fashion the appearance of a new type of piety, which was neither civic nor ritualistic but rather a piety of a Greek type.[16] In consequence of the information laid out above, the Games seem rather to have been restricted to Roman citizens and their families. Moreover, one need only read the descriptions of the celebrations to discover that, far from projecting an individualist, spiritual fervor or some mystical air, one observes little beyond the manifestation of old-fashioned ritual piety. The sacrificial prayer extends the well-being consequent upon the rites to the allies and subjects of the empire, but the celebrants are the priests of the Roman people.

As regards the Megalesian Games, their public and civic status is denied by critics of the model of *polis*-religion, who urge that this holiday concerned only the elite and not the entire community. However, the evidence for this ceremony, although sparse, is nevertheless clear. To suggest that the Games were a holiday simply for the patrician elite, three arguments are advanced: they fell to the responsibility of the curule aediles, magistrates of patrician rank; during performances, senators sat apart from non-senators;[17] and finally, the nobility celebrated *mutitiones*, collective banquets, behind closed doors.[18]

That the festival was organized by the curule aediles is a banality. Roman public games were basically always orchestrated by one of the group of aediles, curule or plebeian, sometimes by the consuls, sometimes by the urban praetor, or sometimes by the priests. This does not signify that this great festival concerned only senators or patricians, but rather that one of the representatives of the Roman people in its totality had the annual duty of celebrating these games. It would never occur to anyone that a religious service celebrated by a catholic priest or a pastor was directed exclusively at the clergy, or the nobility if the celebrant were of aristocratic origin. As with all acts that concerned the Roman people, the conduct of religious affairs belonged to the magistrates or the priests. Representation of the people was assured, at Rome, by senators and patricians. This amounted in no way to an exclusion of the ordinary citizen, and it is notable that no indication is given about the numerical participation of citizens who did not belong to the elite. On the contrary, we know that the Roman plebs rushed to the games.

The second argument that is taken to demonstrate the closed nature of this festival, that regarding the separate seating for senators, is even more nonsensical to relate.[19] That senators should occupy separate places from non-senators in public spaces was quite simply the custom, the social etiquette of a community articulated in distinct juridical ranks, among whom senators and likewise Roman equestrians had separate seating. This has no implication for any so-called aristocratic character of games or religious rites in which they took part. At the circus, too, senators, magistrates, priests, equestrians, and so on always benefited from separate seating. But this did not make chariot races or wild animal hunts or gladiatorial games into events exclusively for aristocrats. Nor did the fact of separate seating shock the Roman plebs. An anecdote from Tacitus proves this.[20] One day, Frisian ambassadors attended a festival at the Theater of Pompey and asked that the system of seating in the building be explained to them. When the banks of seats for senators were pointed out to them, they saw some men in foreign dress seated there. On being told that these were ambassadors from nations most distinguished for their bravery and friendship, the Frisians went and seated themselves as well in the seats for senators. Their boldness was taken in good spirit by the attendants, as the mark of an ancient frankness and the product of a spirit of emulation, or so comments Tacitus. Apparently no one was surprised that the system of seating at spectacles should, by virtue of legal regulation, reflect social distinctions. The narrative shows that the audience might rather be shocked by the presumption of the Germans, which shows on the one hand that no one questioned the Roman system of social ranks and, on the other, that everyone observed rather carefully the scruples associated with that social system.

As for the *mutitationes* described by Aulus Gellius,[21] the issue concerns invitations that patrician families issued to one another to their respective homes. The topic therefore concerns the oldest Roman families—the "Trojan" families, one might say; it was, in other words, a social practice among a restricted group of aristocrats, and the banquets in question were closed. What one must understand is that these invitations belonged to the totality of rituals connected with the celebration. Cybele, the Great Mother, had been introduced for her mythical connection to the Trojan origins of Rome and to Aeneas in particular. To him she had furnished the wood to construct the fleet with which he had been able to flee Troy and reach Italy.[22] In the ritual device of the Megalesian Games, these intimate narratives of the great families who called themselves Trojan recalled one of the reasons for the introduction of the Great Mother to Rome. One can imagine that these invitations, even if they took place exclusively among the so-called Trojans, contributed to the grandeur of the occasion. One of the attractions of the holiday was to see these families pay their respects to one another; and although the actual fulfillment of the ritual requirement for banquets was closed to public scrutiny, it formed part of the obligations of the festival, under the same title, as it were, as the public sacrifice to Cybele and the games, which parts were accessible to all. We cannot say more, because of the gaps in our knowledge. However, the end of the passage of Aulus Gellius that cites the *mutitationes* and shows the ritual side of these invitations also reports that the Roman plebs did the same thing during the festival of the Cerealia. Where, then, is the exclusively aristocratic side of civic religion?

None of these arguments therefore convinces. On the contrary, the very examples that are invoked by critics of the civic model in fact show that civic religion was a form of cult shared among all citizens, under different modalities, and that the beneficiary and authority with final responsibility for the rites was the Roman people, in all its aspects. How in these conditions can one refuse to admit that the agent in cult and the object of its actions is the civic community, with its earthly goals, and not the individual with his metaphysical aspirations? This can be maintained only by denying altogether the existence of an institutional religion of the sort clearly attested by the sources.

One can thus see that the overall presentation of the Megalesian Games is immediately marked by contradiction and misunderstanding. It is the same for the second argument, which seeks to show that collective religion could never contribute to the constitution of identity, insofar as there was no exclusionary rule in Roman religion.

An attempt has been made to demonstrate the inefficacy of excluding slaves from public cult by citing the reproach addressed by Cicero to his enemy Clodius. Clodius had disturbed the games of the Great Mother in 56 BCE, over which he had presided as curule aedile, by allowing slaves to manifest themselves noisily there.[23] To establish the basic impiety of Clodius, Cicero denounces him, during a hearing several weeks or months after the event, with the claim that, previously, when Clodius's own father and uncle celebrated these games, they ordered slaves to leave the theater and separated them from free men through the voice of heralds. With the consent of their descendant, behold, hordes of slaves chased the free away with their fists and attended the games. Stefan Krauter believes bluntly that the adverb *antea*, "formerly," can mean nothing other than that, in the age of Cicero, slaves were not excluded from the Games of the Great Mother. The only thing that is correct in this deduction is that, in the generation of Clodius's immediate ancestors, the exclusion of slaves concerned the Megalesian Games and that this evidence is not sufficient to extend this rule to the full ensemble of games. Is it possible to conclude that, in the age of Cicero, the ritual of exclusion had no place? Perhaps, but not for the reasons imagined. The profanation of the Megalesian Games and the hearing about the response of the haruspices took place in 56 BCE, therefore during a period of agitation that more and more closely resembled a civil war. It is therefore in every way difficult to perceive the normal functioning of Roman religion under exceptional circumstances. And it is not impossible that the religious restoration undertaken by Augustus addressed itself to rules such as this one, neglected for a generation or two, and this would explain its renewed attestation during the Secular Games. Also, one must pay attention to the context of the hearing. In his argument, Cicero takes pains to refer to the immediately prior generation of Clodius's family but does not actually say anything about the present. He intends to contrast, in the very family of Clodius, those who showed themselves pious and had respected custom, on the one hand, with Clodius himself on the other, who had conducted himself so inappropriately. In any event, if one must juggle texts in this way in order to prove that slaves were no longer ritually excluded from the games, I fear that the conclusions will inevitably be extremely fragile. From these texts I retain only the datum that, at least in the preceding generation, around 99 to 91 BCE, when the father and uncle of Clodius were curule aediles, that is to say, when they organized the games, the exclusion still existed. And as we investigate Roman religion in the historical period, this datum seems to me important. Whether in the age of Clodius the rule had been forgotten or was violated is in fact merely anecdotal knowledge and was treated as an aberration.

Beyond this episode, other arguments are invoked in favor of the hypothesis of the non-exclusion of slaves from public cult. The first concerns information ostensibly about the conservatism of the emperor Claudius, who was seriously deformed. In his *Life of Claudius*, Suetonius wrote: "Touching religious ceremonies and civil and military customs, as well as the condition of all classes at home and abroad, he corrected various abuses, revived some old customs or even established new ones."[24] He provides three examples in the religious domain: his taking of an oath, following ancient custom, when nominating a candidate for election to a priesthood; the announcing of propitiatory rites before the People's assembly by the urban praetor when the earth shook; and finally, the passage that concerns us. Suetonius writes: "[He carefully observed the scruple] of offering a supplication whenever a bird of ill-omen was seen on the Capitol. This he supervised himself in his capacity as pontifex maximus, dictating the form of the words to the people from the *rostra*, after the crowd of laborers and slaves had been removed."[25] Krauter urges that the crowd of laborers and slaves would have been removed above all in order to produce calm in the Forum.[26] Once again, this interpretation errs by virtue of superficiality and so misses an opportunity to craft an argument in favor of the collective practice of civic religion. First, unless one imagines a work site before the rostrum, I do not see how laborers and slaves would have troubled the peace of the Forum—no more than the merchants, who were certainly more numerous and more noisy. What's more, all the laborers were certainly not slaves. Finally, I know of no work site in the forum under Claudius. Why, therefore, this precaution on the part of the emperor? I would seek an explanation in the area of a regulation that had fallen into general disuse, as Suetonius wrote: it is this that the anecdote must aim to prove, and not that Claudius was crazy about silence.

The exclusion of slaves could be a return to or reintroduction of compliance with an old custom, to wit, of celebrating cult among free persons. As the entire chapter is concerned with a conservative restoration of customs, there is no reason to exclude this interpretation, if the noise caused by slaves was not in fact the cause. But the laborers? There's the rub: to interpret Roman religion, one must know it well. In this case, one needs to know that during celebrations of cult, work must cease, at least within the environment of the religious action. We know the rules concerning the obligatory cessation of all work on the basis of texts concerning certain priesthoods—for example, the flamen of Jupiter and the so-called king of rites (*rex sacrorum*). We also know that the days of great festivals were holidays, and likewise the period of celebration of public rites, at least within the immediate perimeter of the ritual scene. This was because the times and places in question were assigned to the gods and activities that concerned them, and not to mortals and their affairs. The propitiatory prayer was an important public rite: the very fact that the pontifex maximus participated is a strong indication of its importance. The people were therefore called together in the forum at the appointed hour and, at the moment of the prayer, Claudius caused an announcement to be made, out of respect for sacredness of the hour and for the exclusion of laborers, be they slaves or free men. What's more, this proclamation corresponded to an ancestral tradition, like the neglected rite of seeking signs in response to an ill-omened augury. We cannot analyze these exclusions further than this, because the text says nothing more.

However, what has not explicitly been raised in regard to this text is that it offers a very fine example of a civic religious rite, in the heyday of the imperial period. The propitiatory prayer was pronounced by all the citizens present who responded to the summons; the pontifex maximus in person dictated the wording to them, according to the rite of public prayer. Just as for Claudius, an ill-omened augury occurring on the Capitol concerned the Roman people and appeared a serious matter, so, too, he held that the Roman people should pronounce the formula of propitiation itself, without intermediation. Please note: as always, it was not the person who dictated the prayer whose action was held efficacious, but those who repeated after him. In other words, it was the citizens assembled in response to the official summons who pronounced the performative formula. One is reminded at this juncture of the famous episode of the *ver sacrum*, the sacred spring.[27] In 217 BCE, after the Roman military disaster at Lake Trasimene, where Hannibal annihilated a Roman army, the Senate ordered, among other rites and dedications at temples, the votive consecration to Jupiter of "all that the spring would produce from herds of pigs, sheep, goats and cattle," if in five years the *respublica* of the Roman people and the Quirites had been preserved safe and sound in its present wars. According to the long votive formula, which is impassioned and appears in its substance to be authentic, the citizens are obliged to sacrifice victims individually. However, once consulted, the pontiffs specified that what was at issue in this vow was the individual property of all Roman citizens and not their common, public patrimony. They therefore recommended that the votive formula be approved by all citizens. The people were therefore summoned to the forum, and the formula in question was there approved by a vote.

Moreover, in this same formula, amid various details concerning the fulfillment of the votive contract, which mentioned among other things that all sacrifices were to be held valid, whatever might be the form in which they took place, one finds the following stipulation: "whether offered at night or by day, by a slave or a free man." I can conclude only one thing: just as normally a sacrifice to Jupiter the Best and Greatest could be celebrated only by day and not by night, so a sacrifice to the supreme god of the Romans ought to be celebrated by a free man and not a slave. But in those exceptional circumstances, given the urgency and complexity of fulfillment, in terms that had to be honored by all Romans, the formula added these specifications: even if the father of a family caused the sacrifice in question to be celebrated in the manner of a domestic rite, and thus by his *vilicus*—the manager of his farm, who would have been a slave—the rite was valid.

Finally, let us consider one other argument raised against the rule of excluding slaves, which is based on the interpretation by Hermann Diels of the term *aristóphilos* in a Sibylline oracle concerning hermaphrodites, reported as having been cited in deliberations on the sacred at Rome.[28] The interpretation may be correct, but one should not press too hard from a desire to draw general conclusions. Diels wondered in a footnote if the terms *aristóphilos* and *nêpistos* might not signify, very simply, *impius*, "impious."[29] However, in a passage elsewhere in the same book, he suggests that these terms designate the foreigner and the slave who, being of foreign origin and therefore of another religion, were excluded from sacrifices.

A more direct argument against the rule limiting *polis*-religion to the citizen body relies on the formula reported in the eighth century by the Benedictine Paul the Deacon, in his abbreviation of the second-century *Dictionary* of Festus. The entry concerns the injunction *exesto*: "Let it be outside. For thus the lictor proclaimed during certain sacred rites—'Alien, conquered, woman, virgin, be outside!'—for it was forbidden for them to be present."[30]

Is it enough to conclude that one does not know to which cults this formula applied, or why the particular persons mentioned were excluded? As Paul the Deacon does not provide relevant detail, critics of the model of civic religion believe the question should remain open, on the ground that the sources do not permit one to establish that foreigners were systematically excluded from cult. I do not intend to perform a critique of this text all over again, because there is nothing to add to what our predecessors have written. Instead, I would like to underline that no one has ever intended to use this passage to claim that the *Dictionary* of Festus proves that all foreigners were always excluded from cult. Here arises a problem of method that intervenes often in this debate. Our sources are notoriously inadequate. To address this lack, which is characteristic of ancient history, we try to extract the maximum from what exists and to exploit these sources as judiciously as possible, by bringing together fragments of similar texts and comparing the situations therein described with other examples drawn from homologous societies. This critical and comparative method itself constitutes one of the methodological strengths of ancient history. And no historian would have the audacity to claim that he or she knows everything that one ought about the subject in order to address it. In the event, as regards the problem that occupies us, one is reminded that in certain cults, women were effectively excluded; that, in others, there were cases where slaves were excluded, as we have seen; and one must admit that the same thing could occur in the case of foreigners. One can then seek to corroborate this conclusion by examining texts that invoke this type of interdiction. To use the isolated and fragmentary character of the evidence in order to conclude that one cannot reach any firm conclusion is not only to deny the historical method of the critique of documents, but further to call into question all of ancient history; and beyond that, to question history as a scientific pursuit. But if we enter into the same game, we could just as easily conclude that the opposite position is just as unable to prove anything whatsoever. What, then, would be the point of practicing history with sources, none of which suffices to draw a historical conclusion of any validity, however defined? As it happens, we shall see that the lacunose character of the evidence is one of the arguments that is advanced by critics of the model of civic religion in order to propose in its place a philosophical and theological doctrine of religion. In point of fact, ancient history draws inspiration not only from the rules of historical and philological games but also from the teachings of social anthropology.

Let us continue. Another passage has been cited in this context and set in relation to the preceding ones in order to prove that there were in fact rules of exclusion. The passage is the narrative of the arrival of Aeneas at Rome, in book 8 of Vergil's *Aeneid*, and the ancient commentary on this passage. Here is what Evander says when welcoming the Trojans, in the midst of a sacrifice to Hercules: "Meanwhile, since you have come here as friends, in good will celebrate with us these annual rites that it is wrong to defer, and even now grow accustomed to the tables of your allies."[31] In the fifth century of our era, the grammarian Servius comments in the following way on these words: "'Since you have come here as friends': If indeed you have now come as friends. For it was not permitted to associate foreigners in rites. But he associates these to the rites as if joined by ancient friendship, whence he adds, 'and even now grow accustomed to the tables of your allies.'"[32] Krauter refuses to give any credit to the commentary, suggesting that Servius could have invented this claim ad hoc.[33] This is possible, although that only occurs as a general rule in the etiological narratives. In any case, the argument is weak, because we know that women were effectively excluded from the cult of Hercules, and it is perfectly possible that this was also true of strangers, whether as regards this particular cult or as regards public cult more generally. In any event, it is not useful to argue for long about Servius's commentary, when the text of Vergil, which one cannot disallow with a flick of the wrist, clearly implies the exclusion of foreigners who were not allies. Note: Evander's invitation was motivated. He does not simply summon Aeneas and his companions to join the sacrificial banquet. He specifies that it is as allies that he welcomes them to his table, when he had already benefited from the friendship of Anchises, the father of Aeneas. And he announces that he will immediately grant Aeneas the alliance that he seeks. In consequence, the sharing of the sacrificial banquet is made possible insofar as it occurs among allies. If they were not such, they could not participate so simply in the rites. Nothing is therefore truly conclusive in the objections made to the current interpretation of this passage. I skip over the other testimonials cited, concerning which Krauter is right to denounce hasty conclusions.[34]

Authorization to Practice a Cult at Rome

Beyond the few texts that show the restriction of cult to citizens, there is a series of documents that show that, in order to sacrifice on the Capitol, it was necessary to ask permission from the Senate. Livy gives nine explicit examples.[35] One finds similar, direct evidence elsewhere in the treaties of friendship between Rome and the city-states of Astypalaia and Stratonikeia, as well as in the privileges granted by Rome to Mytilene.[36] A trace is likewise preserved in the decree of the Senate that grants diverse privileges to three individuals who had done well by Rome; it notably authorizes them to place an inscription with the relevant decree on the Capitol and to sacrifice there.[37] Several Greek documents of this kind, emanating from allies of the Roman people, were in fact displayed on the Capitol.[38]

These documents are very clear. When official authorization was required to sacrifice on the Capitol and to deposit offerings to Jupiter there, it is logical to suppose that these acts were normally forbidden to foreigners, even if they were kings. One must remember that treaties do not announce norms; they do not reflect the rule. They grant privileges to friends and allies, and thus constitute exceptions. Therefore, when one grants authorization to sacrifice and to dedicate to Roman gods for the well-being and victory of the Roman people, this implies that this is a matter of a wholly exceptional right. For this reason, to conclude that this evidence cannot be used for other Roman sanctuaries, insofar as the Capitol was a special case,[39] as it was the central sanctuary of the empire and so possessed great political and diplomatic importance, is an act of sophistry. We are once again confronted by a manipulation of the sources: since we know only examples relative to the Capitol, the rules could not apply to other cults. Yet Vergil attests the same principle in operation for the *Ara Maxima* (the sacrifice to Hercules), as we have seen, and other evidence confirms this equally well. In consequence, it is more reasonable to think that some such custom apparently existed than to speculate on the basis of silence. Moreover, it should be noted that in Greek states, we know full well that similar interdictions forbade non-citizens to participate in cult and there existed an obligation for individuals to apply to *proxenoi*, officials who supervised relations with foreigners, to obtain this privilege—unless, that is, Philippe Gauthier and his colleagues who have written on these matters are all the victims of a collective hallucination.[40]

Finally, one should add that it is normal not to find allusions to other sanctuaries in such documents: it is precisely because all these examples concern international relations that the decisions contained in them were delivered in written form, from which only some survive to this day. To dismiss this evidence, in its many and diverse forms, which provide that even friends of the Roman people were not permitted to sacrifice for the good of that people without having first sought and received authorization: that seems to me to betray a bias against the ritualistic and poliadic religion of the Romans. The cult on the Capitol cannot be disqualified in a discussion about the nature of religion at Rome because of its clearly political nature. Even Krauter admits that it is actually the Romans' most important cult and temple. In this case, what could better testify to the religion of the Romans than this temple? Of course, one could argue that it was the place where the discourse and practice of the elite most particularly expressed themselves—in brief, that it was a place of non-religion. But arguments of this kind appear to me to give evidence of a certain religious bad faith, so overdetermined as regards the conclusions one might reach as to disallow further scientific conversation.

Moreover, the Capitoline cult is not an isolated case. Let us go to the other extreme. One might, for example, cite the case of the Caristia,[41] one of the rites of private funerary cult, to give evidence that the same type of exclusion existed between families, since only the *cognati* (parents by blood) and *adfines* (parents by marriage) of the deceased had the right to participate in these rituals. Does domestic cult in its turn betray a discourse of patriarchy, such that fathers of families were able to arrange private religion to the advantage of their families?

One more word about the debate concerning the exclusion of foreigners. The famous edict of the emperor Caracalla that granted citizenship to all free aliens in the Roman world contains a religious argument, although sadly the condition of the papyrus does not allow us to understand it completely. On any reading, Caracalla argues that, in virtue of the right of citizenship that will henceforth be theirs, aliens can join themselves to the Romans in praying to the gods, or, rather, to the Roman gods. Let us turn to the papyrus of Giessen that appears to preserve a copy of the edict.[42] If we allow, with all other historians, against Hartmut Wolff, that the papyrus transcribes this constitution well,[43] we learn that the emperor, in giving thanks for being rescued from danger, gave the right of Roman citizenship to all free persons of the emperor while preserving all the rights of their city-states of origin. Moreover, the emperor ascribed the motivation for his action to the fact that thus "he will lead to the [sanctuaries?] of the gods [these other people,] who join themselves to my subjects." As Christa Frateantonio has already emphasized,[44] there is not the least indication, neither in the papyrus nor in the rest of the evidence, that this edict officially recognized all cults attested in the empire and integrated them in the cult of the state, as Robert Muth supposed.[45] It merits attention that one part of the edict specifies that the rights and obligations held by those receiving citizenship toward their city-states of origin are to be preserved. This is a stipulation that we find in identical terms in the documentary records of grants of citizenship to individuals, as, for example, in the tabula from Banasa, which dates to 178 CE.[46] Among the obligations one owed to one's city, as we have already recalled, were fiscal ones, as well as participation in local political office, but also religious obligations. Also, contrary to the claim of Hartmut Wolff,[47] there is no need to believe that Roman citizenship became in this era some sort of personal status and was no longer bound to the legal framework of a local city. We have already seen that, from 89 BCE, it was Roman citizenship that anchored citizens to their little fatherland, their city of origin. There can be no question of there being a "citizenship of the empire," any more than there can be of a "religion of the empire." The only cult of the empire that joined all Roman citizens was that which was celebrated in their name and for them at Rome, on the banks of the Tiber, by means of the conduct of the magistrates and priests of the Roman people. All other religious obligations were tied to local contexts.

To return to our discussion, it is clear that, whatever the details of its formulation, the Antonine Constitution gives the impression that, formerly, aliens could not simply assimilate themselves to Romans in order to pray to the gods. And if that was not possible, it was because they were not Roman citizens. As Cicero says, "Every *civitas*, city or citizen body, has its own religious obligation, as we have ours."[48] No one was supposed to celebrate the rites of another city. It was possible under certain circumstances, and no one opposed it, so long as the rules of admission were respected, but to imagine that everyone could simply participate in obedience to some personal impulse goes against everything that our evidence tells us.

I am not going to examine the topic of priestly responsibilities, since the debate borders on the absurd.[49] To maintain that the sources indicate in no way that a priest ought to be a Roman citizen and to dismiss the case of the priestesses of Ceres, who had come from Greece or Sicily but immediately received Roman citizenship, on the grounds that the cult of Ceres would have had great political importance for the plebs, or that Cicero would have exaggerated the importance of this custom in the context of a hearing about a contested case of citizenship, amounts once again to playing with the sources. On the one hand, the priestesses of Ceres were not attached to the cult of Ceres, Liber, and Libera: that was the cult tied to the plebs, and it was celebrated by the flamen of Ceres. The priestesses of Ceres rather concerned themselves with the cult of Ceres-Demeter and Proserpina-Kore, which was not the same thing as the plebeian triad Ceres, Liber, and Libera. And on the other, the political importance of a cult does not determine whether it is religious or credible. As for being surprised that the sources do not explicitly say that priests ought to be Roman citizens, one could say the same about magistrates, senators, equestrians, legionaries, judges, or the plebeians who received free grain: the claim, which I have already cited, is so absurd that it does not merit response.

In short, to argue that in all the evidence nothing proves that the possession of rights in the community was necessary to participate in cult or to organize cult activities, but that every occasion where this necessity is attested is an isolated case and thus not relevant to a general inquiry, amounts to a denial of historical method and comes very close to an argument *ex silentio*. The critics nevertheless argue thus: the important thing was to belong to the social and political elite—though they rarely take the trouble to specify or investigate what this claim might amount to—and the mass of citizens would never have access to cultic functions. Even in the rare cases when the totality

of the population was summoned to participate in cult, as during the Secular
Games, it was all free persons and not citizens who would have been summoned.[50] In consequence, citizenship would never have played a determinate
role in the practice of religion in the city of Rome. In sum, civic cult, civic
religion, was a fantasy. Moreover, it is concluded that in the multiform, daily
cult that existed to one side of the official religion of the elite, rights in the city
were not important. What of themes like the acquisition of material goods,
sickness, health, or the family? In what way did they contribute to the definition of collective political identity?

As always, the conclusion reveals the operation of sophistry. One wants
to prove that civic religion and the religious community to which citizens
belonged did not exist, or in any case that no decisive proof would allow one
to claim otherwise. But why not? No scholar of antiquity shrinks from check-
ing the sources, and I am the first to recognize that our general interpretations
are sometimes daring and that our evidence is often insufficient or obscure.
In this case, however, matters are different. Here, the sources are incompletely
interpreted and used with an eye toward partial or erroneous conclusions. In
this case, the twisting of the evidence has for its sole aim to allow the conclusion that those who celebrated cult did not feel in the least bit concerned with
civic religion and that their actual interests were not in politics or the city, but
the family, their personal health, or their affairs.

I do not want to enter into the argument that the needs of individuals were
not taken into account by civic religion. I will content myself first by recalling
that the healing cults of Apollo and Aesculapius were introduced by the magistrates and the Senate, and that they were civic cults. Next, I will cite once again
Minucius Felix, who emphasizes through the figure of the pagan Caecilius that
it is in "the temples and sanctuaries of the gods, which protect and adorn the
city and community of Rome," that "our seers, in communion with the god and
filled with its presence, have a foretaste of the future; warning they furnish for
danger, remedy for disease, hope for suffering, help for affliction, relief for hard-
ship."[51] In other words, that which individuals are thought to seek elsewhere—at
least, according to the critique of official cult—is procured, still at the beginning
of the third century CE, in the great civic temples of Rome.

The idea that it might be through the framework of the city, or in a community that functions like a city, that private cult ordered itself is not even
considered. The reason for this is that the people who look down on the civic

model of religion want above all to maintain that religion is something else entirely. For them, it was not a formalist ritualism that filled the mold, as it were, of Roman institutions and society, but some personal feeling that concerned exclusively the individual and his or her bond with a divinity.

In suggesting that anyone could participate in cult and that no one was excluded, the critics of *polis*-religion seek to convince us that the contours of civic religion were completely fluid, to the point of rendering them nonexistent. By then reducing civic religion to some political rites celebrated by the elite and to a discourse maintained by aristocrats anxious to justify their domination, the critics seek to assert the notion that such a "religion" could never respond to the demands that individuals addressed to gods.

It is not that simple. What about religious repression? If it existed, official religion was not as soft and fluid as is claimed. Repression therefore traces the limits of collective religious practice.

Chapter 7

Religious Repression

The study of breaches of piety is important for the understanding of Roman religion. This is so not only because it allows one to establish that the ancients paid attention to religious matters and had a clear perception of them, but also because it tells us something about the religious community itself, which was affected by those breaches. For critics of the model of civic religion, the attested rules and norms prove only that repression was effective within the religious space that the city directly controlled. For the rest, Rome would have been too big for anyone to be able to regulate religious practice effectively. However, those critics fail to consider the possibility that the city did not have control over all aspects of religious practice because not all communities were relevant to its self-understood role. Nuance is essential. Let us consider first the sources concerned with *piacula*, expiations for religious infractions.

Thirty-five years ago, I employed this means to ascertain in what measure systems of blame in religious matters permitted one to circumscribe the responsibility of citizens.[1] My point of departure was certain documents, which I in part reinterpreted: these showed that the citizen was responsible only for his personal acts, not for those of the collectivity. But, in the framework of public religion, religious practice was the sole responsibility of the city and its representatives. In public cult, religious initiative was delegated exclusively by the Roman people. Fundamentally, no one could sin, not even a magistrate of the Roman people. Religious actors could only temporarily trouble relations between the city and its gods, up until the moment when the authorities perceived the impiety and proved the goodwill of the civic community. It seemed to me important to observe that similar rules obtained in the framework of religious misdeeds as existed in the realm of criminal law: if a misdeed was involuntary, it could be repaired without problem by the agent of the infraction himself. But in the case of willful misconduct, the culprit was immediately excluded from civic and religious life, while the city for its part restored good relations with the divinity harmed.

To understand this aspect of civic religion well, compare this understanding of impiety with Christian sin. The latter concerns exclusively the guilty individual. Whether voluntary or involuntary, culpability rests with the individual alone. A priest can indicate to the person a penalty to allow him or her to try to redeem the fault, but in no case does the fault alone place the rest of the religious community in danger. For that, it would be necessary for all the individuals in the community to conduct themselves badly. That was not the case at Rome. It was enough that a commander of troops, even of subordinate rank, pillage a place of cult for the entire Roman people to be at risk of guilt for sacrilege. Once the crime is discovered, the Roman authorities immediately expiate the involuntary impiety of the *respublica* of the Roman people and take the necessary measures to repair the harm. The immediately guilty party is arrested and imprisoned with an eye to judgment, but there was never a question of rehabilitation nor even of punishment for impiety. The eventual punishment was supposed to focus on the material harm caused to the Roman people. The narrative to which I have just alluded is that of Quintus Pleminius during the Second Punic War: he punished the Locrians in a terrifying fashion for having aided Hannibal and pillaged the sanctuary of Persephone that was located in their city.[2] Contrary to what one might think, narratives of this type were not merely edifying examples of ancestral piety, but affirmations of the norms that the Romans and, as it happens, the new master of Rome, Augustus, wished to restore at the beginning of our era. In my study, I tried to show, against Mommsen and Wissowa, that this attitude prevailed under the empire, and that it did not yield to a softer or more lenient practice as regards impiety, as they had argued.[3] Stefan Krauter questions my interpretation, and I must briefly return to the documents on which I based my reflections.

The sources that inform us agree about the principle that a deliberate act of impiety immediately rendered the guilty party impious and excludes him or her from the community. Consider some examples. The famous pontifex maximus Quintus Mucius Scaevola, who held office at the end of the second century BCE, decided, for example, that a praetor who had given ritual formulas for a trial during a holiday would be the object of the following sanction: "The praetor who then spoke, if he did it unintentionally, can be expiated by the sacrifice of an expiatory victim; but if he spoke intentionally, Quintus Mucius said that, being impious, he could not be expiated."⁴ The expiatory sacrifice transmits an excuse to the gods and thus relieves the person who offers the sacrifice of responsibility. Another series of responses of the pontifex maximus Scaevola is cited by Macrobius:

> The priests [to wit, the pontiffs], moreover, used to claim that religious festivals [*feriae*] became polluted if any work was undertaken once they had been proclaimed and formally scheduled. The priest in charge of sacrifices and the flamens were also forbidden to observe any work being done during festivals: that's why their approach was announced by a herald, so that any such activity would cease, and anyone who ignored the announcement was fined. Indeed, besides the fine there was the rule that a person who out of ignorance performed some work on such occasions was obliged to offer expiation with a pig. Scaevola the pontiff used to claim that one who intentionally acted thus could not offer expiation, though Umbro denies that pollution is suffered by one who undertook a task that served the gods or their sacred rites or performed some action that met a vitally pressing need. Scaevola, finally, when asked what one was permitted to do on a holiday, replied, "What would cause harm if neglected."⁵

These jurisprudential principles are also visible at work in historical narratives as well as in the *Laws* of Cicero. According to Cicero, a religious infraction committed in an impious fashion cannot be expiated—which is to say, the guilty party would be considered as impious. Cicero continues his prescriptions as follows: "Let the public priests expiate what can be expiated."⁶ He adds that the impious should not have the audacity to want to appease the gods with gifts. The deliberate sacrileges committed by Pleminius in 205 BCE at Locri and by Fulvius Flaccus in 174 BCE in the temple of Juno Lacinia at Croton, in Calabria, led equally resolutely to a judgment of impiety against those who committed them and to an expiation by the pontiffs, which relieved the Roman people of responsibility. I concluded that the individual responsible for the transgression, even if he were a high magistrate, did not have the power to directly implicate the civic community. Its responsibility extended only to its own actions. An individual who deliberately offended the gods would alone suffer the consequences. By considering the person impious, the Roman authorities freed the civic community from divine punishment following the principle of *noxae datio*, according to which the response to offenses was directed toward the party responsible for the offenses, in order not to arouse a blind or blanket action by the offended group. I will not dwell on this aspect of the topic, as I have treated it at length elsewhere.[7] What needs emphasis is that, fundamentally, religious offense is not an individual act. It is incapable of attracting divine attention to the offending party; if intentional offenses had been understood to attract the attention of the gods directly to the person who committed them, no collective action would have been necessary. Religious offenses therefore threatened above all the sole entity responsible for collective relations with the gods—namely, the civic community. In this regard, one might cite a parallel from international relations: a deliberate illegality committed against a state by an actor from another state, even an official representative, could be resolved through the expulsion and forfeit of the actor to the offended party. Guilt was understood to belong to the collectivity, which was threatened with reprisal, and it might be lifted only by a collective decision to enact reparation for the offense.[8] All this appears to me to prove that in Roman public cult the civic community, the *respublica* of the Roman people, alone possessed a religious personality, and that it possessed this collectively. Offense against the gods, if it was serious, could not be resolved except at this level.

That said, a normative text of the third century BCE appears to call into question the rigor with which punishments for impiety were enforced. At issue are two inscriptions discovered on the territory of the Latin colony of Spoleto, founded in 241 BCE. The inscriptions give the same regulation protecting the integrity of a sacred grove.[9] The sanction against infractions that concludes the text appears to call into question the procedure that I have just described. And as the evidence arises from normative texts of a public nature, it is important. It reads as follows:

> If someone has violated [sc. "this sacred grove" or "this regulation"],
> let an expiatory sacrifice of an ox be given to Jupiter [*Iove bouid*
> *piaclum datod*],[10] to whom the sacred grove belongs. If someone has
> violated [sc. "this sacred grove" or "this regulation"] deliberately

and with malice aforethought, let an expiatory sacrifice be given
to Jupiter [*Iove bouid piaclum datod*], and let there by a fine of 300
bronze coins. Let responsibility for the offering of the expiatory sacrifice and the collection of the fine belong to the *dicator* [the local
magistrate, who officiates in the name of the collective].[11]

Mommsen, followed by Wissowa, saw in these sanctions evidence of a more
gentle attitude to impiety.[12] In their view, in both cases—the one of uninten-
tional and the other of intentional misdeed—the *piaculum* was offered by the
impious party, who in the case of an intentional violation could pay a fine for
having violated the rule of the colony. Hence, this is how they translate the
phrase *Iove bouid piaclum datod*: "he shall offer through an intermediary a cow
as expiatory sacrifice to Jupiter."

This interpretation was called into question in a Dutch thesis completed
in 1921 by Sebastian Tromp.[13] In conclusions that appear to me always precise,
Tromp argues that the offense performed *scie(n)s dolo malo*, "deliberately and
with malice aforethought," disturbed the peaceful relations of the entire community with the gods, as I have just suggested. And he calls attention to the
examples and norms that I have cited.

For his part, Stefan Krauter seems to have understood the importance of
this representation of impiety, according to which the guilty individual is actually in some way an event or an offense that extends beyond him- or herself,
since, in cases where the fault is found to be serious, the guilty party is effaced
in one way or another.[14] Wissowa, on the other hand, rejected Tromp's interpretation of the rule from Spoleto because he believed that grammar rendered
it impossible.[15] Krauter repeats this critique in order to prove that city-states
did not exercise strict supervision over religious matters. Let us take a closer
look at the alleged grammatical incorrectness of our interpretation. Wissowa
and Krauter think that, in the phrase just cited, the subject of *datod*—the crucial verb of the prescription—ought to be the same as that of the subordinate
conditional phrase that precedes it: "If someone has violated [sc. 'this sacred
grove' or 'this regulation'] deliberately and with malice aforethought." To want
to change the subject of the verb *datod* and in its place recognize the *dicator*
runs counter to elementary rules of language and renders the phrase incom-
prehensible, since there would be a change of subject.

It is possible that my explanation is not clear enough. In spite of my long-standing and profound admiration for Georg Wissowa, who certainly knew Latin better than I do, I will allow myself to repeat my interpretation. I do not want to linger over the difficulty of Latin texts, especially such as involve technical matters; they do not contribute to my interpretation. My understanding of the phrase is simply different than Wissowa's. As I signaled in a text that I presented at a roundtable in 2004,[16] I take the verb *datod* not as active imperative, but as passive, as I have just done in my translation: "let an expiatory sacrifice be given." This way of reading the sanction poses no problem to the reading of the sentence. The sentence contains a second verb, *suntod*, whose subject is also different from the subject of the conditional proposition. If he had wanted not to mislead at this point, the editor ought to have written again *a(sses) (trecentos) datod*: "Let him give 300 bronze coins." I therefore understand that, in the two types of situations, a *piaculum* is offered, with the rule specifying who should make the offering. That detail is given at the end of the rule: the *exactio*—literally, the levying of the *piaculum* and the fine—falls to the *dicator*. Applied to the *piaculum*, the term *exactio* does not mean "performance," as I wrote in 1980, but "levying of an obligation." The *piaculum* is regarded as something owed to the gods under the same legal title as a fine is owed to the colony. One must suppose, therefore, that the *dicator* offered the two sacrifices, or he constrained the guilty party to do it. One can be no more precise.

Understood in this way, the rule does not contradict in any way the other rules applied in the same era or later. For his part, Krauter is not able to admit this. He cannot imagine that a society as open as that of the Romans of the second century BCE could act repressively. Otherwise, according to him, we would not know of but a single case of exclusion from civil society being imposed as a punishment on someone guilty of intentional religious misdeed.

Once again, we meet the assertion that the stated and published rules of cult would have been nothing more than the object of debates that magistrates and legal academics found it amusing to conduct, but outside their circle, these principles would not have been applied. The more-or-less contemporary affairs of Pleminius and Flaccus are accepted by Krauter.[17] But they are simply bracketed by him, on the grounds that they concerned persons of high rank whose sacrilegious acts might have provoked international conflict. Everyone understood, in Krauter's view, that there was no common measure that also applied to individuals who violated the integrity of small sacred groves. By way of a response, one might insist on some details: at the time of the forfeit of Pleminius, the city of Locri, an ancient ally of the Romans, had submitted and was occupied; for its part, Croton was then nothing but a shadow of its former self; it had at most two thousand inhabitants. One cannot speak of an international conflict between Rome and this village. Some years later, moreover, in 194 BCE, it became a Roman colony, and so, in 174 BCE, the sacrilege of Flaccus was a matter purely internal to Rome. In addition—and this is crucial in these affairs—in the debate in the Senate in 174, the sentiment was clearly voiced that the gods would hold the Roman people to account: it was they who were responsible.[18] The rule at Spoleto sanctions precisely the consequences of a sacrilege committed, as had Pleminius and Flaccus in the sanctuaries at Locri and Croton. And nothing prevents one from understanding the colonial rule as a transposition of the principles at stake in the affair at Croton.

It is also necessary to take account of the fact that the rule from Spoleto does not mark an end to the severe treatment of cases of impiety. Through Cicero and beyond, the same principles are always affirmed. I am of course willing to acknowledge that all was not right at Rome and in the world. That said, even if Cicero has to admit that impiety is often not punished during the life of the guilty party, that has no consequence for the norm that he affirms. A little before Cicero, the pontifex maximus Scaevola and other jurists had expatiated on these same principles, without changing anything. And after Cicero, they are once against reaffirmed by the emperors Tiberius, Severus Alexander, and Justinian.

The three cases of impiety known from the imperial period concern perjury. In his treatise *On the Laws*, Cicero states that the divine penalty for perjury is death, and the human penalty is dishonor.[19] The same definition is placed on the lips of the emperor Tiberius in the *Annals* of Tacitus, in narrating a case of anonymous accusation.[20] According to Tacitus, someone accused a certain Rubrius of having committed perjury in taking an oath on the power of the divine Augustus, the *numen Divi Augusti*. It is essential to understand that perjury was a grave offense that affected the honor of a divinity, insofar as it had served as witness and guarantor of the oath taken. When the emperor Tiberius learned of this accusation, he wrote to the consuls to the effect that Augustus had not been divinized so that the honor might operate to the harm of citizens. As for the rest, Tiberius decided that this perjury ought to be assessed as if Jupiter had been insulted. Where the gods were concerned, it was their job themselves to punish offenses of which they were the object. In so writing, Tiberius made two decisions. To my eye, the first is the refusal to condemn for acts contrary to the majesty of the divine Augustus; the second situates the false oath by the power of a divinized emperor on the plane of ordinary perjury. That is to say, Tiberius treated the false oath by Augustus like an offense against a divinity and, indeed, the supreme divinity, Jupiter. Finally, and in conclusion, Tiberius reaffirmed the old principle according to which the gods themselves took charge of impious persons. We know that this principle was referred to once again in the third century of this era by the emperor Severus Alexander, and that text was cited and excerpted in the sixth century by the emperor Justinian in his Code.[21]

The treatment of intentional impiety is not a sign of relaxation in the observance of rules or the affirmation of individual religious desires in the face of the obligations and traditions of ancestral religion. Once more, everything depends on what the modern historians mean by the punishment of impiety. If Mommsen and Wissowa ignore the later evidence, and see in the rule from Spoleto the first sign of a softening of custom, that is because they thought Roman religion was falling bit by bit into decadence, while the authorities became more and more cynical about religious matters. But the system of norms, supervision, and punishment persisted in a consistent fashion for centuries beyond that text, and nothing suggests a "softening." Acts adjudged impious were expiated by the appropriate rites at the level of the city or community. The impious party was himself abandoned to divine vengeance. It would be interesting to know how this surrender of the guilty party to the relevant divinity was managed in practice. Perhaps it occurred through the designation and description of the impious person in some official fashion, by a notation on the part of the censor, by a denunciation on the part of the pontiffs, or merely by rumor.[22] As with the official sanction of bad repute, impiety may have meant exclusion from public offices and religious services, or simple juridical incapacity. In certain exemplary stories reported by ancient historians, the perjurer is assimilated to persons subject to forfeit, which is to say, the perjurer is expelled from Rome. But as always in the city, enactment required consensus, and if this did not obtain, the affair might rest where it was. There is in any event no reason to be surprised if, in the final instance, perjurers or other impious persons appear to have gotten off lightly. Even if their notion of responsibility and personal stakes is very different, the various

Christianities do not appear to me to have devised very different treatment for sinners. Earthly powers intervene only in cases of impiety that concern them as representatives of the civic community, and sometimes to punish an infraction of rules they have themselves pronounced. But this occurs only in very serious cases, rightly or wrongly—namely, those that seem to call into question public order or the very foundations of society and the civic community, so that the earthly power launches a violent reaction.

We will not analyze local or general repressive actions, as these are not our subject. It is important for us at this stage to refine the dominant model of collective religion in the Roman world, of which civic religion is in fact only one face.

Chapter 8

Civic Religion, a Modality
of Communal Religion

We have already observed that a civic community was not an aggregation of individuals each pursuing his or her own whim. The religious obligations of the civic community are independent of the persons living at any given moment, in the same fashion that public properties do not belong to the individuals who contingently enjoy the status of citizen, but to an indissoluble totality. The religion, the patrimony, and the other rights and obligations of civic communities belong to the abstract juridical personality of the collective, which endures beyond the life of its citizens.[1] So, religion depends on the abstract totality of the collectivity, represented by those persons to whom the collective delegates its powers. Those persons are its magistrates, Senate, and their advisers, the priests. An object is not sacred; which is to say, it does not belong to the gods, unless the supreme authorities in this world have consecrated it. That which an individual consecrates by individual right in the sanctuaries of the civic collective can, at the margins, be considered inviolable, but such objects do not participate in the juridical category of the sacred.[2] The civic community also has divine partners. Caecilius, the defender of ancestral religion against the "champions of the truth," as the Christians name it, is made by Minucius Felix to say, "in empires, provinces and city-states, we see that each community has its own ritual modalities and venerates its fellow citizen gods."[3] I do not translate *dei municipes* by "municipal gods," which corresponds rather to *dei municipales*, but by "fellow citizen gods," which conforms to the strict meaning of the term *municipes*. Communities always venerate the gods of their ancestors, those that their ancestors have chosen. For Minucius

Felix, that choice is explained, in the tradition of Euhemerus, by the diviniza-
tion of ancient benefactors and kings. But it is essential for us that he regards
the gods of the Romans as members of their community, their fellow citizens.

These are the relations civic communities had with their gods, on earth
and in view of earthly objects, such as victory, success, or health here and now,
which constitute civic religion, and not relations with far-off gods in view of
the afterlife. As the figure of Caecilius proclaims at the start of the third century, civic religion had not disappeared by that date. Once again, Minucius
Felix evokes not only the *convivia publica*, public banquets, but the prayers
and public cult that the crowd addresses to the statues of the gods.[4] What's
more, if, in order to describe pagan cult, Augustine himself used the *Divine
Antiquities* of Varro, who insisted on the preeminence of public cult,[5] that is
apparently because this principle was always the reality in a pagan milieu. Nor
does this evidence reveal some hidden trace, gesturing at a discourse sustained
by a minority. They speak to a daily reality that one might poke fun at, from
the margins, but which nonetheless existed.

That the public religious institutions did not function under the empire
as they had in the fifth century BCE is obvious. But this evolution did not
affect either the necessity of ritual obligation or the modalities of cult. Only
the mode of participation was transformed, within the limits that I have indicated. No regular prescription either forced or invited all citizens to attend; it
sufficed that the required number of celebrants united. Even in the republican
era, not everyone attended. What changed little by little alongside growth
in the citizen body, especially after 89 BCE, is the ability of a majority of Romans physically to attend public religious services at Rome. The religion of
the Roman people was celebrated for the collective totality of Roman citizens,
and even for their allies, whether they were present at Rome or not, just as
the grand rites at Saint Peter are celebrated on behalf of the entire Catholic Church. Even if the majority of Catholics cannot attend these rites, their
validity is not in question. As a result of the enlargement of the civic body,
the majority of Romans did not know religious life at the metropole except
through books and images. It was the same for great cultural and political
events at Rome. One can ask whether, over the long haul, this evolution did
not play some role in the gradual opening of minds to a religion of the book,
to a religion that one came to perceive exclusively through books and written
documents. But, for the questions that preoccupy us, this evolution brought

no change to the functioning of public religion at Rome itself. In this regard, it is necessary also to recall that citizens were integrated into the political community of Rome by means of their city of origin. From a religious point of view, participation in the cults of one's municipality or colony amounted to participation in the piety of Roman people.

This is precisely what the critics of the civic model of religion forget. The religious life of the citizen did not concern solely the rites that were celebrated on the Capitol or in the forums of Rome. In the same way that cult practice was addressed to a plurality of gods, it possessed many sites of anchorage, independent of one another and yet convergent in their aim: the conduct of Roman piety. Moreover, the inhabitants of the Roman world, whether they were citizens or not, all practiced cult of a poliadic type in their city of origin. As these cities were generally smaller than Rome, the material framework of religious practice in those city-states had not changed to remotely the same degree since the republican period. And of course, in those city-states, it was the magistrates and local Senate, advised by some priests, that exercised authority and discharged religious obligations. This last fact is almost never taken into account by critics of the civic model. The exercise of religious power belonged always, in the final instance, not to an autonomous clergy that was accountable only to God, but to a temporal power, which clearly signals the public and civic character of the religion of the city-states.

Beyond the city-states of Italy and the provinces, individuals were involved in multiple communal networks, which obeyed the same logic as a *respublica*. Each of these communities had its own religion, which is to say, its own gods, its own ritual obligations, and its religious authority belong to the temporal authorities of these groups. It is for this reason that the overall rubric of studies devoted to Roman religion at the École pratique des hautes études in Paris was called "Religions of Rome," in the plural, a formulation taken over by Mary Beard, John North, and Simon Price as the title for their handbook.[6] Among these communities, one must first cite the family, which constituted an autonomous religious group. Contrary to what one often reads, the priests of the city did not have the power to intervene in domestic practice. Religious authority and the organization of ritual fell to the father of the family or his son, possibly assisted by his wife: they were the priests of the family. The public priests, the pontiffs, constrained themselves within this system to recommending the conduct to be observed in cases where private obligations overlapped with public ones. There is still the question of administrative aspects of religious practice. Thus, the pontiffs oversaw the cadaster of the public necropoleis, authorizing the installation of a tomb and afterward protecting its integrity. The funerary rites themselves could not in any case be celebrated by the pontiffs, who were not even allowed to see a corpse. It was the father or sons in the family who officiated.

The only public interventions into familial religious communities or, more broadly, in any private religious community, were determined by the desire on the part of authorities to maintain order. It is in this context noteworthy that the controls placed on so-called voluntary associations were provoked by a suspicion that these were sites of political protest and conspiracy: the controls placed on them had nothing to do with religion and, indeed, exemptions were occasionally allowed precisely for them to fulfill religious functions. As regards maintaining order: the Bacchanalian affair of 186 BCE or, likewise, the occasional repression enacted against philosophers, fortune tellers, or the Jewish or Christian communities show the pattern clearly. When we look closely, these result from denunciations, even local pogroms, into which the temporal authorities of the city intervene. Subsequent prosecution could be based on a claim of religious perversion, as in the case of the Bacchanalia or Christianity, but these measures in no way resembled the Inquisition. It was the secular arm of the Roman state—or, in the family, the father of the family—who oversaw such matters, to the exclusion of all priests, and the measures undertaken struck at the persons accused and only very rarely at the cults themselves. After the violent repression of the Bacchanalia, for example, the Senate and consuls were content to allow the cult of Bacchus to continue in its ancestral form. One could say that Roman society was occasionally intolerant, but its religions were not.

In any case, all religious communities of private status, whether families or professional associations or communities paying cult in the districts of Rome, had their gods and their own rites, which they conducted in the same fashion as a city. One ought therefore recognize that the civic model is not some sort of isolated vestige of ancient practice. Rather, it constitutes a model of religious life that extended beyond the community of citizens and which functioned under the empire at all levels of society, a society that was much more fragmented than modern societies. Religious life corresponded to this fragmentation. The only observable developments are the new features of religious practice owed to the massive increase in the size of the civic body and the number of Roman city-states.

Alongside these communities of citizens, all Romans and foreigners were involved in private communities of the same type: families, districts or quarters of city-states, *collegia*, of which they became members by birth or adoption, through manumission or some form of social pressure, in the same fashion that one became a member of the religious community of the Roman people. In all these cases, it was not due to an individual decision or, for example, a conversion that one took on religious obligations to one of these communities.

It was not so much entry into a religious community that posed a problem or compelled a personal choice, but exit from one. One became a member of a religious community by birth or by virtue of social reasons, to a point automatically. Religious belonging was corollary to situations and professional choices. To disengage from religious obligations therefore signified a repudiation of social belonging, and such a decision is never easy.

To demonstrate the social and topographic divisions that characterized Roman religions, one need only read the *Metamorphoses* of Apuleius. This famous "novel" of the second century recounts the adventures of a certain Lucius, who was transformed by magic into an ass. After many trials and tribulations, Lucius is rescued by the goddess Isis, and he becomes one of her devotees. After having been initiated into her religion in Greece, where the plot unfolds, Lucius leaves for Rome. His first action in Rome involves his savior, in her great temple on the Campus Martius. So, in order to participate in cult, what did Lucius need to do? He got himself initiated once again, at Rome, in the Isaic religion.[7] Thus this religion, which is described as universal in modern handbooks and which, by virtue of this, is thought to address itself to individuals and their private feelings, reveals itself to be as local as those other religions and subordinates access to the cult to the observance of specific rites.

The communal model that one attributes to the city is thus a fact of the culture, which one can observe at every level of social organization. It is not a question of separating some practices from those of the city in its totality, from what the ancient calls public cult (*sacra publica*). To the extent that the culture of the city-states continued to offer a framework for daily life—contrary to theories of civic decline—the objections against the civic model are missing the point.

Is it necessary to associate the formation of a collective identity with these communal cults? After a fashion, yes. To the extent that all communities in the Roman world were autonomous, their religious institutions, and most notably the gods to whom they paid preeminent recognition, distinguished one from another, in the same way that names distinguished families, or professions distinguished voluntary associations. *Collegia*, roughly "guilds," defined their members by the gods who were their earthly partners: we know, for example, of guilds of the worshippers of Silvanus or of Mithra.[8] Families invoke their Penates, the gods that they venerate in particular, and great aristocratic families at Rome had specific associations with the cult of particular gods, such as Sol for the Aurelii or Veiovis for the Julii. A given cult could also characterize an entire region. In the *Octavius* of Minucius Felix, Caecilius observes that "the Eleusinians worship Ceres [Demeter], the Phrygians the Mother of the gods, the Epidaurians Aesculapius, the Chaldaeans Bêl, the Syrians Astartes, the peoples of Tauris Diana, the Gauls Mercury, and the Romans, all of these."[9] Taking a Roman perspective, Caecilius can describe by a single characteristic divine name the habits of this or that city or province; and by way of affirming the status of Rome as metropole, it claims that all the gods are worshipped there. Earlier we argued that access to a given cult was never completely open except for members of its specific community. For domestic cults or public ones, it was necessary to obtain specific authorization to participate, if one did not belong in one fashion or another to the community in question.

However, one should not push to the point of absurdity claims about the role of cult in the formation of identity, as certain theoretical formulations might lead one to do. I am not unaware of the claims of Fustel de Coulanges and Durkheimian sociology, according to which society is the origin, source, and objective of religion: as summarized by Corinne Bonnet, "God exists as an expression of social power: one could nearly say that God is society, and vice versa."[10] A century later, such theories have undoubtedly influenced researchers taking their inspiration from social anthropology. However, since Alfred Radcliffe-Brown, social anthropology has itself moved away from evolutionist and old-fashioned functionalism. I thus consider these formulas more as summary generalizations, of the same type as that advanced by Caecilius in the *Octavius*, who said that the Syrians worship Astarte. Of course, there were communities in Syria that did not worship Astarte, and those that did also worshiped at the same time a crowd of other divinities that were just as important. When foreigners suppose that the French wear berets and love red wine and camembert, it is the same type of generalization. When Roman authorities devised identity controls, they certainly asked whether a person subject to those checks was a Roman citizen or not; they asked about his origin and rank, but they did not seek to know what gods he worshipped. By contrast, the fact that a person could openly participate in a sacrifice in a given community means that the person is a member of that community. That person was taken to be in conformity with the collective identity of the group, whether this was as a citizen of full right, as an alien resident, as a permanent resident, or in certain cases merely as a traveler.

I have the impression that this entire debate concerning civic identity is distorted. It seems to me to go back to a study published by Mary Beard in 1987.[11] In this article, Beard examined the relationship between the rite of the Parilia, an old pastoral festival on 21 April that commemorated the founding of Rome, and the interpretations that learned scholars and Roman poets gave to it. Beard observes that the numerous explanations furnished by learned Romans do not reveal an ultimate meaning of the ritual; they constitute, rather, a series of reflections about what it meant to be Roman. The rite itself was thereby reduced to gestures to be accomplished and an ancestral obligation to be celebrated, but the signification of the festival changed over time. Beard's conclusions are drawn in so rigid a fashion as to pay a price in plausibility. To want to deduce from this example the notion that that the objective of civic religion was to establish Roman identity makes no sense, since the etiological myths associated with Roman rites did not furnish the ultimate reason for religious obligations. The myths were more-or-less erudite reflections about the rite; they generally had no place in it and fulfilled no normative function to provide meaning for it. Neither civic religion specifically nor the religions of the ancients more generally functioned in this fashion. What Beard achieved was precisely to bring to light the diverse forms that such interpretations might take.

This point leads us to cult itself and to the meaning of religious practice, which is never taken into account in critiques of civic religion. To my mind, this lacuna is very revealing of the ongoing life of a very traditional prejudice, according to which civic cult is incoherent and hollow. In the perspective of such criticism, civic religion offers nothing to anyone but functionalist anthropologists or those interested in the interpretations of poets and grammarians. The peculiar narrowness of their reflections is then set in contradistinction to the beautiful metaphysics of the philosophers and the "authentic" religious sentiments of individuals, who display a more transparent and satisfying vision of the divine. Let us therefore now turn to the relationship among religious practice, emotion, and belief.

Chapter 9

Emotion and Belief

The opponents of the model of civic religion always insist on the necessity of treating piety as an expression of individual and sincere emotion, independent of every social context. I will not address again the profoundly Christian basis that motivates this claim, which rejects, as Franz Cumont did, ritual as profane and secular.[1] It is hardly surprising that this position has exercised profound influence on psychology, psychoanalysis, irrationalism, and phenomenology.[2]

Was Roman religion therefore a religion without emotion and deprived, by virtue of this, of all religiosity, in Schleiermacher's sense of the term? This question appears to me to call for two responses. First, one must show that there was indeed emotion in the religious practices of the Romans, but its place is not the same as that which emotion occupies in Christianity. The second aspect of the question, and the reproach, concerns the notion of "belief." Was Roman ritualism tied to some interiorized belief, or was it reducible to a set of administrative rules? Let us begin with the first question.

The Place of Emotion in Roman Religions

Contrary to what is often said, emotion is not absent from Roman religions. Only its place is different. On the one hand, the absence of emotion or, rather, the control of it, was considered a preeminent religious virtue. On the other, emotion did not form the basis or origin of belief and practice, but was potentially a consequence from excessive or poorly performed practice. Let us consider these points.

King Numa, successor to the wild Romulus, is treated by mythology as the creator of Roman religion. In addition, there are anecdotes that narrate his perfect piety. Two of these anecdotes bear upon the topics of faith and emotion. The first shows us the good king in the process of sacrificing, surrounded by his people, when enemies attack.[3] His companions, in the grip of fear and panic, demanded that he do something; Numa was content to reply, "But I am sacrificing!" The moral of the story is that the pious Roman, and above all the perfect magistrate, ought not be anxious before a threatening phenomenon. In contrast to his cowardly entourage, Numa had confidence in divine assistance, and he gives the reason: I am fulfilling my obligations with respect to the protectors of Rome, and I will not interrupt this task to busy myself with trivial problems. Numa's behavior illustrates precisely what the Romans meant by the notion of *fides*, which is the ancestor of our word "faith," and which was the object of a foundational study by Émile Benveniste.[4] The literal meaning of *fides* is "trust" and designated the aid or benefit that one could expect from someone who maintained a relationship of exchange and reciprocity. The Roman had relations of trust with his *patronus*, with his protector, to whom he was bound by often hereditary obligations. By fulfilling all the actions and gestures of respect and support that the social code demanded, the *cliens*, the protected individual, was confident that he would receive the support of his *dominus*, and the inverse was equally true. The same reciprocity existed between the Romans and their gods. To respect, gifts, sacrifices, and systematic consultation on the part of humans, the gods were thought to respond with gestures of goodwill and support. Whence the confidence of Numa, which could be translated by *fides*.

The mutual confidence, or trust, that regulated relations between mortals and their immortal *patroni*, and which was expressed in the day-to-day by diverse religious obligations, focused on earthly benefits: victory, success, health, riches. And these relations were so institutionalized that when the Romans were persuaded that they had fulfilled all their obligations to the gods, they refused to discharge their vows if they had not been met.

A second anecdote concerning the piety of Numa illustrates the specificity of relations between Romans and their gods.[5] Once he became king, Numa put an end to the Romulean savagery of the Romans by establishing justice and piety. Please observe that justice and religion are equivalent social virtues, of which one is directed toward humans, the other toward the gods. Peace is established on earth, but Jupiter continues to terrify his mortal partners by thundering and flashing lightning more and more violently. Numa had the courage to confront him. By the appropriate means, he arranges to meet with the Most Great. Emotion is naturally present. Like any mortal, the king is afraid when Jupiter appears: his hair stands on end and his blood freezes. But, being a perfect magistrate, the king masters his fear and interrogates the god. He desires to know why the god continues to torment the Romans when rites, respectful of the rank of the gods, have been established and are regularly celebrated. The terror, the emotion, that Numa felt before the immense superiority of the god betrays a feeling of absolute dependence before Jupiter. However, this sentiment does not give rise to an abandoning of self to one's emotions or a desire to join god in heaven, but to a reaction against his hostile demonstrations. Conditions of perfect piety being met, the king wishes to know why the god does not respect *fides*, civic reciprocity. Numa clearly makes reference to a civic manifestation of authority and superiority: in Roman society, a social superior did not treat his fellow citizens like slaves. He followed a code of conduct that rested upon proportional equality, itself founded upon exchanges of respect and benefits. When a god becomes angry, the citizen and above all the magistrate do not immediately submit themselves by casting themselves as penitents. The nature of religious obligations, which is to say, *religio*, demands that one first perform a check, because relations with immortals were founded upon a feeling of interdependence and not upon servile submission. To yield to anxiety and thus to grant to the gods power without limit or justification would be to fall into *superstitio*, which amounted to a feeling and form of conduct that was the inverse of true piety.

The *fides* of the king commits Jupiter still further. The god decides to test the little mortal by soliciting an emotional response anew. When Numa ventures to ask him what might still be lacking from their religious obligations in order to appease his anger, Jupiter responds in an ambiguous fashion. He makes it appear that he seeks a human sacrifice. The king, however, resists, deflecting these distressing claims three times with a trick. After the exchange, the god announces himself reassured and promises to help the Romans.

The anecdote demonstrates perfectly that, for the Romans, emotions always governed relations with the gods, but in a different fashion than we might expect. It was for them to dominate their emotions, to channel them in an institutionally and contextually appropriate way, with the goodwill of the gods, who were supposed to be in the image of their fellow citizens. Like them, the gods decline the exercise of tyranny. And it is the *fides*, the confidence or trust of Numa in the goodwill and loyalty of the gods, that explains his constancy of soul. We find this behavior in Roman divination, particularly when disquieting signs and prodigies were seen. Rather than become upset right away and throw themselves into some disorder of superstition, the Romans began by dominating their fear and examining the signs. One needed first to determine whether and in what way the gods might have addressed them. Strong because of their trust in the gods, they invariably conclude that their social relations with their heavenly protectors had been disturbed; they seek and naturally find the infraction. Thus the terrible defeat at Lake Trasimene in 217 BCE was due to divine anger aroused by the impiety of Flaminius, who had violated an ancestral, institutional code. In response, without becoming excessively emotional, the authorities instituted a number of new cults to reestablish good relations with the immortals.

It is not only in the conduct of the state that these behaviors are attested. We find them equally in the private sphere. Thus, one of the funerary rites consisted in firmly opposing the spirits of the dead who had not received burial or who had died early. During the Lemuria in the month of May,[6] the father of the family confronts them in their space, the darkness of midnight, by offering them a gift of food and by guarding against any link with them. Then he expels them from the house by making noise. The father of the family therefore dominates his fear of ghosts that torment humans and, by fulfilling his duty in respect of them, which is to say, by honoring them with a gift of food, he earns their quietude.

The mystery cults are often cited in this debate because, in this supposedly new religious practice, it is claimed that the ancients experimented with a piety founded upon religious emotion. But, as Walter Burkert has emphasized in an excellent small book on the mysteries, far from being a novelty in Greece, these were ancient cults, and the practices in which they participated were not in any way free from ritualism.[7] On the contrary, as Philippe Borgeaud specified long ago, the mystery rites make use of and channel emotions more than they lead to them.[8] He says this because the emotional phase of the mysteries, which is perfectly attested, was, according to the ancients, an educational and cathartic stage of the experience, and was not valorized in itself.

The Roman sources contain also numerous testimonies to the opposite conduct. The crowd, women, barbarians, but also magistrates and even bad emperors yield easily to anxiety and terror. One can certainly regard the effort to control the emotions as a posture of the aristocracy, which was eager to maintain its preeminence on all levels. But I am not confident that this theme, which is certainly tied to a social position and a model of the citizen in which not all could share, and which perhaps did not always surmount the existential anxieties of individuals, was nothing more than a discourse limited to a few. I believe that it is a principle that was shared by the majority of Romans and that it defined their particular form of "religiosity." An example shows this. In 213 BCE, in the midst of the Second Punic War, after a new series of military disasters, notably that of Cannae, Rome found itself in the grip of doubt and anxiety.[9] Magistrates and Senate seem to have lost their *fides* and fallen into inaction. Suddenly, the Forum was invaded by women, the people of the working-class neighborhoods, and the fortune-tellers, who celebrated rites that ancestral norms regarded as superstitious. Note that in this passage, Livy contrasts two spaces of Roman cult: "it was now not only in secret and in the interior of home [i.e., in private] but also in public, in the Forum and on the Capitol [i.e., in public] that Roman rites were neglected." In the face of the apathy of the authorities, it was the Roman citizens described as *boni*, the right-thinking people, who react and demand that the Senate intervene, to chase away this superstition and reestablish ancestral religious customs.[10] The Senate finally does act, criticizing the lower magistrates for their inactivity and demanding that the urban praetor, who was the head of the executive, free the people from these religious fears. On this occasion, the mass of the citizens therefore reacted in a correct fashion to catastrophe. While the elite appears to have lost its *fides*, which is to say, its confidence in the goodwill and support of the gods, it was the simple citizens who recalled with passion the ancestral form of piety. In this anecdote, emotion is doubly present, negatively in the cultic form claimed for itself by the crowd, and positively in the anger that the abandoning of ancestral rites arouses in the citizens. One is free to regard Livy's narrative as an invention. However, it does not relate to the archaic period, but to an era from which there survived archives and narratives. For my part, I believe that one can accept the fashion in which the substance and spirit of the event are presented. Livy could grant this episode more space than it deserved because he wanted by this example to illustrate ancestral piety, in the same way that he made a set-piece of the scandal over the Bacchanalia, which also was reported to the magistrates by individuals. To admit this does not amount in any way to thinking of the anecdote as purely rhetorical.

In any case, like the repression of the Bacchanalia or the treatment of religious infractions, this reaction attests an aspect of religious emotion that Claude Lévi-Strauss evoked clearly in his book on totemism.[11] The anthropologist recalls that, in traditional societies, what one feels depends very closely on the manner in which it is permitted or prescribed for one to conduct oneself. Customs are given, like external standards, before internal feelings are engendered. Cult is above all conventional. There was nothing spontaneous, and the individual had no other explanation to put forward, no other reason to assign for his or her behavior, than tradition. Fervor was not revealed in obedience and practice. It manifested itself on those occasions when custom was violated. It is not emotions that provoke rituals, but rituals that engender and sustain the emotions. This is exactly the type of alterity that one finds in Roman religion.

Ritual and Belief

Fides, confidence in the goodwill and support of the gods, as it was expressed in Roman religion, leads us to the notion of belief. Among the Romans, belief appears to focus above all on the necessity of rites. But was it only that? Did the rituals have no other meaning? What should we make of the multiple and often contradictory or even useless interpretations that were given for rites? Did the Romans thus believe in nothing else? Was there no interiorization of the meaning of rites and therefore no "religiosity"?

We have seen that the opponents of the civic model of religious practice have insisted since Hegel and Mommsen on the emptiness or incoherence of Roman rites and privileged religions of interiorized spirituality. I have already responded to these critiques by emphasizing the separation that existed between religious practice and the metaphysical speculations that theologians and phenomenologists inspired by the Tübingen school of religious history consider as the mark of true "religiosity." This was so at all levels of Roman society. Let us take an example from the end of pagan antiquity, from the milieu of the Neoplatonist philosophers, who worked out speculations that many Christians have not disowned. And yet, according to one of the most learned scholars of that tradition, John Dillon, the philosophers of late antiquity did not differ from the thinkers of classical Greece—or Cicero or Varro, for that matter: they continued to practice cult in a traditional manner, which did not prevent them from interpreting their own observances in a more metaphysical, allegorical fashion, much as Philo of Alexandria had done with traditional Judaism.[12]

But what was the ritual? Was there some meaning to religious practice other than its necessity? Did all rites conform to this model?

It is tempting to want to find, in the practice of certain grand figures, traces of a more elevated ritualism. Some have interpreted an anecdote related about Scipio Africanus along these lines.[13] Scipio had the habit of going to the temple of Jupiter on the Capitol to meditate and speak with the god. Scipio would thus have practiced on his own initiative an interiorized religion of the Christian type, that one might assimilate to his philosophical inclinations or a dream he had had.[14] I am not sure, however, that one needs to interpret his dialogue with Jupiter in this way. Let us skip over the historicity of this anecdote. As Jörg Rüpke has emphasized, at the very least it proves that in the era when it was inserted in the charges leveled against the royal ambitions manifested by Scipio, one could conceive the existence of a prayer of this kind, a prayer addressed to a god independent of any ritual.[15] However, I am not sure that we have read this anecdote correctly. As always, it is not sufficient to summarize the ancient sources, which allows one to assimilate them to whatever model one wants. One must be attentive to the details in which the information one wants is embedded. So, the text of Livy specifies that Scipio did this on the days on which he had to take a public or private decision of some importance.[16] Hence, his conduct becomes intelligible and it may be understood within the framework of traditional ritual practices. It amounts first to a private approach, concerning Scipio's own affairs. At the end of the night, before the start of the day, which is to say, before the break of day on the day he had to make a decision, Scipio went to consult Jupiter. It is essential to know that this was always the hour when magistrates took the auspices and consulted Jupiter. Together with Aulus Gellius, I would therefore identify the approach of Scipio to Jupiter as a private divinatory consultation.[17] The fact that he came to consult Jupiter in his Capitoline temple, as if to emphasize the privileged relations he enjoyed with the Most High, would have been proof of his pretension. To go to inquire of a god in his temple was not in itself an exceptional act. An anecdote related by Cicero reveals it to have been common in private divination.[18] A practice of honoring a divinity whose temple one approaches with a small offering and a prayer is equally well attested.[19] In any event, the texts that tell us about the visits of Scipio to the Capitol do not permit us to know how his dialogue with Jupiter unfolded: was it a simple oracular consultation, as was performed by sitting in a temple waiting for a sign,[20] or did Scipio make an offering of wine and incense in order to greet Jupiter and pray that he send him a sign? I prefer to interpret the conduct of Scipio in line with one of these traditions, rather than to see in it evidence of mystical meditation, a phenomenon that seems to me to be clearly much later.

Whatever might be the case, these private consultations did not prevent Scipio in any way from celebrating the ancestral rites with rigor and precision. As adepts of philosophical doctrines, we do not know what they truly believed, but the sources teach us what they practiced, and that they recommended one practice above all, the ancestral rites. I have already cited the case of Varro. He, for example, interpreted the Capitoline triad in the Platonizing Stoic way, as God (which is the say, the active principle of the universe), Matter (the passive principle), and Form (the Logos).[21] Elsewhere, however, he practiced the rites of public religion as a senator, praetor, and legate. We also learn that in private, he was a Pythagorean, and that he had himself buried according to the recommendations of the Pythagorean sect, surrounded by leaves of myrtle, olive, and black poplar.[22] Is this to say that he combined philosophy and practical choices in his private life? Perhaps. However, one needs to emphasize that he had every right to do so, because he was the sole authority in his domestic religion, and what we know of his funeral does not contradict ancestral rites in any way. Those prescribed only to bury the dead and to effect a separation from him by offerings of food. Cremation came to be predominant in the age of Varro's death, but nothing forbade inhumation. At that date, one finds both types of funerary practice. One might imagine that Varro ordered a vegetal offering to his shades in order to respect a Pythagorean rule that was opposed to blood sacrifice. A vegetal offering was perfectly possible in funerary rites. But I have already passed beyond the content of the passage that I have cited, which teaches us only that he was buried and that his body was surrounded by different kinds of leaves. It is therefore not certain that a sow was not sacrificed, the form of sacrifice described by Cicero. It is of little importance. One can already see that Varro did not modify rites except in the private domain, where he had the right to do so. And still, we do not know if he lived according the rules of what we call Pythagoreanism. If we read the writings of Varro, we learn that in fact he referred at least occasionally to nearly all the doctrines and interpretations about the gods that existed. I have mentioned Pythagoreanism and the Platonizing Stoicism of his teacher Antiochus of Ascalon, but one also finds in his work etymological, mythological, historical, and moral interpretations, without any clear hierarchy among the references. Certainly, following the pontifex maximus Quintus Scaevola, Varro repeated the tripartite model of representing the gods: the mythic way, that of the poets, which found expression in the theater or mythology, which was vulgar and useless; the physical way, which is to say, that of the philosophers, which the crowd did not need to know; and finally the political way, that of the city-states, which is to say, that which found expression in the rites of civic cult. Only the last could be the object of practice according to ancestral custom. Varro ranked the three types of discourse about the gods, but the reader of his work, or that of Cicero or the other poets and learned individuals, rapidly discovers that he constantly used all three modes of representation. It is for this reason that we can and should conclude that we do not know what Varro truly believed.

This observation leads us to the conclusion that the notion of belief among the ancients was not the same as that of modern times. There was no normative requirement that all should believe, let alone believe the same thing. Truths were multiple, and they varied according to point of view. The rituals, the gods, and the other institutions allowed for a wide range of knowledge, which reflection revealed from different angles. None of these explanations delivered an ultimate truth. The notion of truth could not have the same meaning in Roman civilization as in a Christian one, where truth is revealed by God, diffused by a book, and codified in dogmas. Nothing of the sort existed at Rome, where the truth was plural and depended on the point of view of the person who formulated it. The only truth shared by the collectivity was precisely ritual truth, which consisted in the obligation to perform the rites.

At this point in our reflection, we can ask ourselves whether the rituals had a meaning. Given their importance, did they not provide an ultimate explanation for the way of things, the ultimate truth about relations between humans and gods? I have already explained Roman ritual conduct many times by extracting information from rituals about the position of the gods in the Roman conceptual universe. I have said that they were represented as members of the earthly community and not as metaphysical powers. This conclusion stems from a close reading of divinatory or sacrificial rites. Specifically, sacrifice can give a precise definition of divine nature. If one takes apart the components of the rituals at the start of a sacrifice,[23] the offering of incense and wine, and the rituals of division and offering,[24] we can understand the sacrifice as a formal greeting to the gods as immortal and superior partners occupying the first place in the Roman universe, in which mortals take second place. The libation and sacrifice therefore constituted a sort of *credo*. It is for this reason that I titled a book devoted to sacrifice *Quand faire, c'est croire* [When to Do Is to Believe]. In a study of rituals and the names of gods, we are also in a position to reconstruct the identity of different gods, as well as the relationship that existed between divinities. Some years ago, for example, I examined a series of expiatory sacrifices and a vow for the success of the emperor Trajan and highlighted the particular conception of the gods that the Romans crafted for themselves.[25] In fact, the Romans considered their gods to be active powers, but they did not group all aspects of divine action into a single agent. On the contrary, rather than attribute the responsibility for the totality of the phases of action to a divinity thought to realize them, the Romans divided them into multiple segments: the will to action, the modality of action, and its effect. One can thus speak of an ancestral Roman theology, which corresponds to an incapacity on the part of the Romans to think about an act and its unfolding in a unified way.

The Romans were in no way ignorant of this way of reading rites. The interpretations offered by learned individuals or priests often provide the implicit explanation that underlies them. So, the secretary of the Arval college calls an offering to a divinity *cena*, "dinner," as if to underline the homology between a sacrifice and a meal. We know, too, that the pontiffs thought about the literal meaning of the segments of rituals when they had to engage in sacral jurisprudence. And when the Romans restored a rite, they often used ancestral ritual material, by analyzing its meaning in a way that permitted the construction of a new ritual. The implicit meaning of rites, which is so indispensable to us for understanding them, was therefore not ignored by the Romans. But did they consider it the true meaning of religious practice?

There lies a paradox. The meaning of a rite: they knew rites had meanings, and they sought after and used such meanings, at times self-consciously, in order to restore or describe rituals, but in their eyes, no given meaning amounted to anything more than one interpretation among many. The ritualism and the literature of Vedic India as Charles Malamoud has explicated them can help to clarify this paradox.[26] Clearly, the Romans regarded the literal interpretation of a rite as one of its components rather than as the reason behind the rite. It did not provide aid to belief; it was simply a ritual fact, like the gesture or prayer that accompanied it. A prayer never says more than a gesture; it is an oral gesture. Prayer confers on gesture its perfection, but it never provides its unique and binding explanation. The only binding given in practice is the ritual obligation itself. As for the rest, it suffices to know and to believe that "the rites become intelligible when one has understood that they are that which renders the world intelligible," to quote Charles Malamoud.[27] Ancestral rites offer in some way a corpus of gestures and behaviors that can then be used, in speculation, to interpret all aspects of life and the system of things. The rites themselves are not empty, as the Indologist Frits Staal says;[28] rather, they are silent in the sense that their implicit significance does not extend beyond the ritual action.[29]

It is this separation between religious practice and meaning, of religion and "religiosity," that is the preeminent characteristic of the religion of the Greeks and Romans, much more than its civic and communal character. The latter is simply a corollary.

How indeed might one assign universality to a religion composed of silent collective acts, which were a precise obligation, situated in space and time, and constituted in no way by abstract belief? These ritual acts were rooted in a set of communities and belong to the institutional heritage of those communities, whether public or private. The universalization of Roman religion took place not by reference to a private individual and his or her adherence to a unified belief (which did not in fact exist), but through the general granting of citizenship to free persons, which process extended Roman ritual obligations to all. We can also conclude that a religious system of multiple roots and founded on a silent ritualism was much more capable of integrating new members than a confession founded upon an explicit and binding doctrine. Without wanting to say that the rigor of Roman ritualism amounted to a will or disposition, which to my mind would require a functionalism that I cannot endorse, it is certain that this ritualism was connected to the open nature of Roman society and its imperialism. Or perhaps I should say that the rigor of its ritualism was not an obstacle to imperialism. And this openness brought

into being a society so large, so diverse, and so heterogeneous as to make ancestral ritualism appear as the only possible common religious reference, to the
point where institutional change was viewed as impossible.

We often hear the ancients insist that the desire of mortals to be able
to know the true nature of the gods is vain. The only knowledge possible
derives from the earthly institutions of cult. Some years ago, I compared this
understanding, attested from Plato to Minucius Felix, to the understanding
of Jewish observances held by Maimonides, in order to underline that other
ways of explaining ritualism were possible, and that there were other forms of
"religiosity," too.[30]

Chapter 10

Why Did Roman Religion Change?

These reflections bring us to the last point that we must examine, the reasons for religious change. In fact, we have already emphasized that the model of *polis*-religion is capable of explaining how city-states managed the arrival of new cults, but not why religious change occurred. Often, the underlying idea in scholarship is that expressed by Franz Cumont and Richard Reitzenstein, to wit, that it is "individual religiosity" that was the origin of new beliefs. The adoption of the new religion was imposed on everyone precisely at that moment when city-states—and the public religion of the elite—faded out.

However, the matter is not so simple as this. I am not going to return to the question of the supposed decline of the city-states in Greece at the end of the fourth century BCE and later, with the advent of empire, throughout the Mediterranean world. This historiographical model, founded upon Hegelian dialectic and shaped by the aspiration to unify Germany, nourished by the great thinkers and historians of Germany in the nineteenth century, has long since been revealed as false. The city and its civilization remained the framework of life and thought for the ancients until late antiquity. This entire patchwork of reasoning by the adversaries of the civic model ought therefore to be revised. This is all the more true, insofar as the communal framework of religions is not simply an aspect of the political organization of individuals, but also of the functioning of private communities. This dimension amounts to more than just an aspect of what we call civic religion. It is further characterized by ritualism. If one rereads the criticisms made of Georg Wissowa by his contemporaries[1] and by certain contemporary authors, one realizes that the question of change is often accompanied by, or merely a proxy for, another concern, to wit, that rigorous ritualism would not have been able to respond to the aspirations of individuals or a people with true "religiosity." On this view, a religion based on ritualism, like Judaism, Shinto, or Taoism, to name only a few, would not merit the name of religion.

Healing Cults

Back to the issue of religious change. What are the religions that are thought to incarnate this change? There is little surprise in the arguments of Wissowa's adversaries and the critics of civic religion. Clearly, above all it is Christianity, preceded by precursors like the mystery cults, the cults of the Egyptian gods, those of Cybele and Mithra, in short, those that one calls "oriental cults." Often, one adds also the so-called healing cults, whether these are cults of Aesculapius or sanctuaries associated with springs.

First, a general remark, which is not drawn from theories of communication or theology, but which is a fundamental theory of history: no event can be explained by its consequences. One cannot give an account of the advent of Christianity by postulating that humanity had long since been longing for it. The adversaries of the model of *polis*-religion are nevertheless adepts of this approach. In their eyes, it should suffice to look for the traces of this aspiration and, like Ulrich von Wilamowitz-Moellendorff or Richard Reitzenstein, to find them in the high "religiosity" of Greek tragedy, in Platonism and in the oriental cults.

By proceeding in this way, the researcher projects, onto actions earlier than the change he or she studies, the characteristics that he or she attributes to the later phenomenon. But the later phenomenon, in the form in which it is conceived, is often itself a construction clearly posterior to the period of supposed change. In consequence of this reflection, one might ask, for example, which version of Christianity one should one have in mind. The doctrinal history of the first centuries of Christian religion is complex, and it is only gradually that a certain unity emerges. Again, it is essential to remember that the model employed in the inquiries that I have discussed derives from the era after the Reformation. In short, from a historical point of view, this approach poses numerous problems. It is not a question of denying that Christianity is the child of its era and that one finds in it elements that preexisted it. It is the use that is made of a modern understanding of Christianity to reconstruct its history that one must denounce.

Let us turn to religious change, keeping the evidence of upheaval in the religious sphere in chronological order. I will not dwell on the mysteries. Walter Burkert and others have long since explored the ancientness, the ritualistic character, and the thorough integration of the mysteries into their contexts, at Athens as in the Roman world.[2] Here, we must perform a very selective reading of the sources, sufficient to challenge certain historical observations. Take the healing cults. We are told that the state and the elite restrained religion in order to control society and to preserve their own preeminence,[3] and that the people, for their part, had very different needs and aspirations, touching on their individual existence: health, healing, and success. The healing cults reflect these aspirations, with their thousands of ex-votos of every type. Is this correct? Two objections can be raised against this argument, which is related to the concept of *Volksreligion*, the religion of the masses, passionate and simple, who (according to Hegel) smoldered beneath the ashes of official cult, even if they did so without aim or order.[4]

Allow me to cite a few significant passages, in order to recall where these theories come from. Hegel writes in the *Lectures on the Philosophy of History*: "The Romans, by contrast, remained satisfied with a dull, stupid subjectivity; consequently, the external was only an Object—something alien, something hidden."[5] He continues: "Among the Romans, the religious thrill of awe remained undeveloped; it was confined to the mere subjective certainty of its own existence."[6] In other words, the Romans understood piety, but they did not know in whom, or in what, to believe. As far as institutional religion goes, he said a few pages earlier, regarding the conflict between the patricians and plebeians for control of religious institutions in the early republic, that in the fifth and fourth centuries BCE the domination of the patricians had a religious justification: "since the patricians had the *sacra* in their hands, while the plebeians would have been godless, as it were, without them. The plebeians left to the patricians their hypocritical stuff (*ad decipiendam plebem*, Cic.) and cared nothing for their *sacra*."[7] The tone is indicative of a disdain for Roman ritualism, respect for which is attributed only to the patricians, which is completely false. Finally, regarding evolution, he writes: "The element of subjectivity that was wanting to the Greeks, we found among the Romans: but as it was merely formal and in itself indefinite, it took its material from passion and caprice;—even the most shameful degradations could be here connected with a divine dread."[8] Hegel refers at this juncture to the Bacchanalia, and the passage leads to remarks on the evolution of the importance of the individual. But let us return to our subject. The simple people therefore would have had their own religion, tied to that which interested them: health, healing, and success. This is the context in which the healing gods are then highlighted. Such arguments call forth two objections. First, the divinities that are targeted by this devotion of the people were in fact always introduced by the elite. Second, the cult of the so-called healing gods is itself often wrongly reduced to this function by the moderns who claim merely to study them.

What about the popular divinities, the divinities of the individual? In the fifth century BCE, the Roman authorities introduced to Rome a god of Greek origin, Apollo, who received an altar outside the city. Writing much later, Roman historians attribute his installation to a desire to react to an epidemic,[9] but, when writing about the foundation of the Apollinarian Games in 212 BCE, Livy specifies that the games were instituted for a warrior rather than healer god, although in the eyes of his contemporaries, the name *medicus* (doctor; healer) seemed to belong to him.[10] Moreover, much later a temple to Bellona was constructed next to that of Apollo; according to Georges Dumézil, Bellona patronized the pains of war.[11] Much later, Apollo became a political god, protector of Octavian-Augustus, and assumed the heritage of Apollo of Delphi and of the Muses. There is much one could say about the exaggerated interpretations of Palatine Apollo, such as were put forward by Richard Reitzenstein and Jean Gagé, who made of him a symbol of a novel mysticism.[12] I am content to observe that these conclusions rest upon an erroneous understanding of the Secular Games, which were anything but a mystical celebration of some religious revival.[13] It is enough to read the protocols of the ceremony to discover that one prayed there vigorously for the health and victory of the Roman people and their legions, and also for the permanent subjection of the subjects of the Roman people, which appears to me more imperialist than mystical. What is more, the Secular Games were in no way an Apollonian festival. They were concerned with a multiplicity of gods, of which the pair of Apollo and Diana constituted but one part.

However, it is undeniable that in the Latin-speaking provinces—for example, in Gaul—Apollo was often worshipped in the company of a consort who evoked medicine and therefore physical health. Georges Dumézil tried to show that healing characteristics belonged to a regular mode of divine action, which was capable of spreading epidemic as well as reestablishing harmony.[14] Whatever the case may be, the introduction of Apollo was the work of the Roman elite and not the result of popular pressure, and the same is true of the installation of Aesculapius in 293 BCE. According to what we know, that god was installed at Rome by the Senate and magistrates, in order to provide aid to everyone against illness. The later evidence shows that, in Rome, Italy, and the provinces, his was a healing cult, attested by numerous anatomical ex-votos. However, it is essential to recall once again that this was a cult instituted by the elite, anxious to attach to itself the goodwill of a divinity that was celebrated in the Greek world. Moreover, as Olivier de Cazanove had shown, the cult of the god did not diffuse as an effect of the aspirations of individuals, but through the foundation of Roman colonies.[15] It is once again in the framework of city-states that a god was installed in the Roman world, as a figure of their pantheons. At Rome itself, one should likewise remember, Aesculapius was the object of public cult, whose anniversary fell on 1 January, a celebration performed by the community. The fact that the god did not possess a flamen or *sacerdos*, a priest, does not need to compel the conclusion that his cult was in some way financed by the offerings made by individuals in search of healing, as Greg Woolf has suggested for the sanctuaries of Asclepius at Epidauros or Pergamon. Individuals paid taxes and provided donations in all public temples. No one would think to transform these into symbols of individual religiosity or a system of financing. The fact that we still do not have inscriptions or texts that teach us how the temple of Tiber Island was administered, or who held responsibility for it, does not prove that it was a new cult, practiced and financed solely by individuals.

As regards sanctuaries associated with springs, which are often cited (for example, in Gaul) as seats of immemorial and continuous popular cult, I think that I have shown elsewhere that this is in part of a modern historiographical myth, with deep roots in Romantic folklore about the status of popular religion as hostile to sacral institutions.[16]

Spring sanctuaries are far from all being healing sites, and when they were such, the agents credited with therapeutic properties are generally not the gods of the spring but other divinities, who ultimately use the water but who heal and preserve health through their own action, whether one is talking about Apollo, Aesculapius, or Hercules. Moreover, the waters often offer well-being and salubriousness that ensures *salus* for all. Still further, such cults were generally creations of the local elite, of the city-states or members of the Roman military, and not sites of pilgrimage financed by the modest offerings of the sick poor.

To base a theory of religious change on these cults therefore seems to me quite daring. Healing cults always existed at Rome, and all gods participated in them. From the third century BCE, a gradual growth in the number of pre-served documents allows us to identify the desire of the authorities to attach to the civic community the protection of the partners best qualified to preserve health, especially the skilled Apollo and Aesculapius, but this documentation does not reveal any change in individual piety. It is pointless to dissent by contrasting ex-votos in terra-cotta or wood with monuments in marble and gold. That is so first because the sanctuaries with ex-votos do not contain only objects in terra-cotta. They preserve equally objects in precious metals emanat-ing from the elite, though these are generally dispersed, thanks to the value of their metal, but they are perfectly well attested, at least through inscriptions. Second, it is pointless because ex-votos in terra-cotta or wood cannot neces-sarily be traced back to non-elite visitors. As one sees in the fourth century BCE mime by Herondas, who describes a vow fulfilled by two ladies at the Asklepieion at Cos, the ex-voto was generally a sign attesting the celebration of a religious service—a sacrifice, for example—and one can imagine that these objects were mass produced for such occasions, to serve as an instrument of cult for everyone. Finally, one should be prudent about interpreting ex-votos. Ton Derks has been able to show that in the public temple of Lenus Mars, at Trier, the ex-votos of infants are not attributable to a healing or an individual act of devotion, but to a rite of passage that allowed one access to this or that age class.[17] Like the sacrifices to Jupiter on the Capitol at Rome by males reaching majority, the ex-votos representing infants arise, according to Derks, from a col-lective rite celebrated by parents in a great public temple of Trier, without doubt in fulfillment of a vow. Where is the new form of devotion?

The So-Called Oriental Cults

The same observation can be made regarding the cults often cited as examples of the deepening of "religiosity," those of Isis and Mater Magna, the Great Mother. But these cults seem to me to provide evidence of exactly the opposite.

Documents relevant to Delos and to the Italian traders there show that, from the second century BCE, the cult of the poliadic gods of Alexandria, Isis and Serapis, were constitutive of the community of grain traders, who were linked to Egypt as major traders in Egyptian grain. It is through this connection that the cult developed in Italy and at Rome, within a private but collective framework. Small religious buildings and private temples are attested from the end of the second century at Rome, but the cult was not publicly celebrated there. One of those temples, the Iseum Metellinum,[18] was, however, linked to a great senatorial family. Despite this support, the cult of the Egyptian gods did not become public under pressure from initiates of Isis, but for political and military reasons.

In keeping with their position as poliadic divinities of Alexandria, the Egyptian gods always had a political existence at Rome. The events of 58, 53, 50, and 48 BCE give evidence of the politicization of the cult, which was tied to a violent group of the *populares* inspired by the tribune Clodius.[19] Their provocations led to a temporary repression of the cult, and in particular to the destruction of the altar or small building that was located in the precinct of the temple of Jupiter Capitolinus. In the age of Caesar or during the first years of the triumvirate, the question was raised over several years of whether there should be a public temple of Isis and Serapis in Rome, in order to strengthen the friendship between Rome and Egypt. This project was forgotten in consequence of the war between Octavian and Cleopatra and after the latter's defeat. For a long time, there were only private cults of Isis, which perpetuated ancient traditions, albeit at the mercy of events and scandals. So, under Tiberius, one of the private temples was destroyed by way of punishment, and the cult was repressed to the first milestone from the center of Rome. The community that practiced this devotion was, however, firmly implanted, and so it continued, in spite of everything, to rebuild its sacred buildings and temples as soon as the storm had passed. It should be emphasized that the repression was due in the one case to the political provocations of the 50s BCE and in the other to an act of fraud under Tiberius. On the other hand, pressure from worshippers of Isis was not enough to make the cult a public one. That this happened, and that it spread through Roman city-states, was for a very traditional reason: Isis and Serapis were the official and protective deities of the city where Vespasian was proclaimed emperor in 69—namely, Alexandria. Vespasian made this the cult of the Flavian party in the civil war and, after his victory, he caused the construction of the great Iseum of the Campus Martius at Rome. I have tried to show that it was not Caligula but Vespasian who created the public cult of Isis and Serapis.[20] The Iseum undoubtedly constituted an ex-voto, the fulfillment of a vow undertaken by Vespasian at Alexandria for his victory. The procedure was utterly traditional. Practically all the temples on the Campus Martius are due to this type of vow, fulfilled by important leaders in war after a triumph. If the proclamation of Vespasian had not taken place at Alexandria, if the Egyptian gods had not immediately announced his victory to him, and if Vespasian had not chosen to sleep in the proximity of the new temple that had begun to rise after his victory on the night before his triumph, then I could accept the attribution of his choice to a Flavian family tradition or to personal choice. But the data are sufficiently numerous to exclude any choice inspired by "religiosity" in the Romantic sense: it is in consequence of a military and political choice that Isis and Serapis became divine fellow citizens of the Romans. And, as always, the cult then spread into Roman city-states that had not yet known it, initially without doubt in order to honor the Flavian victory.

The example of the Great Mother, Mater Magna, also known as Cybele, will not keep us for long. Introduced in 204 BCE by the authorities of the Roman republic on the recommendation of the Sibylline books and the oracle of Delphi, the cult of Cybele was from the start eminently public.[21] I have long campaigned against the subtle distinctions that others wish to introduce between the Roman cult of the goddess, on the one hand, and the unbridled "religiosity," supposedly typical of Asia Minor, of her clergy proper, on the other. In fact, I have found nothing in the sources that supports the drawing of these distinctions or the interpretive claims that others base on them. I believe that the maternine rite (from *mater*) had henceforth become public cult of Rome, even if the self-mutilation prescribed by its first adepts was forbidden to Roman citizens, at least for a while. Above all, what interests us here is that this cult—of which one part of its savage rites, that leading to self-castration, reflected the complete alienation of the celebrant—was celebrated on behalf of the health of the Roman people. Again, it is crucial to remember that public cults were an obligation that lay on the totality of the Roman people, and which was imposed at Rome as upon its colonies. It is highly probable that the Roman city-states that had a temple and cult of Mater Magna had installed them in consequence of the oracle of 204 BCE and the edicts that followed. It is for this reason that we still see, at the end of the third century CE, that the quindecimviri, the college of priests responsible for the Sibylline books and all cults derived from them, still supervised the clergy of Cybele's cult in the colony of Cumae in Italy.[22]

It is therefore not as an effect of the private devotion of individuals, but for collective, public, and especially military reasons that this cult was installed at Rome at the end of the Second Punic War. It signals a public choice and a public volition, as well as the opening of Rome to the eastern Mediterranean. Likewise with the famous cults celebrated according to the Greek modality (*ritus Graecus*), which proclaimed Roman multiculturalism: they are a marker of Roman imperialism and not evidence of a new spirituality. I do not exclude the possibility that some people, having been illuminated by the rites, subsequently allowed themselves to be seduced by the special tyrannical piety of the Phrygian cult of the Mother. What I wish to say is rather that, without the political decision emanating from the *respublica*, the cult of Cybele would never have been officially introduced at Rome and would never have known such growth. A relative expansion, however: one must never forget that if one compares all the rites celebrated at Rome and in the Roman world, the so-called oriental cults played only a marginal role.

The cult of Mithra, whose traces are rather easily reconstructed by virtue of the distinctive organization of its cult sites, does not contradict this claim. It was introduced into Italy, as it seems, and the western world by the Flavian army (once again), since it was one of the cults practiced in the Roman legions stationed in Syria. What is more, the cult of Mithra always remained more or less confined to soldiers and members of the Roman administration. As we begin to understand the Mithraic liturgy better, we also discover that it resembles other cults more closely than we had previously thought, as can be seen from the Mithraic cult sites of Martigny, in Switzerland, and Tongres in Belgium.[23] In any case, as Robert Turcan underlined already a long time ago, the cult of Mithra was marginal compared with others, and moreover, it was restricted to a particular professional milieu.[24]

In other words, if it is undeniable that the various Christianities of the ancient world draw on religious practices existing in the Roman world,[25] it is also
misleading to make certain of its beliefs, thought to be more profound and
more individual, into precursors of what Minucius Felix called "true religion"
(*vera religio*). The rituals and representations that these cults could share with
Christianity are often known from patristic sources, to be sure. But one should
not forget that, for the Christians, these gods, even Mithra and Isis, were de-
mons, and their cult was a monstrous superstition. It would therefore be inap-
propriate to reconstruct a linear evolution, because resemblances could signify
merely that the adepts of initiatory cults were, like the Christians, children
of their time. After all, the pope ended up taking the title *Pontifex Maximus*,
greatest pontiff! But who would be crazy enough to regard the pope as a successor to the Roman pontiffs? Nor does any evidence suggest, even today, that
the healing cults or the so-called oriental cults gradually replaced the edifice of
ancestral religion in the Roman world—namely, the communal cults. On the
contrary, we must affirm that the most celebrated of these owed their success
to the civic framework and that this was the result of political choices. As far as
I know, no Roman city ever made Isis or Mater Magna its principal cult, with
the notable exceptions of their city-states of origin, Alexandria and Pessinous.

One can push this conclusion further and recall that Christianity itself
owed its historical success to a decision that a Roman emperor took in a military context: the pattern holds yet one more time. In a struggle for power,
the emperor Constantine trusted in a Christian interpretation of an observed
prodigy and so granted, after the victory on the Milvian bridge, a public existence to the new god and its cult alongside the ancestral religions. My colleague Paul Veyne thinks that Constantine truly believed in Christ and the
new religion.[26] This is possible. Werner Eck has defended the hypothesis according to which Constantine already knew Christian bishops in Gaul and
at Cologne, who impressed him with their personality, their intelligence, and
especially their interpretation of a prodigious halo observed in the sky.[27] It is
this interpretation that the emperor followed. If this hypothesis is correct, it
also carries evidence of a *fides*, of an entirely Roman confidence on the part of
Constantine in the new god. Perhaps. In any case, in 312 CE, his actions were
those of a Roman commander who instituted in public form the cult of the
divinity that had allowed him to bring back victory. It is also possible that
Christianity won by chance. Once again, Veyne makes a valuable observation

in this regard. He notes that the advent of the emperor Julian the Apostate, with his religious politics, raised no outcry among the people or the elite, any more than did, after his death, the advents of Gratian or Theodosius, two radical Christians who definitively put an end to ancestral public cult at Rome and in the city-states of the empire. It is, writes Veyne, as if this historic event, with its immense consequences, came about by chance.[28]

Claude Lepelley has argued in the same fashion that the religion of the *coloni*, the peasants of an African estate, followed the whims of the religious choices made by their master.[29] If he was pagan, they were pagan; if he converted to the Catholic faith, they became Catholic; and if he chose the camp of the Donatist heretics, they became Donatists. In general, one should note that religious reforms or revivals as a whole were always the work either of institutions or of elites, who either contested them or sought to make them more effective. This observation diminishes the force of the claim, according to which civic religion was never more than a discourse of the elite. Of course, one can always assume that the provocation to religious change derives not from custom itself or from traditional religious attitudes, but from the personal rather than institutional "religiosity" of some intellectual or grandee. However, one finds no trace of this anywhere in the sources. Not only did the adepts of the so-called new religious practices play no role in the religious changes that occurred in the Roman world, but they also did not try to change the existing system. On the contrary: as Richard Gordon has written, they confirmed and strengthened it.[30]

Chapter 11

The Gods, the State, and the Individual

Setting in perspective the reflections that have just been offered allows us to formulate some conclusions. We started from the idea that the criticisms that were once directed at the model of civic religion and which are still put forward today by their modern adherents rest upon a series of misunderstandings and errors. We have tried to replace such arguments with others, drawn from a historical rather than theoretical point of view.

The contradictions that have been revealed are multiple, starting with those that related to the evaluation and use of the sources. The critics of the civic model often claim to be surprised at the lack of sufficiently rich and explicit source material, as if they have no experience of historical work, especially as it is conducted on the ancient world. But instead of beginning from the idea that the sources are incapable of proving anything whatsoever, it would have been better to follow the tried and true method that permits one to make the best use of the evidence for ancient history that we have. However insufficient it appears at the start, the evidence reveals itself more rich than expected, especially if one takes the trouble to engage in appropriate comparative work, whether with ancient or non-ancient comparanda.

One also frequently gets the impression that, deep down, theorists of "religiosity" work not on the basis of primary sources but rather from encyclopedia articles. This seems clear when one finds the *Dictionary* of Festus cited from an outdated edition, such as were published before the beginning of the twentieth century. We have had occasion at least once to examine such a source: it had been understood to provide evidence against civic piety, but, correctly interpreted, it in fact provided a particularly explicit example of its practice, so long as one took the trouble to examine the text in question and to read it in the context in which it was inserted. Before launching oneself into producing definitive conclusions or grand theories, it would be best to begin more modestly, with the technical work that awaits the historian, philologist, or archaeologist.

Second, it is perfectly legitimate to call to account the schemas on which the supporters of the civic model of Roman religion are dependent. We have done that, too, for Wissowa as well as his predecessors, contemporaries, and successors. In doing this, one must still avoid succumbing to the false evidence of hackneyed historiographical models. It is essential always to examine oneself, and to grant others the benefit of employing a mode of thought, whether rational or religious, which is their own, even and perhaps especially when they appear to be close to our own perspective. Finally, I have insisted on the fact that the totality of the criticisms directed at civic religion are ultimately dependent upon a hoary theory of the rapid and final decline that struck the world of the city-states. Being committed counterrevolutionaries of the nineteenth century, the founders of this dialectical model believed that the civilization of the city-states exercised a tyranny over the individual, while the latter was supposedly free of the oppressive guardianship of the city. Whether this decline occurred after Chaeronea or after the Roman conquest of Greece, or still later under the empire, one cannot say. No matter: in each case, the individual is supposed to have won autonomy at the expense of the city-state and community.

This outdated theory, which the last generation did much to critique and analyze, contains two errors. The first concerns the notion of the self. Numerous historians, including Peter Brown, for example, have shown that the notions of the individual and of the person alike were not the same in classical antiquity as they became later on.[1] It has been argued that the first individual in the post-classical sense of the term is Augustine. Thus, we do not even know what the ancients who left us the bulk of our evidence really thought or believed. John Dillon, a specialist in late ancient philosophy, confesses to not knowing what the encyclopedist Varro actually believed.[2] We know in any case that, throughout all of classical antiquity, a clear distinction was drawn between religion, on the one hand, and speculations of every type regarding the gods and the nature of the world, on the other. The ancients could fashion for themselves the same ideas as we do about the meaning of the world or the nature of the gods. But the speculations that they developed on these subjects did not affect religious practice. Such speculations did not form the content of some body of doctrine of the *sacra*. Above all, the opinions that the ancients could formulate regarding one and the same cult or one and the same god were never single or definitive. As we have seen, the truth was plural. None of these truths was mandatory.

The other error, still more coarse, consists in subscribing to the old theory of the collapse of the world of city-states. It has been possible for at least two generations to show that this idea had enormous resonance with Hegelian dialectic, but it receives no documentation of any kind in the evidence. In spite of the multiple changes that occurred in the ancient world between the eighth century BCE and the fourth century of this era, city-states continued to form the conceptual and everyday horizon of the ancients. All of ancient civilization was a civilization of the city, if you will. In consequence, civic religion continued to function, and the collective desire to practice the rites was never repudiated. If one looks a little more closely, the sources show that public religion was celebrated until the fourth century CE by and for the citizens of a given city, and for all those who were duly registered as residents. In the new framework of the great city-states of the high empire, participation in public cult became a fact of life for even more persons.

What the critics of civic religion forget completely, when concentrating their fire on public cult, even as the Christian martyrs once did, is that all Romans and, more generally, the entire population of the Roman world was organized into communities. Like members of city-states, members of communities conceived the gods in relation to the groups to which they belonged. Consequently, if one decides to endorse the theory of the detractors of *polis*-religion, it is the totality of religious conduct among Romans and in the Roman world that one puts in doubt. At all levels of society, religious practice conformed to a communal model. To understand this, it is essential to know Roman society in detail and not assimilate it to ours. The otherness of religious conduct deserves neither anathema nor contempt. One need only read the pages, as violent as they are amusing, written about Roman religions by the great historian of ancient Rome Theodor Mommsen in order to understand that his criticism of ritualism and liturgical formalism was in fact aimed at the Catholicism of his day, which he sought to stigmatize as a contemptible relic of the past.

To consider still one more misunderstanding, it is true that slaves did not participate in cult and that slaves were excluded from ritual spectacles. That was the principle. This means that a slave could not attend as someone *sui iuris*, as someone of full rights at law, with the capacity to perform civic acts. And this was true for public rites and for domestic ones. The fact that a slave could serve as an assistant to a priest or magistrate who celebrated games has no value as an objection against this general rule, because in such cases the slave acted in conformity with the subordinate status that was his. His presence brought no taint, and there was no question of impurity. On the domestic front, the treatise *On agriculture* by Cato the Censor teaches us that slaves were capable of celebrating domestic cult, but in the name and at the command of the father of the family, not in the slave's own name. Let us go a little further. If a slave himself possessed a slave, a *vicarius*, a substitute, he could take the same initiative vis-à-vis this slave as his master took in regard to him. In the same way that a *vicarius* could call his owner, himself a slave, *dominus* or "master,"[3] the latter could command the former to celebrate cult for his own *Genius*, his protector deity, by this or that rite. In other words, from the point of view and in function of juridical position, a slave could be excluded from cult, all the while fulfilling roles in cult and even taking the initiative in religious matters. It is true that one could choose to regard the apparent complexity of Roman society as an amusing illusion constructed by jurists or as a discourse of the elite, and so write another history of the Roman world and its religions. But in that case, I am not sure that one would still be speaking of history or of the Romans.

The specificity, the alterity of the Romans, which causes critics of the civic model to shudder, may also be found in the very conception that ancients had of divine presence. Until the Christian era, the Romans regarded the gods as earthly partners maintaining relations with mortals with an eye toward reciprocal earthly benefits: the necessities of life for the humans, and honor and recognition of their superiority for the gods. In no case did they regard their gods as absolute masters requiring from mortals a complete and perpetual submission. Roman gods were seen as *patroni*, as powerful persons who protected and helped their *clientes*, according to a model of social relations shared by all Romans. The contradiction with the Christian way of seeing things is total. This conception was valid for all cults, those that people have assumed were new as well as ancestral ones, public cults as well as private. From this perspective, the religious practices most typical of the private individual, the rites that we call "magic," could never be adduced in this debate, because they reverse completely the normative relationship between mortals and gods, by constraining the latter to enter into the service of a human.

Beyond these misunderstandings regarding the world of the city-states and the Roman inclination toward communal life, one of the most distressing oversights of the deconstructive theorists concerns beliefs and the very heart of religious practice. Against those who are surprised at the absence of emotion or coherent beliefs, we have recalled that Roman religions were truly communal, but they were above all founded upon the preeminence of rites, rites whose meaning remained implicit and which did not impose any belief beyond the necessity of their observance. Emotion was not a prerequisite for a religious act; the practice itself might provoke an emotional response, when the celebration appeared harmonious or, on the contrary, when it was disturbed. Moreover, even if Roman ritualism appears austere, it was unquestionably bound to a particular form of religious thought that reveals itself in sacred jurisprudence. A few years ago, I gave a lecture in which I invoked the concept of spirituality in order to draw attention to this form of thought,[4] but today I prefer to conform to the principle of alterity and to abandon this anachronistic term, which hearkens to the Christianity of the nineteenth century and has no claim to universality. That the rites of the Romans were tied neither to a revelation, nor to a book or dogma, that they were reducible to their literal obligation, is indicative once again of an otherness with respect to that which the modern West, whether agnostic or not, understands by "religion." I refer the reader to the superb study produced by Caroline Humphrey and James Laidlaw, which shows that a practice devoid of beliefs or preparatory emotions belongs to the daily religious life of contemporary India.[5] One does not, however, have to go that far. What do today's disciples of Schleiermacher think of Judaism or Islam?

The objections that are made against a trumped-up version of the civic model are thus not historical, not least because their model does not correspond to religion as it was seen and practiced by the ancients. More seriously, the problem is not merely a deficit at the level of theory or a historical model that needs to be questioned. What the critics of the civic model reject is rather the very idea of the relative alterity of the ancients, such as the literary, epigraphic, papyrological, and juridical sources do not cease to attest, and such as we discover widely in the researches of contemporary social anthropology. Their refusal to credit any such alterity is not based on the refutation of the historical arguments that have aided in the formulation of this vision of ancient religion; it is not based on a contestation of the principles of modern anthropology; it is, at the base, the result of a confessional approach to religious history. Whether one invokes Schleiermacher, Wilamowitz-Moellendorff, Wach, Simmel, or phenomenology, one is dealing with a Christianizing theory. In other words, deconstructionist approaches do not lead to a new construction, to a new approach to Roman religious practice. That would have been exciting. Rather, they lead to reintroduction of a historiographical and theological model from the beginning of the nineteenth century, whose Christian character is obvious. The result is that no place is left for a different "religiosity." Respect for alterity, the foundation of a secular attitude, is abandoned.

For my part, I have tried for thirty years to write history—to write religious history—in conformity with this principle. I do not write Christian theology of history. I see no reason to change my method.

Notes

TRANSLATOR'S FOREWORD

1. Jonathan Z. Smith, *Drudgery Divine: On the Comparison of Early Christianities and the Religions of Late Antiquity* (Chicago: University of Chicago Press, 1990), pp. 1–35.

2. See, e.g., Andreas Bendlin, "Rituals or Beliefs? 'Religion' and the Religious Life of Rome," *Scripta Classica Israelica* 20 (2001): 191–208, or C. Robert Philipps III, "Approaching Roman Religion: The Case for Wissenschaftsgeschichte," in Jörg Rüpke, ed., *A Companion to Roman Religion* (Oxford: Blackwell, 2007), pp. 10–28.

3. Georg Wissowa, *Religion und Kultus der Römer*, 2nd ed. (Munich: C. H. Beck, 1912).

4. Although now somewhat dated, Clifford Ando, ed., *Roman Religion* (Edinburgh: Edinburgh University Press, 2003), provides bibliographic and historiographic introductions to a number of fields of inquiry in Roman religion beyond those described here.

5. A related problem concerns the freighted unpacking of the Roman term *religio*. A recent, excellent contribution to this field, with a thorough review of earlier work, is Giovanni Casadio, "*Religio* vs. Religion," in Jitse Dijkstra, Justin Koesen, and Ymi Kuiper, eds., *Myths, Martyrs and Modernity: Studies in the History of Religion in Honour of Jan N. Bremmer* (Leiden: Brill, 2010), pp. 301–26.

6. Clifford Ando, "Exporting Roman Religion," in Jörg Rüpke, ed., *A Companion to Roman Religion* (Oxford: Blackwell, 2007), pp. 429–45.

7. Landmark studies in this vein include Mary Beard's two articles, "Cicero and Divination: The Formation of a Latin Discourse," *Journal of Roman Studies* 76 (1986): 33–46, and "A Complex of Times: No More Sheep on Romulus' Birthday," *PCPhS* 33 (1987): 1–15; the latter is reprinted in Ando, ed., *Roman Religion*, pp. 273–88. Beard herself offers a stunning display of the integration of the forms of inquiry she has espoused in *The Roman Triumph* (Cambridge, MA: Harvard University Press, 2007). In a large and diverse landscape I might single out Jerzy Linderski, "Roman Religion in Livy," in Wolfgang Schuller, ed., *Livius: Aspecte seines Werkes* (Konstanz: Universitätsverlag Konstanz, 1993), pp. 53–70, and W. J. Tatum, "Roman Religion: Fragments and Further Questions," in S. N. Byrne and

E. P. Cueva, eds., *Veritatis Amicitiaeque Causa: Essays in Honor of Anna Lydia Motto and John R. Clark* (Wauconda, IL: Bolchazy-Carducci, 1999), pp. 273–91, for the cogency of their methodological reflections on the study of religion in particular.

8. This is a theme charted in a remarkable essay by John North, "Conservatism and Change in Roman Religion," *PBSR* 44 (1976): 1–12, but only recently taken up by others. See now Clifford Ando, "The Ontology of Religious Institutions," *History of Religions* 50 (2010): 54–79; Clifford Ando, "Praesentia numinis, Part 2: Objects in Roman Cult," *Asdiwal* 6 (2011): 57–69; John North, "Disguising Change in the First Century," in Jörg Rüpke, ed., *The Individual in the Religions of the Ancient Mediterranean* (Oxford: Oxford University Press, 2013), pp. 58–84; Clifford Ando, *Religion et gouvernement dans l'Empire romain*, Bibliothèque de l'École des Hautes Études (Turnhout: Brepols, 2015), chapter 4; and Jörg Rüpke, "Historicizing Religion: Varro's *Antiquitates* and History of Religion in the Late Roman Republic," *History of Religions* 53 (2014): 246–68.

9. On this topic, see now Greg Woolf, "Ritual and the Individual in Roman Religion," in Rüpke, *The Individual*, pp. 136–60, and Clifford Ando, *Religion et gouvernement dans l'Empire romain*.

10. Gordon's arguments in this regard are elaborated in three splendid articles, "From Republic to Principate: Priesthood, Religion and Ideology," "The Veil of Power: Emperors, Sacrificers and Benefactors," and "Religion in the Roman Empire: The Civic Compromise and Its Limits," all published in Mary Beard and John North, eds., *Pagan Priests: Religion and Power in the Ancient World* (Ithaca, NY: Cornell University Press, 1990), pp. 179–255. Recent essays that include significant literature reviews include Brent Nongbri, "Dislodging 'Embedded' Religion: A Brief Note on a Scholarly Trope," *Numen* 55 (2008): 440–60, and Clifford Ando, "Subjects, Gods and Empire, or Monarchism as a Theological Problem," in Rüpke, *The Individual*, 86–111.

11. John Scheid, *Romulus et ses frères: Le collège des frères arvales, modèle du culte public dans la Rome des empereurs* (Rome: École Française de Rome, 1990). Among the essays on ritual and its interpretation, I would single out M. Linder and J. Scheid, "Quand croire c'est faire: Le problème de la croyance dans la Rome ancienne," *Archives de sciences sociales des religions* 81 (1993): 47–62; J.-L. Durand and John Scheid, "'Rites' et 'religion': Remarques sur certains préjugés des historiens de la religion des grecs et des romains," *Archives de sciences sociales des religions* 85 (1994): 23–43; J. Scheid, "Hiérarchie et structure dans le polythéisme romain: Façons romaines de penser l'action," *Archiv für Religionsgeschichte* 1 (1999): 184–203, which is translated in Ando, *Roman Religion*, pp. 164–89, and also reprinted, with a number of other splendid essays on ritual, in Scheid, *Quand faire, c'est croire: Les rites sacrificiels des Romains* (Paris: Aubier, 2005). I published a review article on this volume, with extensive consideration of Scheid's output to that date in its international context, under the title "Evidence and Orthopraxy," *Journal of Roman Studies* 99 (2009): 171–81.

12. A kindred historical survey is available in Woolf, "Ritual and the Individual."

13. J. North, "Religious Toleration in Republican Rome," *PCPhS* 25 (1979): 85–103, reprinted in Ando, *Roman Religion*, pp. 199–219; see also North, "The Development of

Religious Pluralism," in J. Lieu et al., eds., *The Jews Among Pagans and Christians in the Roman Empire* (London: Routledge, 1992), pp. 174–93.

14. G. Woolf, "Polis-Religion and Its Alternatives in the Roman Provinces," in H. Cancik and J. Rüpke, eds., *Römische Reichsreligion and Provinzialreligion* (Tübingen: Mohr Siebeck, 1997), 71–84, reprinted in Ando, *Roman Religion*, 39–54. An idiosyncratic and valuable contribution with similar aspirations is Ramsay MacMullen, "The Unromanized in Rome," in S. J. D. Cohen and E. S. Frerichs, eds., *Diasporas in Antiquity*, Brown Judaic Studies 288 (Atlanta: Scholars Press, 1993), 47–64.

15. A. Bendlin, "Peripheral Centres—Central Peripheries: Religious Communication in the Roman Empire," in Cancik and Rüpke, *Reichsreligion*, 35–68; A. Bendlin, "Looking Beyond the Civic Compromise: Religious Pluralism in Late Republican Rome," in Ed Bispham and Christopher Smith, eds., *Religion in Archaic and Republican Rome and Italy* (Edinburgh: Edinburgh University Press, 2000), pp. 115–35; and Bendlin, "Rituals or Beliefs?" See also Nongbri, "Dislodging 'Embedded' Religion."

16. A celebrated and controversial work in this vein is Rodney Stark's *The Rise of Christianity: A Sociologist Reconsiders History* (Princeton, NJ: Princeton University Press, 1996). The literature engaging Stark is enormous. A particularly valuable essay, in part because it reads Stark alongside contemporaneous literatures in ancient history, is Roger Beck, "Religious Market of the Roman Empire: Rodney Stark and Christianity's Pagan Competition," in Leif Vaage, ed., *Religious Rivalries in the Early Roman Empire and the Rise of Christianity* (Waterloo, Ontario: Canadian Corporation for Studies in Religion, 2006), pp. 233–54.

17. Ando, "Monarchism."

18. See, e.g., John Bodel and S. M. Olyan, eds., *Household and Family Religion in Antiquity* (Oxford: Blackwell, 2008); Rüpke, *The Individual*.

19. For another attempt to understand the positions of Scheid and his prominent anglophone interlocutors, see Ando, "Evidence." That essay also sketches important theoretical statements by Scheid not elaborated in this book but relevant to its themes, perhaps the most prominent being his remarkable efforts to demonstrate that select forms of household and non-statal cult (especially as connected with the dead) exhibit powerful forms of structural and gestural affinity with statal cult.

20. The metonymic reach of *civitas* is an important topic in my own study of Roman political and legal language: Ando, *Roman Social Imaginaries: Language and Thought in Contexts of Empire* (Toronto: Toronto University Press, 2015).

PREFACE

1. Fontenelle, *Histoire des oracles* (Paris, 1687).

2. See the analogous remarks of Robert Parker, *On Greek Religion* (Ithaca, NY: Cornell University Press, 2011), pp. 1–63.

3. *Le Monde des religions* 5 (2012): 5.

INTRODUCTION

1. Georg Wissowa, *Religion und Kultus der Römer* (1902; Munich: Beck, 1912).

2. On this point, see also Clifford Ando, "Evidence and Orthopraxy," *Journal of Roman Studies* 99 (2009): 171–81 at 174.

3. John Scheid, "L'impossible polythéisme: Les raisons d'un vide dans l'histoire de la religion romaine," in Francis Schmidt, ed., *L'impensable polythéisme* (Paris: Éditions des Archives contemporaines, 1988), pp. 425–57 ("Polytheism Impossible; or, the Empty Gods: Reasons Behind a Void in the History of Roman Religions," *History and Anthropology* 3 (1987): 303–25).

4. Minucius Felix, *Octavius* 38.6: *Fruamur bono nostro et recti sententiam tenemus: cohibebatur superstitio, impietas expietur, uera religio reseruetur.* "Let us enjoy our good and hold to this view of what is right: let superstition be curbed, impiety expiated, and true religion preserved and sustained."

CHAPTER I. THE CRITIQUE OF *POLIS*-RELIGION

1. Georg Wilhelm Friedrich Hegel, *Leçons sur la philosophie de l'histoire* (1822–30; repr. Paris: Vrin, 1963); Hegel, *Leçons sur la philosophie de la religion*, IIe partie, 2 (1821–31; repr. Paris: Vrin, 1959). On this influence, permit me to refer to Scheid, "L'impossible polythéisme: Les raisons d'un vide dans l'histoire de la religion romaine," in Francis Schmidt, ed., *L'Impensable polythéisme* (Paris: Éditions des Archives contemporaines, 1988), pp. 425–57 ("Polytheism Impossible; or, the Empty Gods: Reasons Behind a Void in the History of Roman Religions," *History and Anthropology* 3 (1987): 303–25).

2. Ulrich von Wilamowitz-Moellendorff, *Der Glaube der Hellenen*, 2 vols. (Berlin: Weidmann, 1931–32); Theodor Mommsen, *Histoire romaine* (1854; repr. Paris: Robert Laffont, 1985); G. Wissowa, *Religion und Kultus der Römer* (1902; repr. Munich: Beck, 1912); Franz Cumont, *Les Religions orientales dans le paganisme romain* (1906; repr. Paris: Ernest Leroux, 1929; repr. Turin: Nino Aragno Editore, 2006) (see Corinne Bonnet, Vinciane Pirenne-Delforge, and Danny Praet, eds., *Les Religions orientales dans le monde grec et romain: Cent ans après Cumont (1906–2006)* [Rome: Institut historique belge de Rome, 2009]); Jules Toutain, *Les Cultes païens dans l'Empire romain*, part 1: *Les provinces latines*, vol. 2: *Les cultes orientaux* (Paris: Ernest Leroux, 1911).

3. Mircea Eliade, *Traité d'histoire des religions* (1949; repr. Paris: Payot, 1974).

4. John Scheid, *Religion, institutions et société de la Rome antique* (Paris: Fayard, 2003).

5. Such is the nickname given to a group of British scholars who, between the end of the nineteenth century and the start of the twentieth, undertook to relate the origin of mythology and of classical drama to the practice of ancient rituals. See William M. Calder III, ed., *The Cambridge Ritualists Reconsidered* (Atlanta: Scholars Press, 1991).

6. Émile Durkheim, *Les Formes élémentaires de la vie religieuse* (1912; repr. Paris: PUF, 1968); William Warde Fowler, *The Religious Experience of the Roman People* (1911; repr. New York: Cooper Square, 1971).

7. Henri Hubert and Marcel Mauss, "Essai sur le sacrifice (1899)," in Marcel Mauss, *Œuvres. I. Les fonctions sociales du sacré*, ed. Victor Karady (Paris: Minuit, 1968), pp. 193–307. On this text, see Marcel Detienne and Jean-Pierre Vernant, *La Cuisine du sacrifice en pays grec* (Paris: Gallimard, 1979), pp. 24–28.

8. G. Wissowa, *Religion und Kultus der Römer*, p. viii: "When someone with warm acquaintance of my achievement feels the need to rebuke my representation for a certain exteriorization of religious concepts and forms, arising, one supposes, from its adopting the point of view of pontifical law, or for a one-sided legalistic perspective that betrays a small conception of religiosity, then the question may legitimately be posed, whether 'religiosity' truly is a concept wholly fixed and constant for all times and peoples and whether that which has been identified as a lacuna in the work is not better referred to the object of study."

9. U. von Wilamowitz-Moellendorff, letter of 31 December 1901: "You have treated the *religio* of the Romans and left religion, subjective feeling, to one side. That is fully justified, especially in this study. It should also not be said, that anyone could truly know anything about that. But the curious will ask, above all if he has the habit of posing such questions." For the text, see Francesco Bertolini, "Inediti: Wilamowitz a Wissowa e Praechter," *Quaderni di Storia* 4 (1978): 185–210 at 191–92.

10. Johann Gottfried von Herder, *Idées sur la philosophie de l'histoire de l'humanité*, 3 vols. (1784–91; repr. Paris: Levrault, 1827–28).

11. Scheid, "L'impossible polythéisme"; John Scheid, *Religion et piété à Rome*, 2nd ed. (Paris: Albin Michel, 2001), pp. 20–21.

12. Theodor Mommsen and Wilhelm Henzen, eds., *Corpus inscriptionum latinarum*, vol. 1 (1863); Theodor Mommsen, Wilhelm Henzen, and Christian Hülsen, *Inscriptiones Latinae antiquissimae ad C. Caesaris mortem*, 2nd ed. (Berlin: Reimer, 1893), pp. 283–339.

13. On this topic, see John Scheid and Eckhard Wirbelauer, "La correspondance entre Georg Wissowa et Theodor Mommsen (1883–1901)," in Corinne Bonnet and Véronique Krings, eds., *S'écrire et écrire sur l'Antiquité: L'apport des correspondances à l'histoire des travaux historiques* (Grenoble: J. Millon, 2008), pp. 155–212.

14. Theodor Mommsen, *Le Droit public romain*, 7 vols. (Paris: Thorin, 1889–96). The original was published in two editions between 1871 and 1888.

15. See Mommsen, *Le Droit public romain*.

16. Wilhelm Mannhardt, *Wald- und Feldkulte*, 2 vols. (Berlin: Borntraeger, 1875–77); James Frazer, *Le Rameau d'or* (1890–1915; repr. Paris: Robert Laffont, 1981).

17. Wissowa, *Religion und Kultus der Römer*, p. 409, n. 4. The author expresses reticence about the ideas of Salomon Reinach, Albert Dieterich, and Ada Thomsen on the origin of sacrifice.

18. Christiane Sourvinou-Inwood, "What Is *Polis* Religion?" in Oswyn Murray and Simon Price, eds., *The Greek City from Home to Alexander* (Oxford: Oxford University Press, 1990), pp. 295–322, reprinted in Richard Buxton, ed., *Oxford Readings in Greek Religion* (Oxford: Oxford University Press, 2000), pp. 13–37. This article will be cited from the latter publication. See also Christiane Sourvinou-Inwood, "Further Aspects of *Polis*

Religion," in *Annali dell'Istituto Universitario Orientale di Napoli, Sezione di Archeologia e Storia Antica* 10 (1988): 259–74, also reprinted in Buxton, *Oxford Readings*, pp. 38–55.

19. One might cite by way of example the article of Richard Gordon, "Religion in the Roman Empire: The Civic Compromise and Its Limits," in Mary Beard and John North, eds., *Pagan Priests: Religion and Power in the Ancient World* (London: Duckworth, 1990), pp. 235–55.

20. Gordon, "Religion in the Roman Empire," p. 251: "The justification for the authority of ascetic priests lay properly in personal purity and religious learning, which together formed a revalued conception of piety; and their authority was conceived as a private matter, without public implications."

21. One might refer by way of example to the article of Greg Woolf, "*Polis*-Religion and Its Alternatives in the Roman Provinces," in Hubert Cancik and Jörg Rüpke, eds., *Römische Reichsreligion und Provinzialreligion* (Tübingen: Mohr Siebeck, 1997), pp. 71–84.

22. Louise Bruit Zaidman and Pauline Schmitt-Pantel, *La Religion grecque* (Paris: Armand Colin, 1989); Sourvinou-Inwood, "What Is *Polis* Religion?"

23. For a famous articulation of this argument, see John North, "The Development of Religious Pluralism," in Judith Lieu, John North, and Tessa Rajak, eds., *The Jews Among Pagans and Christians* (London: Routledge, 1992), pp. 174–93, notably p. 178: "So the basic story proposed by this chapter is one of development from religion as embedded in the city-state to religion as choice of differentiated groups offering different qualities of religious doctrine, different experiences, insights or just different myths and stories to make sense of the absurdity of human experience."

24. See, for example, Philippe Gauthier, *Études d'histoire et d'institutions grecques: Choix d'écrits* (Geneva: Droz, 2011).

25. See Andreas Bendlin, "'Une perspective trahissant un piètre sens de la religiosité': Émotion et Orient dans l'historiographie religieuse romaine de l'époque moderne,» *Trivium* 4 (2009), unpaginated electronic edition, translated by Anne-Laure Vignaux from *Archiv für Religionsgeschichte* 8 (2006), pp. 227–256.

26. On the importance of anti-Catholicism to this strand in the historiography of religion, see Jonathan Z. Smith, *Drudgery Divine* (Chicago: University of Chicago Press, 1990), pp. 1–35.

27. Friedrich Schleiermacher, *Die christliche Glaube nach den Grundsätzen der evangelischen Kirch im Zusammenhang dargestellt*, 2nd ed. (Berlin, 1930); English translation: *The Christian Faith*, ed. H. R. Mackintosh and J. S. Stewart (London: T&T Clark, 1999).

28. Schleiermacher, *Christian Faith*, section 3, pp. 5–12.

29. Richard Reitzenstein, *Werden und Wesen der Humanität im Altertum: Rede zur Feier des Geburtstages seiner Majestät des Kaisers am 26. Januar 1907 in der Aula der Kaiser-Wilhelms-Universität Straßburg* (Strasbourg, 1907), p. 20 (regarding the Secular Games of 17 BCE): "We perceive it: the age of humanism is over; an age of religiosity is again coming to be."

30. Jerzy Linderski, "Roman Religion in Livy," in Wolfgang Schuller, ed., *Livius: Aspekte seines Werkes* (Konstanz: Universitätverlag Konstanz, 1993), pp. 53–70 at 54, regarding

an article of P. G. Walsh: Walsh describes Livy as "attempt[ing] to sift from the mass of superstitious myth a central doctrine of the relationship between men and gods which will lend order and significance to human life. . . . This is the fundamental force of Livian *pietas*—a reverence for the godhead which ensures the right ordering of men's lives." Linderski comments: "This makes out of Livy a member of a protestant church; but his history is not about god in men's lives, but about the rise of Rome, *dis auctoribus* [with the gods as motivating agents]."

31. Andreas Bendlin, "Looking Behind the Civic Compromise: Religious Pluralism in Late Republican Rome," in Edward Bispham and Christopher Smith, eds., *Religion in Archaic and Republican Rome and Italy: Evidence and Experience* (Edinburgh: Edinburgh University Press, 2000), pp. 115–35.

32. Bendlin, "Civic Compromise," p. 120. The passage continues: "Religion was, for the first time in the history of humankind, exclusively presented as an internalised belief system detached from any non-private religious institutionalisation; it was removed from the realm of societal communication."

33. Bendlin, "Civic Compromise," p. 121: "Despite the fact that the traditional Schleiermachian notion of religion is a creation of the eighteenth century, no one has doubted its validity when it is applied to, for instance, Christian belief systems in the Middle Ages."

34. Nicole Bourque, "An Anthropologist's View of Ritual," in Bispham and Smith, eds., *Religion in Archaic and Republican Rome and Italy*, pp. 19–33.

35. Stefan Krauter, *Bürgerrecht und Kultteilnahme: Politische und kultische Rechte und Pflichten in griechische Poleis, Rom und antikem Judentum* (Berlin: De Gruyter, 2004).

36. Gustav Mensching, *Sociologie religieuse* (1947; repr. Paris: Payot, 1951); Joachim Wach, *Sociologie de la religion* (1951; repr. Paris: Payot, 1955).

37. Krauter, *Bürgerrecht und Kultteilnahme*, p. 264: "One should rather commence from an always already extent religious, from a tension between individual and collective religion, between change—better: many tendencies toward change, which are always compatible with one another—and persistence."

38. Krauter, *Bürgerrecht und Kultteilnahme*, p. 426: "In reality they show that ancient religion cannot be reduced to the constitution of collective identity. That it had this function, should in no way be contested. But beyond this, it opened for persons in antiquity multiple further dimensions of meaning."

39. Georg Simmel, "Religion," in *Essays on Religion*, ed. and trans. Hörst Jürgen Helle in collaboration with Ludwig Nieder (New Haven: Yale University Press, 1997). On Max Weber, see Volkhard Krech, "Religiosität," in Hans G. Kippenberg and Martin Riesebrodt, eds., *Max Webers "Religionssystematik"* (Tübingen: Mohr Siebeck, 2001), pp. 51–76.

40. Simmel, *La Religion* (Paris: Circé, 1998), p. 103: "All explanation of the 'origin' of religion—that it grew out of fear or love, out of need or the self's supraindividual consciousness, out of piety or a sense of dependence, or whatever other ideas." On Simmel's debt to Schleiermacher, see Patrick Watier's postscript to the French translation of Simmel's *Religion: La Religion* (Paris: Circé, 1998), pp. 135–81 at 135ff. To get a sense of the profoundly

theological character of Simmel's arguments, English readers may wish to read Simmel's essay, "Fundamental Religious Ideas and Modern Science: An Inquiry," published three years after *Die Religion*, also translated in *Essays on Religion*, pp. 3–6.

41. Simmel, *La Religion*, p. 103.

42. Bendlin, "'Une perspective trahissant un piètre sens de la religiosité'": "La recherche *doit* en revanche chercher à surmonter cette dichotomie traditionnelle sujet/objet et à réintégrer les domaines de la culture et de l'émotion, plus précisément, de la religion institutionnalisée et de la dimension psycho-émotionnelle de l'acte et du sentiment religieux."

43. Bendlin, "'Une perspective trahissant un piètre sens de la religiosité,'" p. 16: "Le besoin du latiniste Wissowa de défendre son propre objet d'étude et sa propre discipline comme un domaine distinct et autonome de l'activité scientifique intervient sans doute."

CHAPTER 2. *POLIS* AND REPUBLIC

1. For example, Greg Woolf, "*Polis*-Religion and Its Alternatives in the Roman Provinces," in Hubert Cancik and Jörg Rüpke, eds., *Römische Reichsreligion und Provinzialreligion* (Tübingen: Mohr Siebeck, 1997), p. 73: "The spread of the city state in Greece, through the Mediterranean basin and in Hellenistic and Roman empires, led to the extension of *polis*-religion. Yet as the autonomy and integrity of poleis were weakened by those same imperialisms there was a marked growth in alternative forms of religion—Bacchic cult, Judaism, Mithraism, Christianity among others—which paid less respect to *polis* boundaries and the social order."

2. Andreas Bendlin, "Looking Behind the Civic Compromise: Religious Pluralism in Late Republican Rome," in Edward Bispham and Christopher Smith, eds., *Religion in Archaic and Republican Rome and Italy: Evidence and Experience* (Edinburgh: Edinburgh University Press, 2000), pp. 123–24: "For as the advocates of the model of civic religion surmise, it is a result of the differentiation of religious choices in the Mediterranean world from the fourth century onwards at the latest that civic religion, no longer sufficiently able to incorporate new choices, would itself disintegrate."

3. See, for example, Stefan Krauter, *Bürgerrecht und Kultteilnahme: Politische und kultische Rechte und Pflichten in griechische Poleis, Rom und antikem Judentum* (Berlin: De Gruyter, 2004), pp. 401–2.

4. Yan Thomas, "Citoyens résidents dans les cités de l'Empire romain: Essai sur le droit d'origine," in Laurent Mayali, ed., *Identité et droit de l'autre* (Berkeley: University of California, 1994), pp. 1–56; Yan Thomas, *"Origine" et "commune patrie": Étude de droit public romain (89 av. J.-C.–212 apr. J.-C.)* (Rome: École française de Rome, 1996).

5. Fernand De Visscher, *Les Édits d'Auguste découverts à Cyrène* (Louvain: Bibliothèque de l'Université, 1940); Vincenzo Giuffré, Paul Frédéric, Girard Senn, and Félix Senn, *Les lois des Romains* (Naples: Jovene, 1977), pp. 408–21; Adrian N. Sherwin-White, *The Roman Citizenship* (Oxford: Clarendon Press, 1973), pp. 297ff., 334ff.

6. A. N. Sherwin-White, "The *Tabula* of Banasa and the *Constitutio Antoniniana*," *Journal of Roman Studies* 63 (1973): 86–98; William Seston and Maurice Euzennat, "Un dossier de la chancellerie romaine: La 'Tabula Banasitana,' étude de diplomatique," *Comptes rendus de l'Académie des inscriptions et belles-lettres* 3 (1971): 468–90; see *L'Année épigraphique*, 1977, 871 = *AE* 1995, 1801 = *AE* 1999, 1860 = *AE* 2003, 2035 = AE 2006, 1655.

7. Christopher P. Jones, "A New Letter of Marcus Aurelius to the Athenians," *Zeitschrift für Papyrologie und Epigraphik* 8 (1971): 161–83.

8. Aulus Gellius, *Attic Nights* 16, 13, 8–9, trans. J. C. Rolfe (1927; rev. ed. Cambridge, MA: Harvard University Press, 1946): "But the relationship of the colonies is a different one: for they do not come into citizenship from without, nor grow from roots of their own, but they are as it were transplanted from the State and have all the laws and institutions of the Roman people not those of their own choice. This condition, although it is more exposed to control and less free, is nevertheless thought preferable and superior because of the greatness and majesty of the Roman people, of which colonies seem to be miniatures, as it were, and in a way copies. At the same time, because the rights of the municipal towns have become obscure and invalid, and from ignorance of their existence, the townsmen are no longer able to make use of them."

9. Aulus Gellius, *Attic Nights* 16, 13, 6: "*Municipes* [municipal citizens], then, are Roman citizens from free towns, using their own laws and enjoying their own rights, merely sharing with the Roman people an honorary *munus* or 'privilege' (from the enjoyment of which they appear to derive their name), and bound by no other compulsion and no other law of the Roman people except such as their own citizens have officially ratified."

10. For all this, see the excellent pages written by François Jacques in François Jacques and John Scheid, *Rome et l'intégration de l'Empire (44 av. J.-C.–260 apr. J.-C.)*, vol. 1: *Les structures de l'Empire romain* (Paris: PUF, 1990), 209ff., and Patrick Le Roux, *Romains d'Espagne: Cités et politique dans les provinces, du iiᵉ siècle av. J.-C.–iiiᵉ siècle apr. J.-C.* (Paris: Armand Colin, 1995). More generally, see also Clifford Ando, "Was Rome a *Polis*?" *Classical Antiquity* 18 (1999): 5–34.

11. Claude Lepelley, *Les cités de l'Afrique romaine au Bas-Empire*, vol. 1: *La permanence d'une civilisation municipale* (Paris: Études augustiniennes, 1979); Lepelley, "Un éloge nostalgique de la cité classique dans les *Variae* de Cassiodore," in Michel Sot, ed., *Haut Moyen Âge, culture, éducation et société: Études offertes à Pierre Riché* (Nanterre: Publidix, 1990), pp. 33–47; Lepelley, "Universalité et permanence du modèle de la cité dans le monde romain," in *Cité et communauté civique en Hispanie aux IIᵉ et IIIᵉ siècles apr. J.-C.* (Madrid: Casa de Velázquez, 1993), pp. 9–23; François Jacques, *Les cités de l'Occident romain: Documents traduits et commentés* (Rome: École française de Rome, 1992), pp. 241–44.

12. Aulus Gellius, *Attic Nights* 18, 7, 5.

13. Ernst Kornemann, "Civitas," RE suppl. 1, 1903, col. 300–301; see also Wilfried Nippel, "Republik, Kleinstaat, Bürgergemeinde: Der antike Stadtstaat in der neuzeitlichen

Theorie," in Peter Blickle, ed., *Theorien kommunaler Ordnung in Europa* (Munich: Olden-bourg, 1996), pp. 225–47.

CHAPTER 3. THE INDIVIDUAL IN THE CITY

1. Michael H. Crawford, ed., *Roman Statutes,* vol. 2 (London: Institute of Classical Studies, 1996), pp. 781–86.

2. Acts 16:11–39.

3. Acts 22:22–32.

4. Seneca, *De clementia* 1.24.1 (in *Moral Essays,* trans. John W. Basore [London: Heine-mann, 1928]): "A proposal was once made in the Senate, to distinguish slaves from free men by their dress; it then became apparent how great would be the impending danger if our slaves should begin to count our number."

5. *Lex coloniae Genetivae,* cited from *Roman Statutes,* ed. and trans. M. H. Crawford (London: Institute of Classical Studies, School of Advanced Study, University of London, 1996), no. 25, chapter 126: "Whoever as IIvir, aedile, or prefect shall organise stage shows for the colonia Genetiva Iulia, or if anyone shall organize stage shows for the colonia Gene-tiva Iulia, he is so to lead to sit the colonists of (the colonia) Genetiva Iulia, *incolae,* guests and visitors, and he is so to grant, attribute and assign a place as the decurions shall have decreed."

6. *ILS* no. 1374, Aquileia, 105 CE: "[That it be known] that the very sacred *princeps* Trajan Augustus decreed, on his motion, that *incolae . . .* should fulfill municipal duties among us."

7. *Lex Flavia municipalis,* cited from J. González, "The *Lex Irnitana*: A New Flavian Municipal Law," *Journal of Roman Studies* 76 (1986): 147–243 (here, text from Malaca), chapter 53 (trans. M. H. Crawford): "Whoever holds an election in that *municipium* for choosing *duumviri,* likewise aediles, likewise quaestors, is to draw one of the *curiae* by lot, in which *incolae* who are Roman or Latin citizens may cast their votes, and the casting of their vote is to take place in that *curia.*"

8. *Lex coloniae Genetivae,* chapter 126.

9. *Lex Flavia municipalis,* chapters 77 and 79; *ILS* no. 3395 (Menjibar, Baetica): "Dedi-cated to Pollux. Sextus Quintius Fortunatus, freedman of Sextus Quintius Successinus, be-cause the honor of the sevirate . . . a banquet having been given to the citizens and resident aliens and games having been held."

10. *ILS* no. 6916 (Lora del Rio, Baetica): "To Lucius Lucretius Severus, Patriciensis and decurion in the *Flavian Municipium* of Axati on the basis of his residency, this statue, which he ordered in his will to be put up to himself."

11. I cannot enter into all the details here. See the exposition by François Jacques in François Jacques and John Scheid, *Rome et l'intégration de l'Empire (44 av. J.-C.–260 apr. J.-C.),* vol. 1: *Les structures de l'Empire romain* (Paris: PUF, 1990), pp. 209ff.

12. Ulpian, *Ad edictum* bk. 2 = *Dig.* 50.1.27.1 (trans. M. H. Crawford, in A. Watson,

ed., *The Digest of Justinian* [Philadelphia: University of Pennsylvania Press, 1985], ad loc): "If anyone possesses lands in a colony, but does not conduct his business in this colony, but in a municipium, where he usually resides, where he sells, buys and contracts, frequents the forum, bath and entertainments, celebrates festivals, in fact enjoys all the facilities of municipality and none of those of colonies, he is regarded as having his domicile there rather than where he goes in order to cultivate [the land]."

13. Modestinus, *Regulae* bk. 3 = *Dig.* 50.1.34 (trans. M. H. Crawford): "An *incola* who has been designated for the performance of public *munera* cannot renounce his position unless the *munus* has been completed."

14. On this topic, see Yan Thomas, "La valeur des choses: Le droit romain hors la religion," *Annales HSS* (November 2002): 1431–62.

15. Jürgen Habermas, *The Structural Transformation of the Public Sphere: An Inquiry into a Category of Bourgeois Society*, trans. Thomas Burger with the assistance of Frederick Lawrence (1962; repr. Cambridge, MA: MIT Press, 1989).

16. Cicero, *De domo sua* 136 (from Cicero, *Orations*, translated N. H. Watts [Cambridge: Harvard University Press, 1923], ad loc): "Again, when Licinia, a Vestal Virgin of noble birth, distinguished by the most sacred of priestly offices, dedicated an altar, a small temple and a sacred couch at the feet of the Rock [i.e., the Aventine Hill], in the consulship of Titus Flaminius and Quintus Metellus (120 BCE), did not Sextus Julius the praetor, on the Senate's authority, refer the question to this College [i.e., the college of the *pontifices*]? On that occasion Publius Scaevola, the supreme pontiff, answered on behalf of the College that that which Licinia, the daughter of Gaius, had dedicated in a public space was not deemed by them to be sacred."

17. Wilfried Nippel, "Von den 'Altertümern' zur 'Kulturgeschichte,'" in François de Polignac and Pauline Schmitt-Pantel, *Public et privé en Grèce ancienne: Lieux, conduites, pratiques, Ktèma*, vol. 23 (Strasbourg, 1998), pp. 17–24.

18. François Hartog, *Le xixe siècle et l'histoire: Le cas Fustel de Coulanges* (Paris: PUF, 1988), pp. 30–31.

19. Jacob Burckhardt, *Histoire de la civilisation grecque,* 4 vols. (1898–1902; repr. Vevey: Éditions de l'Aire, 2002), 4:474–77, 737–39.

20. Jesper Svenbro, "Decolonizzare l'antichità" (entretien), *Dialoghi di archeologia*, n.s. 1, 1 (1979): 98–106.

CHAPTER 4. CIVIC RELIGION

1. Richard Gordon, "Religion in the Roman Empire: The Civic Compromise and Its Limits," in Mary Beard and John North, eds., *Pagan Priests: Religion and Power in the Ancient World* (London: Duckworth, 1990).

2. See, for example, Greg Woolf, "*Polis*-Religion and Its Alternatives in the Roman Provinces," in Hubert Cancik and Jörg Rüpke, eds., *Römische Reichsreligion und Provinzialreligion* (Tübingen: Mohr Siebeck, 1997), pp. 71–84; Stefan Krauter, *Bürgerrecht und*

Kultteilnahme: Politische und kultische Rechte und Pflichten in griechische Poleis, Rom und antikem Judentum (Berlin: De Gruyter, 2004), p. 25.

3. Krauter, *Bürgerrecht und Kultteilnahme*, p. 25.

4. See, for example, Andreas Bendlin, "Looking Behind the Civic Compromise: Religious Pluralism in Late Republican Rome," in Edward Bispham and Christopher Smith, eds., *Religion in Archaic and Republican Rome and Italy: Evidence and Experience* (Edinburgh: Edinburgh University Press, 2000), p. 122.

5. Ulrich von Wilamowitz-Moellendorff considered him a Latinist removed from the language. See William M. Calder III and Alexander Kosenina, eds., *Berufspolitik innerhalb der Altertumswissenschaft im wilhelminischen Preußen: Die Briefe Ulrich von Wilamowitz-Moellendorffs an Friedrich Althoff (1883–1908)* (Frankfurt: Klostermann, 1989), p. 45.

6. See, e.g., Moses I. Finley, "Generalizations in Ancient History," in *The Use and Abuse of History* (New York: Penguin, 1975), pp. 60–74, or "The Ancient City: From Fustel de Coulanges to Max Weber and Beyond," in *Economy and Society in Ancient Greece*, ed. Brent D. Shaw and Richard P. Saller (London: Chatto & Windus, 1981), pp. 3–23.

7. Paul Veyne, *Foucault, sa pensée, sa personne* (Paris: Albin Michel, 2008), p. 14. Readers of English may be referred to Veyne's essay "Foucault Revolutionizes History," translated by Catherine Porter, in Arnold I. Davidson, ed., *Foucault and His Interlocutors* (Chicago: University of Chicago Press, 1997), pp. 146–82. Veyne there wrote of Foucault on madness: "When I showed the present text to Foucault, he responded roughly as follows: 'I personally have never written that *madness does not exist*, but it can be written; for phenomenology, madness exists, but it is not a thing, whereas one has to say on the contrary that madness does not exist, but that it is not therefore nothing'" (p. 170).

8. Michel Foucault, *Dits et écrits*, vol. 1 (Paris: Gallimard, 2001), p. 77. The quotation is from a note from Foucault to Daniel Denfert on 7 January 1979 and is quoted by the latter in the chronology he compiled for *Dits et écrits*. Foucault summarizes the opening pages of the first lecture in the course "The Birth of Biopolitics," which he commenced to deliver on 10 January of that year. The relevant passage in the resulting publication is immensely helpful in understanding the aphoristic passage above: "I would like to point out straightaway that choosing to talk about or to start from governmental practice is obviously and explicitly a way of not taking as a primary, original and already given object, notions such as the sovereign, sovereignty, the people, subjects, the state, and civil society, that is to say, all those universals employed by sociological analysis, historical analysis and political philosophy in order to account for real governmental practice. For my part, I would like to do exactly the opposite and, starting from this practice as it is given, but at the time as it reflects on itself and is rationalized, show how certain things—state and society, sovereign and subjects, etcetera—were actually able to be formed, and the status of which should obviously be questioned. In other words, instead of deducing concrete phenomena from universals, or instead of starting with universals as an obligatory grid of intelligibility for certain concrete practices, I would like to start with these concrete practices and, as it were, pass these universals through the grid of these practices. This is not what could be called a historicist reduction, for that would consist precisely in starting from these universals as

given and then seeing history inflects them, or alters them, or finally invalidates them. Historicism starts from the universal and, as it were, puts it through the grinder of history. My problem is exactly the opposite. I start from the theoretical and methodological decision that consists in saying: Let's suppose that universals do not exist. And then I put the question to history and historians: How can you write history if you do not accept a priori the existence of things like the state, society, the sovereign and subjects?" *The Birth of Biopolitics: Lectures at the Collège de France, 1978–1979*, trans. Graham Burchell, ed. Arnold J. Davidson (New York: Palgrave Macmillan, 2008), pp. 2–3.

9. Veyne, *Foucault, sa pensée, sa personne*, pp. 19.

10. On Simmel see Chapter 1, pp. 19–20.

11. Numa Denis Fustel de Coulanges, *The Ancient City: A Study of the Religion, Laws and Institutions of Greece and Rome*, trans. Willard Small (uncredited) (Baltimore: Johns Hopkins University Press, 1980), p. 186: "If we wished to give an exact definition of a citizen, we should say it was a man who had the religion of the city. The stranger, on the other hand, is one who has not access to the worship, one whom the gods of the city do not protect, and who has not even the right to invoke them." This view is not entirely correct: see below, pp. 38–39.

12. Edward Gibbon, *The History of the Decline and Fall of the Roman Empire* (6 volumes, 1776–1788; reprinted in 3 volumes, London: Allen Lane, 1994), vol. 1, pp. 56–61. See Frank E. Manuel, *The Eighteenth Century Confronts the Gods* (Cambridge, MA: Harvard University Press, 1959), pp. 180ff, and David Womersley, *Gibbon and the 'Watchmen of the Holy City': The Historian and His Reputation, 1776–1815* (Oxford: Oxford University Press, 2002).

13. Krauter, *Bürgerrecht und Kultteilnahme*, p. 25: "This is above all evident from the fact that the model effaces from consideration a large domain of ancient religion, the non-public cults." See Hubert Cancik, "Antike," in *Die Religion in Geschichte und Gegenwart*, vol. 1, no. A–B (1998, pp. 536–42, especially p. 541).

14. Augustine, *De civitate Dei* 4.31, trans. Henry Bettenson (New York: Penguin, 1972), p. 174; see also 6.4. For a reading of Augustine's reading of Varro on these issues, see Clifford Ando, "The Ontology of Religious Institutions," *History of Religions* 50 (2010), pp. 54–79, and Ando, *Roman Social Imaginaries* (Toronto: University of Toronto Press, 2015), 53–86.

15. Augustine, *City of God* 6.4.

16. Augustine, *City of God* 6.4.

17. Plato, *Cratylus* 400d–401a; see also Cicero, *On the Nature of the Gods* 1.14.37.

18. Minucius Felix, *Octavius* 5.5, trans. G. W. Clarke (New York: Newman Press, 1974).

19. Symmachus, *Relatio* 3.10.

CHAPTER 5. CIVIC RELIGION AND IDENTITY

1. Christiane Sourvinou-Inwood, "What Is *Polis* Religion?" in Richard Buxton, ed., *Oxford Readings in Greek Religion* (Oxford: Oxford University Press, 2000), pp. 13–37.

2. Mary Beard, John North, and Simon Price, *Religions of Rome*, 2 vols. (Cambridge: Cambridge University Press, 1998), 1:214–15.

3. Stefan Krauter, *Bürgerrecht und Kultteilnahme: Politische und kultische Rechte und Pflichten in griechische Poleis, Rom und antikem Judentum* (Berlin: De Gruyter, 2004), p. 115: "The Romans knew no more than the Greeks a concept for that we designate 'religion.'"

4. Paul the Deacon *apud* Festus, *De verborum significatu quae supersunt*, s.v. *publica sacra* 284L. Rather oddly, Krauter cites the text from the much older edition of Karl Otfried Müller (Leipzig: Weidmann, 1839).

5. Ulpian, *Institutes* bk. 1 = *Dig.* 1.1.1.2.

6. Ulpian, *Institutes* bk. 1 = *Dig.* 1.1.1.

7. See Greg Woolf, "*Polis*-Religion and Its Alternatives in the Roman Provinces," in Hubert Cancik and Jörg Rüpke, eds., *Römische Reichsreligion und Provinzialreligion* (Tübingen: Mohr Siebeck, 1997), pp. 71–84.

8. Krauter, *Bürgerrecht und Kultteilnahme*, pp. 116ff.

9. Voir J. Scheid, "*Græco ritu*: A Typically Roman Way of Honouring the Gods," *Harvard Studies in Classical Philology* 97 (1995): 15–31.

10. Krauter, *Bürgerrecht und Kultteilnahme*, p. 118: "When one examines the different categories according to which the Romans themselves sought to divide their religion, the resulting picture displays a disorienting, self-contradictory multiplicity."

11. Diodorus Siculus, *The Library of History* 14.70.4, 77.4–5.

12. As is maintained, for example, by Woolf, "*Polis*-Religion and Its Alternatives," p. 76.

13. A helpful translation of the entirety of the surviving record of the Augustan Secular Games may be found in Beard, North, and Price, *Religions of Rome*, 2:139–44.

14. *ILS* no. 5466 (Philippi, Macedon).

15. *ILS* no. 3841; see Nacéra Benseddik, *Esculape et Hygie en Afrique*, vol. 2: *Textes et images* (Paris: De Boccard, 2010), 121.

16. The sources refer to numerous actions: in 58 BCE, the altars were removed from public places (Varro, *Divine Antiquities*, fr. 46a–b Cardauns); in 53 BCE and again in 50, some altars were destroyed (Cassius Dio 40.47.3ff.; Valerius Maximus in the epitome of Julius Paris 1.3.4); in 48 BCE, a sanctuary of Isis was destroyed (Cassius Dio 42.26.2).

17. Herbert Nesselhauf, "Neue Inschriften aus dem römischen Germanien und den angrenzenden Gebieten," in *27. Bericht der Römisch-Germanischen Kommission, 1937* [1939], no. 162 (Bonn, second half of the second century CE); *CIL* XIII, no. 11992 (Nettersheim); Nesselhauf, "Neue Inschriften," no. 163 (Bonn, end of the second or start of the third century CE); *CIL* XIII, no. 8042.

18. Nesselhauf, "Neue Inschriften, no. 164 (Bonn, 235 CE); no. 165 (Bonn, 164 CE).

19. E.g., in Krauter, *Bürgerrecht und Kultteilnahme*, pp. 133–42.

20. Pliny, *Natural History* 18.6; Plutarch, *Roman Questions* 99. An exile or prisoner of war lost his civic rights.

21. Krauter, *Bürgerrecht und Kultteilnahme*, p. 119: "As was already established in the overview of Roman classifications for religion, the great majority of 'public' cult acts, the *sacra publica, in no way took place publicly, in the sense that a large public would have been involved.*" (The emphasis is mine.)

22. Jean-Christophe Attias and Esther Benbassa, *Dictionnaire de civilisation juive* (Paris: Larousse, 1997).

23. Cicero, *De haruspicum responsis* 12.

24. The protocols of the Arval Brethren teach us that the ritual assistants summoned the crowd when the priests moved within the cult site. But outside that corpus such notations are rare, since the sources are not everywhere of such quality.

25. See John Scheid, *Quand faire c'est croire: Les rites sacrificiels des Romains* (2005; repr. Paris: Aubier, 2011), pp. 229–31.

26. Pliny, *Ep.* 10.94.10.

27. William Van Andringa, "Du sanctuaire au *macellum*: Sacrifices, commerce et consommation de la viande à Pompéi," *Food and History* 5 (2007): 47–72; Sébastien Lepetz, "Boucherie, sacrifice et marché à la viande en Gaule septentrionale: L'apport de l'archéozoologie," *Food and History* 5 (2007): 73–105.

28. For some reflections on this question, see Scheid, *Quand faire c'est croire*, pp. 213–74.

29. Suetonius, *Domitian* 4.12.

CHAPTER 6. FOR WHOM WERE THE RITUALS CELEBRATED?

1. John Scheid, *Commentarii fratrum arvalium qui supersunt: Les copies épigraphiques des protocoles annuels de la confrérie arvale (21 av.–304 apr. J.-C.)*, École française de Rome, 1998, no. 55 (87 apr. J.C.), col. I, lines 52ff.

2. *ILS* 4907, Salona, Dalmatia, 137 CE.

3. Scheid, *Commentarii fratrum arvalium qui supersunt*, 247, no. 85 (after 169/177 CE).

4. Livy 29.27.1.

5. Bärbel Schnegg-Köhler, *Die augusteischen Säkularspiele* (Munich: Saur, 2002), 26, fr. C, ll. 9–17.

6. Schnegg-Köhler, *Die augusteischen Säkularspiele*, p. 36, l. 92ff.

7. Cato, *De agricultura* 134.2ff., 141.2ff.

8. Zosimus, *History* 2.5.1: "slaves did not participate in this distribution, but only free persons."

9. Schnegg-Köhler, *Die augusteischen Säkularspiele*, p. 33, l. 65; Zosimus, *History* 2.5.1.

10. Cicero, *De haruspicum responsis* 12.26.

11. See Krauter, *Bürgerrecht und Kultteilnahme: Politische und kultische Rechte und Pflichten in griechische Poleis, Rom und antikem Judentum* (Berlin: De Gruyter, 2004), pp. 119–31, opposing Gabriel M. Sanders, "Kybele und Attis," in *Aufstieg und Niedergang der römischen Welt* II, 17, 3 (Berlin: De Gruyter, 1981), pp. 1500–1535, esp. p. 1515, and Garth Thomas, "Mater Magna und Attis," in Maarten J. Vermaseren, ed., *Die orientalischen Religionen im Römerreich* (Leiden: Brill, 1981), pp. 264–97, especially p. 276.

12. Protocols of the Augustan Secular Games (17 BCE), Schnegg-Köhler, *Die augusteischen Säkularspiele*, 28, ll. 7ff.

13. Protocols of the Severan Secular Games (204 CE), Giovanni Battista Pighi, *De ludis saecularibus Populi Romani Quiritium* (Amsterdam: Schippers, 1965), p. 145, II, l. 4.

14. Giovanni Battista Pighi, *De ludis saecularibus Populi Romani Quiritium*, p. 148, ll. 22–24.

15. Giovanni Battista Pighi, *De ludis saecularibus Populi Romani Quiritium*, p. 148, ll. 17–18.

16. I think in particular of Richard Reitzenstein: see above, p. 17.

17. Cicero, *De haruspicum responsis* 12.24.

18. Gellius, *Noctes Atticae* 18.2.11.

19. Krauter, *Bürgerrecht und Kultteilnahme*, p. 120.

20. Tacitus, *Annales* 13.54.3ff.

21. Gellius, *Noctes Atticae* 18.2.11.

22. Philippe Borgeaud, *La Mère des dieux: De Cybèle à la Vierge Marie* (Paris: Seuil, 1996), pp. 114ff. For the aid given by the Great Mother to Aeneas on Mount Ida, see Vergil, *Aen.* 9.77–92.

23. Cicero, *De haruspicum responsis* 12.26 (Cicero, *Orations*, translated by N.H. Watts (Cambridge: Harvard University Press, 1923), ad loc.)): "When they held the games, they bade slaves depart from the auditorium; you let slaves loose upon one auditorium and ejected freemen from the other. Those who of old were separated from the free upon a herald's proclamation, at your games separated the free from themselves not by proclamation but by force."

24. Suetonius, *Claudius* 22, trans. J. C. Rolfe (London: Heinemann, 1920).

25. Suetonius, *Claudius* 22.

26. Krauter, *Bürgerrecht und Kultteilnahme*, pp. 120–21.

27. Livy 22.10.1–6. On this text, see A. D. Nock, "A Feature of Roman Religion," *Harvard Theological Review* 32 (1939): 83–96, reprinted with translations of all Greek and Latin quotations in Clifford Ando, ed., *Roman Religion* (Edinburgh: Edinburgh University Press, 2003), pp. 84–97.

28. Phlegon of Tralles, *Book of Marvels* 4.10.41–42, William Hanson, trans., *Phlegon of Tralles' Book of Marvels* (Exeter: University of Exeter Press, 1996), ad loc.: "Let no disbeliever be present at the sacrifices, but let him rather stand apart where it is customary for disbelievers to be."

29. Hermann Diels, *Sibyllinische Blätter* (Berlin: Reimer, 1890), p. 96, n. 1.

30. Paul the Deacon *apud* Festus, *De verborum significatu quae supersunt*, s.v. *exesto* 72L. Seer Eduard Norden, *Aus altrömischen Priesterbüchern* (1939; Stuttgart: Teubner, 1995), p. 263. In these old formulas, the foreigner is called *hostis*, "guest," which had earlier had the sense "enemy."

31. Vergil, *Aeneid* 8.172–74.

32. Servius *ad Aen.* 8.172.

33. Krauter, *Bürgerrecht und Kultteilnahme*, p. 126.

34. Krauter, *Bürgerrecht und Kultteilnahme*, p. 128ff.

35. According to Livy 22.37 (in 216 BCE), ambassadors from Hieron give a statue of Victory that the Senate consecrates on the Capitol; in Livy 28.29 (205 BCE), the Saguntines bring a gold crown to Jupiter Optimus Maximus, which the Senate authorizes them to deposit on the Capitol; in Livy 32.27.1 (198 BCE), the deposit on the Capitol of a crown by legates of Attalus; in Livy 36.35.12 (191 BCE), ambassadors from King Philip ask authorization to sacrifice on the Capitol and to deposit a crown in the temple of Jupiter Optimus Maximus; in Livy 42.6 (173 BCE), ambassadors from Antiochus bring, among other things, vases that are deposited in temples by the censors; in Livy 43.6.5 (171 BCE), the Alabandians ask to deposit a crown on the Capitol and sacrifice there; 44.14.3 (169 BCE), ambassadors of the Pamphylians bring a crown, and seek and obtain permission to deposit it in the sanctuary of Jupiter Optimus Maximus; in Livy 45.13.17–14.3 (168 BCE), when Massinissa, the old king of the Numidians and faithful ally of Rome, seeks the same authorization through his son, the Senate responds that he makes a sacrifice among his household gods and allows his son to accomplish the rites at Rome; in Livy 45.44 (157 BCE), King Prusias II asks authorization to sacrifice on the Capitol for the well-being of the Roman people.

36. Treaties and privileges: with Astylpalaia, 105 BCE, *RDGE* no. 16 A–B; Stratonikeia, 81 BCE, *RDGE* no. 18; Mytilene, 45 BCE, *RDGE* no. 26b.

37. Decree of the Senate concerning the privileges of the three Greek naval captains, 78 BCE, *RDGE* no. 22.

38. Luigi Moretti, ed., *Inscriptiones Graecae Urbis Romae*, vol. 1 (Rome: Instituto italiano par la storia antica, 1968), nos. 5–20.

39. Krauter, *Bürgerrecht und Kultteilnahme*, p. 133: "Since at the temple of the Capitoline Triad one is dealing with a special case, the central sanctuary of the Roman empire, with great domestic and international political importance, one can surely not simply transfer relations there to all other Roman sanctuaries."

40. Philippe Gauthier, *Symbola: Les étrangers et la justice dans les cités grecques* (Nancy: Université de Nancy II, 1972).

41. Valerius Maximus 2.1.8.

42. Peter Kuhlmann, *Die Giessener literarischen Papyri und und die Caracalla-Erlasse. Edition, Übersetzung und Kommentar* (Giessen: Universitätsbibliothek, 1994), pp. 217–39, especially p. 222.

43. Hartmut Wolff, *Die Constitutio Antoniniana und der Papyri Gissensis 40 I* (Cologne, 1976).

44. Christa Frateantonio, *Religiöse Autonomie der Stadt im Imperium Romanum* (Tübingen: Mohr Siebeck, 2003), p. 159.

45. Robert Muth, "Vom Wesen römischer 'religio,'" in *Aufstieg und Niedergang der römischen Welt* II, 16.1 (Berlin: De Gruyter, 1978), pp. 290–354.

46. Maurice Euzennat, Jacques Gascou, and Jean Marion, *Inscriptions antiques du Maroc*, II, 1 (Paris: Éditions du CNRS, 1982), n. 94 (=*L'Année épigraphique*, no. 142 [1962]; no. 534 [1971]; and no. 1801 [1995]): "We have read the request of the chief of the tribes of the Zagrenses, and we that he benefits from the high favor of Epidius Quadratus your predecessor; for this reason, and moved by that man's testimony and the merits of the man and the evidence that he submits, we grant Roman citizenship to his wife and children, with the law of his tribe preserved (*salvo iure gentis*)."

47. Wolff, *Die Constitutio Antoniniana*, p. 68.

48. Cicero, *Pro Flacco* 69.

49. Krauter, *Bürgerrecht und Kultteilnahme*, pp. 133–41.

50. On this argument, see above, pp. 80–81.

51. Minucius Felix, *Octavius* 7.5–6, trans. G. W. Clarke (New York: Newman Press, 1974).

CHAPTER 7. RELIGIOUS REPRESSION

1. John Scheid, "Le délit religieux dans la Rome tardo-républicaine," in *Le Délit religieux dans la cité antique* (Rome: École française de Rome, 1981), pp. 117–71.

2. Quintus Pleminius (legate of Scipio in 205 BCE, arrested in 204, executed in 194): Livy 29.6ff., 34.44.

3. Theodor Mommsen, *Le Droit pénal romain*, vol. 3 (Paris: Fontemoing, 1907), pp. 126–27; G. Wissowa, *Religion und Kultus der Römer* (1902; repr. Munich: Beck, 1912), pp. 392–93.

4. Varro, *De lingua Latina* 6.30.

5. Macrobius, *Saturnalia* 1.16.9–11, trans. Robert A. Kaster (Cambridge, MA: Harvard University Press, 2011), with one minor change.

6. Cicero, *De Legibus* 2.22, trans. James E. G. Zetzel (Cambridge: Cambridge University Press, 1999).

7. John Scheid, "The expiation of impieties committed without intention and the formation of Roman theology," in Jan Assmann and Guy G. Stroumsa, eds., *Transformations of the Inner Self in Ancient Religions* (Leiden: Brill, 1999), pp. 331–48.

8. See, for example, the famous cases of the Caudine Forks (Livy 9.5–9.11, 321 BCE), of Regulus (*Periochae of Livy* 18), and of Mancinus (*Periochae of Livy* 56.3).

9. Silvio Panciera, "La lex luci Spoletina e la legislazione sui boschi sacri in età romana" (1994), in *Epigrafi, epigrafia, epigrafisti. Scritti varii e inediti (1956–2005) con note complementari e indici* (Rome: Quasar, 2006), pp. 903–19.

10. The passive imperative in *-to* is very rare. It can be found in the *Lex repetundarum*,

"*censento*" (*Roman Statutes*, vol. 2, ed. Michael H. Crawford [London: Institute of Classical Studies, 1996], p. 74, chapter 77), and in the form *liceto* ("Let it be permitted") in texts from Furfo and Luceria (Attilio Degrassi, *Inscriptiones Latinae Liberae Rei Publicae,* vol. 2 [Florence: La Nuova Italia, 1963], pp. 6ff., nos. 505 and 508). But the explication provided by Sebastian Tromp (*De Romanorum piaculis* [Leiden: n.p., 1921]), that the subject of *datod* in the second sanction is the *dicator,* who offers the *piaculum* and makes amends, cannot be ruled out.

11. Panciera, "La lex luci Spoletina," pp. 911–13.

12. Mommsen, *Le Droit pénal romain,* pp. 126–27; Wissowa, *Religion und Kultus der Römer,* pp. 392–93.

13. Tromp, *De Romanorum piaculis.*

14. Krauter, *Bürgerrecht und Kultteilnahme,* p. 284.

15. Georg Wissowa, review of the thesis of S. Tromp, in *Philologische Wochenschrift* 43 (1923): 80–84.

16. John Scheid, "Oral Tradition and Written Tradition in the Formation of Sacred Law in Rome," in Clifford Ando and Jörg Rüpke, eds., *Religion and Law in Classical and Christian Rome* (Stuttgart: Steiner, 2006), pp. 14–33.

17. Krauter, *Bürgerrecht und Kultteilnahme,* p. 285.

18. Livy 42.3.5–9: *obstringere religione populum Romanum.*

19. Cicero, *De legibus* 2.9.22.

20. Tacitus, *Annales* 1.73.2–4. Tacitus, *Annales* 1.73.2–4.

21. *Codex Justinianus* 4.1.2, a rescript of Severus Alexander from 223 CE: "Neglect of religious scruple in oath-swearing has a sufficient agent of vengeance in the god himself."

22. For some fleeting details on this procedure, see John Scheid, "Les pontifes romains et le parjure," in Christophe Batsch and Madalina Vartejanu-Joubert, eds., *Manières de penser dans l'Antiquité méditerranéenne et orientale: Mélanges offerts à Francis Schmidt par ses élèves, ses collègues et ses amis* (Leiden: Brill, 2009), pp. 183–91.

CHAPTER 8. CIVIC RELIGION

1. Wilhelm Liebenam, *Städteverwaltung im römischen Kaiserreiche* (1900; repr. Amsterdam: Hakkert, 1967), p. 176: "Die Rechte und Pflichten der Geminde sind selbstverständlich unabhängig von dem Wechsel der zeitweise vorhandenen Bürger, weil sie nich an der zufälligen Gesamtheit dieser, sonder an der abstrahierten juristischen Person haften. Zwischen der Gemeinde als solcher und den jeweiligen Gliedern derselben ist scharf zu scheiden; sie kann gegen ihre eigenen Bürger prozessieren. Der Besitz der Gemeinde ist mithin nicht das Eigentum der in gegebner Zeit dieselbe bildenden Bürgerschaft, ebensowenig wie die Schulden und Forderungen einer universitas ohne weiteres Ansprüche an diejenigen Mitglieder begründen, welche gerade diese repräsentieren."

2. See above, p. 41.

3. Minucius Felix, *Octavius* 6.1, trans. G. W. Clarke (New York: Newman Press, 1974).

4. Minucius Felix, *Octavius* 24.5.

5. See above, pp. 50–51.

6. Mary Beard, John North, and Simon Price, *Religions of Rome,* 2 vols. (Cambridge: Cambridge University Press, 1998).

7. Apuleius, *Metamorphoses* 11.26ff.

8. Silvanus: *ILS* no. 3541 (Rome, 108 CE). Mithra: *ILS* no. 4215 (Sentinum, Umbria).

9. Minucius Felix, *Octavius* 6.1.

10. Corinne Bonnet, "'L'histoire séculière et profane des religions' (F. Cumont): Observations sur l'articulation entre rite et croyance dans l'historiographie des religions de la fin du xixe et de la première moitié du xxe siècle," in John Scheid, ed., *Rites et croyances dans les religions du monde romain* (Geneva: Droz, 2007), pp. 1–37, esp. p. 15.

11. Mary Beard, "A Complex of Times: No More Sheep on Romulus' Birthday," *Proceedings of the Cambridge Philological Society* 33 (1987): 1–15 = "Rituel, texte, temps: Les *Parilia* romains," in Anne-Marie Blondeau and Kristofer Schipper, *Essais sur le rituel,* vol. 1 (Louvain: Peeters, 1988), pp. 15–29. The English text is reprinted in Clifford Ando, ed., *Roman Religion* (Edinburgh: Edinburgh University Press, 2003), pp. 273–88.

CHAPTER 9. EMOTION AND BELIEF

1. According to Bonnet, "'L'histoire séculière et profane des religions' (F. Cumont): Observations sur l'articulation entre rite et croyance dans l'historiographie des religions de la fin du xixe et de la première moitié du xxe siècle," in John Scheid, ed., *Rites et croyances dans les religions du monde romain* (Geneva: Droz, 2007), p. 2, F. Cumont felt a sort of "revulsion at ritual, the 'profane and secular' side . . . of ancient religions."

2. Bonnet, "'L'histoire séculière et profane des religions,'" pp. 5–13.

3. Plutarch, *Numa* 15.6.

4. Émile Benveniste, "La fidélité personnelle," in *Vocabulaire des institutions indo-européennes, 1. Économie, parenté, société* (Paris: Minuit, 1969), pp. 103–21; cf. also Georges Dumézil, "Credo et Fides," in *Idées romaines* (Paris: Gallimard, 1969), pp. 47–59; Gérard Freyburger, *Fides: Étude sémantique et religieuse depuis les origines jusqu'à l'époque augustéenne* (Paris: Belles Lettres, 1987).

5. Ovid, *Fasti* 3.229ff. See John Scheid, "Numa et Jupiter, ou les dieux citoyens de Rome," *Archives de sciences sociales des religions* 59 (1985): 41–53.

6. Ovid, *Fasti* 5.419–44; Plutarch, *Roman Questions* 86.

7. Walter Burkert, *Ancient Mystery Cults* (Cambridge, MA: Harvard University Press, 1987).

8. Philippe Borgeaud, "Rites et émotions: Considérations sur les mystères," in Scheid, ed., *Rites et croyances,* pp. 189–229, especially p. 221.

9. Livy 25.1.6–12.

10. Livy 25.1.9–11.

11. Claude Lévi-Strauss, *Totemism,* trans. Rodney Needham (Boston: Beacon Press, 1963).

12. See John M. Dillon, "The Religion of the Last Hellenes," in Scheid, ed., *Rites et croyances,* pp. 117–38, especially p. 120, as well as his reflection in the discussion recorded on pp. 138–40.

13. Livy 26.19.5–8; Valerius Maximus 1.2.2; Aulus Gellius, *Noctes Atticae* 6.1.6; Cassius Dio 16.39 = fr. 57.39; Pseudo-Aurelius Victor, *De viris illustribus* 49.1–3. Allow me also to cite my own essay, "Nouveau rite et nouvelle piété: Réflexions sur le ritus Graecus," in Fritz Graf, ed., *Ansichten griechischer Rituale: Geburtstags-Symposium für Walter Burkert* (Stuttgart: Teubner, 1998), pp. 168–82.

14. Jacqueline Champeaux, "'Pietas': Piété personnelle et piété collective à Rome," *Bulletin de l'association Guillaume-Budé,* no. 3 (1989): 263–79.

15. Jörg Rüpke, *Religion of the Romans,* trans. Richard Gordon (2001; repr. Cambridge: Polity, 2007), p. 13.

16. Livy 26.19.5.

17. Aulus Gellius, *Noctes Atticae* 6.1.6: "in a sort of consultation with Jupiter about the *respublica*" (*quasi consultantem de republica cum Iove*).

18. Cicero, *De divinatione* 1.104; Valerius Maximus 1.5.4.

19. Paul Veyne, "La nouvelle piété sous l'Empire: S'asseoir auprès des dieux, fréquenter les temples," *Revue de Philologie* 63 (1989): 175–94.

20. See the texts cited in note 18 above.

21. Varro, *Antiquitates Divinae,* fr. 206, Cardauns.

22. Pliny the Elder, *Naturalis historia* 35.160.

23. John Scheid, *Quand faire c'est croire: Les rites sacrificiels des Romains* (2005; repr. Paris: Aubier, 2011), pp. 44–57.

24. Scheid, *Quand faire c'est croire,* pp. 255–77.

25. Scheid, *Quand faire c'est croire,* pp. 58–83. The original version of this essay is translated in Clifford Ando, ed., *Roman Religion* (Edinburgh: Edinburgh University Press, 2003), pp. 164–89.

26. Charles Malamoud, "Présentation," *Archives de Sciences Sociales des Religions* 85 (1994): 5–8.

27. Malamoud, "Présentation," p. 7.

28. Frits Staal, "The Meaninglessness of Ritual," *Numen* 26 (1975): 2–22; Staal, *Rules Without Meaning: Rituals, Mantras and the Human Sciences* (Berne: Lang, 1989).

29. On these questions, see Scheid, ed., *Rites et croyances.*

30. John Scheid, "Le sens des rites: L'exemple romain," in Scheid, ed., *Rites et croyances,* pp. 39–71.

CHAPTER 10. WHY DID ROMAN RELIGION CHANGE?

1. See above, p. 7.

2. Walter Burkert, *Ancient Mystery Cults* (Cambridge, MA: Harvard University Press, 1987).

3. See above, pp. 13–16.

4. G. W. F. Hegel, *Leçons sur la philosophie de l'histoire*, trans. J. Gibelin (Paris: J. Vrin, 1987).

5. Hegel, *Leçons*, p. 224 = English translation from Georg Wilhelm Friedrich Hegel, *The Philosophy of History*, trans. J. Sibree (New York: Dover, 1956; repr. Kitchener, Canada: Batoche Books, 2001), p. 308. See also Theodor Mommsen, *Histoire romaine* (1854; repr. Paris: Robert Laffont, 1985), 1:221.

6. Hegel, *Leçons*, p. 224 = Hegel, *Philosophy of History*, p. 309.

7. Hegel, *Leçons*, p. 220 = Hegel, *Philosophy of History*, p. 303.

8. Hegel, *Leçons*, p. 248 = Hegel, *Philosophy of History*, p. 338. See also Mommsen, *Histoire romaine*, 1:222.

9. Livy 4.25.3, 40.51.6; Quintilian, *Institutiones oratoriae* 3.7.8; Augustine, *De civitate Dei* 4.21; Macrobius, *Saturnalia* 1.17.25, 27, trans. Robert A. Kaster, Loeb Classical Library (Cambridge, MA: Harvard University Press, 2011).

10. Livy 25.12.15.

11. Georges Dumézil, *La Religion romaine archaïque* (Paris: Payot, 1987).

12. Richard Reitzenstein, *Werden und Wesen der Humanität im Altertum: Rede zur Feier des Geburtstages seiner Majestät des Kaisers am 26. Januar 1907 in der Aula der Kaiser-Wilhelms-Universität Straßburg* (Strasbourg, 1907); Jean Gagé, *Apollon romain: Essai sur le culte d'Apollon et le développement du "ritus Graecus" à Rome, des origines à Auguste* (Paris: De Boccard, 1955).

13. See John Scheid, "Dell'importanza di scegliere bene le fonti: L'esempio dei Ludi secolari," *Scienze dell'Antichità: Storia Archeologia Antropologia* 10 (2000): 645–57.

14. Georges Dumézil, *Apollon sonore et autres essais: Esquisses de mythologie* (Paris: Gallimard, 1982), pp. 36–42, 155–63.

15. Olivier de Cazanove, "Some Thoughts on the 'Religious Romanisation' of Italy Before the Social War," in Edward Bispham and Christopher Smith, eds., *Religion in Archaic and Republican Rome and Italy* (Edinburgh: Edinburgh University Press, 2000), pp. 71–76.

16. John Scheid, "Épigraphie et sanctuaires guérisseurs en Gaule," in *Mélanges de l'École Française de Rome: Antiquité* 104 (1992): 25–40; Scheid, "Le culte des eaux et des sources dans le monde romain: Un sujet problématique déterminé par la mythologie moderne," in *Annuaire du Collège de France* 108 (2007–8): 621–34.

17. Ton Derks, "Le grand sanctuaire de Lenus Mars à Trèves et ses dédicaces privées: Une réinterprétation," in Monique Dondin-Payre and Marie-Thérèse Raepsaet-Charlier, *Sanctuaires, pratiques cultuelles et territoires civiques dans l'Occident romain* (Brussels: Timperman, 2006), pp. 239–70; Derks, "Les rites de passage et leur manifestation matérielle dans les sanctuaires des Helvètes," in Daniel Castella and Marie-France Meylan-Krause, eds., *Topographie sacrée et rituels: Le cas d'Aventicum, capitale des Helvètes* (Bâle, 2008), pp. 101–204.

18. Filippo Coarelli, "I monumenti dei culti orientali a Roma," in Ugo Bianchi and Maarten Vermaseren, eds., *La soteriologia dei culti Orientali nell'Impero Romano* (Leiden:

Brill, 1982), pp. 55ff.; see also Marietta de Vos, "Iseum Metellinum," in Margareta Steinby, ed., *Lexicon topographicum urbis Romae*, vol. 3 (Rome: Quasar, 1996), pp. 110ff.

19. 1 January 58 BCE: Varro in Tertullian, *Ad nationes* 1.10.18; *Apology* 6.8; Arnobius 2.73; Servius *ad Aen.* 8.698. 53 BCE: Cassius Dio 40.47.3. 50 BCE: Iulius Paris, *Epitome* of Valerius Maximus 1.3.4; Diodorus 1.40; Cassius Dio 40.47.3. 48 BCE: Cassius Dio 42.26.2. See Filippo Coarelli, "Iside Capitolina, Clodio e i mercanti di schiavi," *Alessandria e il mondo ellenistico-Romano: Studi in onore di Achille Adriani* (Rome: Erma, 1984), pp. 461–75; Michel Malaise, *Les conditions de pénétration et de diffusion des cultes égyptiens en Italie* (Leiden: Brill, 1972), pp. 365–77.

20. John Scheid, "Le statut du culte d'Isis sous le Haut-Empire," in Corinne Bonnet, Vinciane Pirenne-Delforge, and Danny Praet, eds., *Les Religions orientales dans le monde grec et romain: Cent ans après Cumont (1906–2006)* (Rome: Institut historique belge de Rome, 2009), pp. 173–86.

21. There is an excellent description of the arrival of the goddess at Rome in the work of Philippe Borgeaud, *La Mère des dieux: De Cybèle à la Vierge Marie* (Paris: Seuil, 1996).

22. *ILS* no. 4175, Cumae, Campania, 289 CE.

23. Mithreum de Martigny: François Wiblé, "Le mithraeum du forum Claudii Vallensium, Martigny (Valais)," *Archäologie der Schweiz* 18 (1995): 2–15; Marleen Martens and Guy De Boe, eds., *Roman Mithraism: The Evidence of the Small Finds* (Brussels: Museum Het Toreke, 2004), pp. 25–56; Marleen Martens, "The Mithraeum in Tienen (Belgium): The Remains of a Feast in Honour of Mithra," in Bonnet, Pirenne-Delforge, and Praet, eds., *Les Religions orientales dans le monde grec et romain*, pp. 215–32.

24. Robert Turcan, *Mithra et le mithriacisme* (Paris: PUF, 1989), pp. 30–43.

25. On this question, see Christophe J. Goddard, "Au cœur du dialogue entre païens et chrétiens: L'*aduentus* des sénateurs dans les cités de l'Antiquité tardive," in Peter Brown and Rita Lizzi Testa, eds., *Pagans and Christians in the Roman Empire: The Breaking of a Dialogue (IVth–VIth Century AD)* (Zurich: Lit Verlag, 2011), pp. 371–96.

26. Paul Veyne, *Quand notre monde est devenu chrétien (312–394)* (Paris: Albin Michel, 2007), pp. 94ff.

27. Werner Eck, *La Romanisation de la Germanie* (Paris: Errance, 2007).

28. Veyne, *Quand notre monde est devenu chrétien*, pp. 186–88.

29. Claude Lepelley, "Trois documents méconnus sur l'histoire sociale et religieuse de l'Afrique romaine tardive retrouvés parmi les *spuria* de Sulpice Sévère" (1989), reprinted in *Aspects de l'Afrique romaine: Les cités, la vie rurale, le christianisme* (Bari: Edipuglia, 2001), pp. 243–77.

30. Richard Gordon, "Religion in the Roman Empire: The Civic Compromise and Its Limits," in Mary Beard and John North, eds., *Pagan Priests: Religion and Power in the Ancient World* (London: Duckworth, 1990), pp. 235–55, especially p. 255.

CHAPTER II. THE GODS, THE STATE, AND THE INDIVIDUAL

1. Pierre Hadot, "De Tertullien à Boèce: Le développement de la notion de personne dans les controverses théologiques," in Ignace Meyerson, ed., *Problèmes de la personne* (The Hague: Mouton, 1973), pp. 133–34; Peter Brown, *The Making of Late Antiquity: Genèse de l'antiquité tardive* (1978; repr. Paris: Gallimard, 1983), pp. 175ff.; Brown, *Society and the Holy in Late Antiquity* (Berkeley: University of California Press, 1989); Brown, *La société et le sacré dans l'antiquité tardive* (1982; repr. Paris: Seuil, 1985), pp. 78ff.; Jean-Pierre Vernant, "L'individu dans la cité" (1986), reprinted in *Œuvres: Religions, rationalités, politique*, vol. 2 (Paris: Seuil, 2007), pp. 1455–71.

2. John M. Dillon, in John Scheid, ed., *Rites et croyances dans les religions du monde romain*, (Geneva: Droz, 2007), pp. 68–69: "I suppose we must admit—following Momigliano!—that we have no idea what a man liked Varro really believed, but we can be sure, from the evidence of his *Antiquitates*, that he was, like Cicero (e.g., *div.* 2.148 . . .), concerned to preserve the traditional rites and ceremonies of the Roman people."

3. See, for example, *ILS* no. 1771 (Rome): "To the Shades of the Dead. [This tomb was made] For Servatus, slave of our Emperor, by . . . Helvius, his *vicarius*, for his well-deserving master."

4. John Scheid, "Religion romaine et spiritualité," *Archiv für Religionsgeschichte* 5 (2003): 198–209.

5. Caroline Humphrey and James Laidlaw, *The Archetypal Actions of Ritual: A Theory of Ritual Illustrated by the Jain Rite of Worship* (Oxford: Clarendon Press, 1994).

Index

Acknowledgments

I would like to thank Christophe Goddard, director of the Centre CNRS–NYU Transitions, for having allowed me to bring this text to completion under ideal conditions. I owe thanks as well to Beatrice Lietz, my assistant at the Collège de France, for her observations on the topic of civic religion. Finally, I would like to express my deep gratitude to my colleague Pierre Rosanvallon for having accepted the French version of this essay, entitled *Les Dieux, l'État et l'Individu*, in his collection.